First Hill, 1908 *Baist's Real Estate Atlas of Surveys of Seattle.* G. William Baist Company, Philadelphia, 1908. Historic Seattle.

Terry Avenue (no date). Apse of St. James Cathedral (right foreground) with Cathedral Hall behind. Sergei Bongart (American, born Ukraine, 1918-1985), oil on Masonite. Frye Art Museum.

TRADITION AND CHANGE ON SEATTLE'S FIRST HILL

PROPRIETY, PROFANITY, PILLS, AND PRESERVATION

| LAWRENCE KREISMAN, EDITOR |

HISTORIC SEATTLE PRESERVATION FOUNDATION

DOCUMENTARY MEDIA, LLC
SEATTLE, WASHINGTON

Tradition and Change on Seattle's First Hill: Propriety, Profanity, Pills, and Preservation

Historic Seattle
1117 Minor Avenue
Seattle, WA 98101
206.622-6952
www.historicseattle.org

First Edition
Printed in China

Produced by Documentary Media, LLC
books@docbooks.com
www.documentarymedia.com
(206) 935-9292

Editor: Lawrence Kreisman
Book Design: Karen Schober
Copy Editor: Judy Gouldthorpe
Editorial Director: Petyr Beck

ISBN: 978-1-933245-38-6

Watercolor of Harvard Avenue retail with Fire Station No. 25 and First Baptist Church. Jule Kullberg (1905-1976). Courtesy Martin-Zambito Fine Art.

Library of Congress Cataloging-in-Publication Data

Tradition and change on Seattle's First Hill : propriety, profanity, pills, and preservation / Lawrence Kreisman, editor.
    pages cm
 Includes bibliographical references and index.
 ISBN 978-1-933245-38-6
1. First Hill (Seattle, Wash.)—History. 2. Seattle (Wash.)—History. 3. Architecture—Washington (State)—Seattle. 4. First Hill (Seattle, Wash.)—Buildings, structures, etc.

 F899.S46F578 2014
 979.7'772—dc23   2014027372

Partial funding from 4Culture
King County Lodging Tax Fund

CONTENTS

ACKNOWLEDGMENTS

THIS PUBLICATION IS THE CULMINATION of significant work undertaken since 1975, when Historic Seattle commenced *An Inventory of Buildings and Urban Design Resources*, a groundbreaking survey of city neighborhoods initiated by consultants Victor Steinbrueck and Folke Nyberg, faculty members in the College of Architecture and Urban Planning (now College of Built Environments) at the University of Washington, with the help of the Seattle Junior League Historic Sites Committee and many student and neighborhood volunteers. Its intent was to identify typical building types and significant buildings, objects, and landscape features that bear importance to the city and also to community residents. Its color-coded maps included sections on the history of particular neighborhoods. One of these maps, completed in 1977, documented First Hill. Thirty-seven years after its completion, that map reveals significant change, particularly in single-family residences and apartments that have made way for higher-density apartment buildings, condominiums, senior housing, retail, medical center expansion, and parking facilities.

In the early 1980s, I developed and conducted a series of architectural walking tours that included First Hill. These tours became the basis for a much larger group of tours offered by the Seattle Architecture Foundation starting in 1990. In 1997, Historic Seattle moved from a Pioneer Square office to the Henry H. Dearborn House at Minor Avenue and Seneca Street. Shortly after that move, I was hired as program director. In order to introduce ourselves to our new neighbors, Historic Seattle did several open houses and initiated tours of the Dearborn House and the Stimson-Green Mansion, now the headquarters of the Washington Trust for Historic Preservation. In recent years, that has expanded to First Hill neighborhood tours. In the process, we realized that few residents had an understanding of the rich heritage of one of the city's earliest residential neighborhoods. Frankly, Historic Seattle didn't know much either.

BELOW: First Hill skyline, 1977, from First Hill map in *An Inventory of Buildings and Urban Design Resources.* Earl Drais Layman, pen and ink. Historic Seattle.

In 1998-99, with support from the City of Seattle's Department of Neighborhoods and training sessions by respected historian Lorraine McConaghy, Historic Seattle staff and volunteers gathered data, identified people who lived on the Hill and had stories to share, and began interviewing them. Thelma Cooney, Phyllis Bannister (deceased), and Constance Schnell were key to this effort. Schnell's inquisitive mind led her to continue interviewing subjects through 2012. Other volunteers reviewed archives and libraries for articles and significant photographs. I mined the office records of famed photographer Asahel Curtis at the Washington State Historical Society library in Tacoma to identify First Hill images he had taken during the first decades of the 20th century, and I had prints made from his glass negatives—some probably for the first time. Our neighborhood project led to a series of three lectures and panels, *Seattle's First Hill: Evolution and Change*, which explored the past, present, and future of the hill.

As Historic Seattle contemplated its 40th anniversary, we decided that a First Hill history publication would be a valuable addition to local scholarship and our gift to the neighborhood and the city. We are grateful that 4Culture Heritage Special Projects funding of $20,000 supported research, writing, copy editing, book design, and photography. We were able to work with an outstanding team of local historians—Paul Dorpat, Dotty DeCoster, Jacqueline Williams, Dennis A. Andersen, Luci J. Baker Johnson, and Brooke Best—who committed a huge amount of volunteer hours to research, write, and review their chapters. Particular thanks go to Brooke Best, who reviewed and organized boxes of files and notebooks of materials collected at Historic Seattle, prepared context documents to get us started, and provided ongoing organizational support, along with authoring a chapter. We are grateful for the staff of Special Collections, University of Washington Libraries, the Seattle Room, Seattle Public Library, the Sophie Frye Bass Library at the Museum of History & Industry, and Washington State Historical Society, Paul Dorpat, Ron Edge, and others who helped us in our photography search. Cory Gooch at Frye Art Museum and David Martin of Martin-Zambito Fine Art gave us access to First Hill related artwork. Executive Director Kathleen Brooker and Historic Seattle staff and its governing Council members were supportive of the project, recognizing that it would take significant staff time and budget allocations to make it a reality.

Documentary Media was supportive from the start, offering guidance and maintaining patience and flexibility as it became obvious that we had unearthed far more information than would fit in the initial size we estimated for our publication. Copy editor Judy Gouldthorpe tackled the inconsistencies of six authors with different writing styles and grammatical prowess. Karen Schober, our book designer, listened to our wish list and came up with a layout that respected and gave adequate space for both the text and images.

Thank you to all of the organizations and individuals who have made this publication a reality. In addition to 4Culture, a number of individuals and businesses provided financial support for this publication, and we are most grateful to them. Some contributions were received after this book went to press and we are unable to acknowledge you here. Nevertheless, you know who you are and we appreciate your support.

Among our lead contributors were Victoria Reed, Kevin and Mary Jean Daniels, Marvin Anderson Architects PLLC, KeyBank Foundation, Jan O'Connor, Wayne Dodge and Lawrence Kreisman, Alan and Terry Axelrod, Lenore Hanauer, Alan and Sally Black, Gilbert Joynt, Exeter House, Richard Bready and Karin Rosenberg, Nostalgic Homes, Tom Speer, Michael and Barbara Malone, Marie Strong, Mary Kae McCullough, and Mimi Sheridan.

Others who supported our work: Karen Allman and Elizabeth Wales, Judith Barbour, Colin and Jennifer Barr, Brooke and Bob Best, Sue Billings, Marta Brace, Kathleen Brooker and Tim McDonald, Adelaide Brooks and Robert Pennell, Frank Chaffee, Shirley Courtois, Lois Crow, Martha Dilts and Ed Schumacher, Sue Drais, Patrick Dunn, Heideh Eftehari, Alvin and Ruth Eller, Richard Engeman and Terry Jess, Mark Failor, Karen Gordon, Fred and Barb Grote, Rhys Hefta, Michael and Julia Herschensohn, Lydia Hillier, Suzanne Hittman, Steve and Leslie Hughes, Doug and Luci J. Baker Johnson, Robert Kahn, Kate and Chapin Krafft, Donn and Patricia Laughlin, Don Luxton and Bruce Grady, Martin-Zambito Fine Art, Glenn and Judith Mason, Mary Kae McCullough, Chuck and Marilyn McKenzie, Dick McKinnon and Mollie Tremaine, Dennis Meier, Richard Mohr, Ron and Lynn Moore, Barbara Morris, Northwestapartments.com, Eileen Piehl, Linda Reisser, Lyn Sauter, Connie Schnell, Marita Sheeran, Mimi Sheridan, Anita Sigel, Claudia Skelton, Miriam Sutermeister, Nancy Talbot Doty, Cathy Taylor, Suzanne Vadman, Richard and Eileen Vincent, Catherine Wilder, Dennis Wilhelm and Michael Kinerk, Jacqueline Williams, Mitchell Wolfson, Eugenia Woo, Gail Yates, and Kathrin Young.

We sincerely hope that the distribution of this book will stimulate interest in citywide understanding of a historically significant and remarkably vital urban neighborhood.

LAWRENCE KREISMAN, EDITOR
PROGRAM DIRECTOR, HISTORIC SEATTLE

ABOUT THE AUTHORS

LAWRENCE KREISMAN, an educator and author in the field of architectural history and preservation, is program director at Historic Seattle. He is author of *Apartments by Anhalt, Art Deco Seattle, West Queen Anne School: Renaissance of a Landmark, Historic Preservation in Seattle, The Bloedel Reserve: Gardens in the Forest, The Stimson Legacy: Architecture in the Urban West, Made to Last: Historic Preservation in Seattle and King County,* and *Dard Hunter: The Graphic Works.* He is coauthor with Glenn Mason of *The Arts and Crafts Movement in the Pacific Northwest.* He also was a contributing author for *King County Collects.* He wrote about historic preservation and home design regularly for the Sunday *Seattle Times* magazine, *Pacific Northwest,* from 1988 to 2012, as well as for national magazines *Style 1900, Old-House Interiors, Old House Journal,* and *Preservation.*

DENNIS ALAN ANDERSEN is a frequent writer and lecturer on regional photographic and architectural history. He has published many articles and coauthored two regional architectural history books, *Shaping Seattle Architecture* and *Distant Corner: Seattle Architects and the Legacy of H. H. Richardson.* A graduate of Pacific Lutheran University, he has pursued graduate studies at the University of Washington, the University of Vienna (Austria), Wartburg Theological Seminary, and the Strasbourg Institute for Ecumenical Research. For seven years prior to his seminary education, he was in charge of photographs and architectural drawings in Special Collections, University of Washington Libraries. He chaired the Seattle Landmarks Preservation Board and was secretary to the board of directors of Partners for Sacred Places, a Philadelphia-based organization. He currently serves as lead pastor at St. James Lutheran Church (ELCA) in downtown Portland.

BROOKE BEST is an architectural historian/historic preservationist who produced a 4Culture grant-funded local history publication, *Celebrating 150 Years, Architectural History of West Seattle's North End: Harbor Avenue, Alki, and South Alki.* She has provided consulting services, including interpretive traveling exhibit panels, a "Haunted History" walking tour for Seattle's Georgetown neighborhood, a historic resource inventory for the Snoqualmie Valley Barn Preservation Initiative, and a survey of Bainbridge Island's Winslow Main Street area. More recently, she served as the preservation liaison for the City of Bothell's Landmark Preservation Board. Brooke currently works as Historic Seattle's office manager.

DOTTY DeCOSTER, a resident of Capitol Hill in the 1960s, 1970s, and 1980s, and more recently of First Hill, has always been an active observer and outspoken participant in these communities, from the Model Cities effort to rescue inner-city neighborhoods, to the Boeing Bust, to changing populations and increasing density, to the strengthening women's movement. She has a fascination for local history and for making new discoveries through primary research. She has written more than a dozen essays on Seattle buildings for HistoryLink, the online "cyberpedia." She has also written articles for the *Capitol Hill Times*.

For more than 40 years, PAUL DORPAT has written books, produced film and video, consulted, acted as curator, and lectured widely, most often on the subject of regional history. Three of his 13 published books, *Seattle Now and Then, Volumes I, II, and III*, were compiled from columns that have appeared weekly in the Sunday *Seattle Times* magazine, *Pacific Northwest*, since 1982. He was coauthor, with Genevieve McCoy, of *Building Washington: A History of Washington State Public Works*, and coauthor, with Jean Sherrard, of *Washington Then and Now*. Other books include *The University Book Store: A Centennial Pictorial* and *Seattle Waterfront: An Illustrated History*. Paul Dorpat is one of the three founders of www.historylink.org, the online encyclopedia of Seattle, King County, and Washington State history, and continues to contribute to it.

LUCI J. BAKER JOHNSON is a freelance writer and historian with wide-ranging interests in family, social, and house histories, and topics that interpret Norwegian settlement and the skills and talents these immigrants brought to the Pacific Northwest. At conferences, she has presented research about the Alaska reindeer project that passed through Seattle in the 1890s, biographical sketches of two early-20th-century Norwegian-American artists who painted murals in Seattle, and information about Norwegian participation at the 1909 Alaska-Yukon-Pacific Exposition. In 2005, she wrote a series of weekly columns—"Immigrant/Emigrant Passages"—for *Western Viking*, a weekly newspaper for Norwegian-American immigrants and their descendants. The immigrant-heritage journal *Budstikken* recently published her article on early Seattle poet and literary critic Thomas O. Stine. She has also conducted seminars and workshops on research skills, including a seminar on how to research a building. A 2000 graduate of the Genealogy & Family History Certificate Program at the University of Washington, she serves on its Advisory Board. She is the Manager of Volunteers and Events at Historic Seattle.

JACQUELINE BLOCK WILLIAMS has been researching and writing about regional topics for nearly 20 years. They range from investigations into food products and cooking, to neighborhood history, to the Jewish presence in the state. In addition to writing many articles for *Columbia: The Magazine of Northwest History*, *Pacific Northwest Quarterly*, and other national and regional periodicals, she is the author of *Wagon Wheel Kitchens: Food on the Oregon Trail, The Way We Ate: Pacific Northwest Cooking, 1843-1900, Family of Strangers: Building a Jewish Community in Washington State* with coauthors Molly Cone and Howard Droker, and *The Hill with a Future: Seattle's Capitol Hill*.

PREFACE

RESIDENTS AND NEWCOMERS TO SEATTLE often dismiss First Hill as that place you have to go for a doctor's appointment, hospitalization, or retirement. Certainly, hospitals, medical centers, retirement homes, and parking lots have obscured much of the traditional residential neighborhood that developed in its heyday when First Hill was synonymous with good living, exclusive private clubs and social gatherings, and religious pageantry. But it was much more than that. Steve Sheppard, a planner with the City of Seattle, is quick to remind us, "First Hill was never the archetypal wealthy suburb/residential enclave that was a segregated area where only the rich resided. The area was a wonderful, eclectic mix of middle, upper, and lower income residents all living together. This eclectic tradition and neighborhood character continues today." It is the purpose of this publication to reveal the Hill in all its diversity.

Occupying one of Seattle's seven hills, First Hill is the first hill one encounters traveling east from downtown. Rising 366 feet above Elliott Bay, the once-forested slope has witnessed several stages of development since 1852 and, over the years, has

BELOW: View toward Elliott Bay shows the Dearborn Cut, the dip between Beacon Hill (left) and First Hill (right), ca. 1935. Towers are (left to right): U.S. Marine Hospital, King Street Station, Smith Tower, Harborview Hospital. Ruth Warren, watercolor. Dodge/Kreisman Collection.

been known by several names. It also has confounded residents and visitors trying to come up with a sense of where it starts and where it ends. Sometimes the local press completely ignores it, assuming it is simply a part of Capitol Hill to its north and east.

WHAT'S IN A NAME?

In the beginning, it was simply known as "the hill." By the 1890s, the southern edge had gained the nickname "Profanity Hill." By 1883, the crest of the hill entered a new era as the first retreat of its "first families," including mayors, judges, industrialists, timber barons, and art collectors. As First Hill, this promontory flourished as an exclusive enclave of fine homes. It offered a choice location—close to downtown, but removed from the rowdiness of the waterfront. This utopian neighborhood provided commanding westerly views of the city, Elliott Bay, and the Olympic Mountains beyond. Of the 40 or more large residences that once dominated First Hill, only four remain—the Stimson-Green, Dearborn, Stacy, and Hofius residences.

Over the years, numerous churches, apartment buildings, workers' housing, hotels, social clubs, and hospitals added to the area's architecture, creating a visual, cultural, and economic tapestry and a unique sense of place.

Since the 1960s, the hill has been severed from the downtown by the freeway. Its once commanding views and exclusive residential blocks have been supplanted by retail, multifamily high-rises, medical centers, and clinics. The hill earned its frequently used nickname "Pill Hill" for being home to Harborview, Swedish, Virginia Mason, and other medical facilities.

Observing development and change on Seattle's First Hill provides a mirror by which people in all densely built American cities can look at and evaluate their own

RIGHT: Boren Avenue and Spring Street, ca. 1905. The copper, brick, and terra-cotta W. D. Hofius mansion is a distinctive presence. The Daniel Kelleher residence is behind it to the right (east), and Dr. George Horton's house is to the left (north). SHS 12189 Seattle Historical Society Collection, MOHAI.

ABOVE: Open-air automobile vies with a cable car on Madison Street, view west to Perry Hotel, ca. 1910. Courtesy Dan Kerlee.

changes. What happened on First Hill was not unique. It reflects typical urban expansion and the rise and decline of inner-city neighborhoods. As Seattle grew from a fledgling seaport town to "the Gateway to the Orient" in the late 19th and early 20th centuries, it underwent great physical changes, reflected in the growth of its waterfront and downtown, the regrading of hills and filling in of tide flats to accommodate commercial development, and the establishment of new residential neighborhoods. The city experienced an influx of immigrants seeking opportunities, fresh starts, and freedom from persecution or poverty or conservative traditions. Seattle offered the promise of a better life to all.

First Hill was the first "neighborhood" to be settled. Rich and poor children went to Central or Summit schools. Roman Catholics lived close to St. James Cathedral, and other congregations took root on the hillside. There were no city parks, so children played ball in whatever open spaces they could find. First Hill was close to the heart of the city's commercial district—an easy downhill walk in the morning and a short climb home in the evening. The Sorrento Hotel promoted itself as "near enough to be convenient, but away from the noise and confusion of the busy streets."

This book captures the changing character, purpose, and rhythm of a dense urban neighborhood—through maps, photographs, postcards, advertising, paintings, written accounts, and oral interviews conducted from 1999 to 2012 with longtime residents who lived, worked, socialized, and worshipped on First Hill. It documents the neighborhood's colorful and diverse past, and poses some key questions about First Hill's contemporary identity.

These snapshots of the past are valuable for newcomers who seek to understand what may appear to be a fragmented neighborhood. It has few prominent historic and architecturally important mansions left. Its post-World War II apartments and hospital buildings are generally monolithic structures that are architecturally uninspiring. Demolition of the neighborhood's original housing stock made way for larger-scale apartment buildings, condominiums, hospital expansion, and parking lots. Much of the community's design integrity and scale were supplanted, making it difficult to envision the historic significance of First Hill.

This book provides an understanding of First Hill's origins, how and why it changed, and the potential that exists for future development of this historic neighborhood. There is, in fact, a First Hill cultural body with a heart that still beats.

HILL BOUNDARIES

First Hill's northern boundary is generally considered to be East Pike Street, although when Victor Steinbrueck and Folke Nyberg conducted their groundbreaking survey of urban neighborhoods for Historic Seattle beginning in 1975, they drew its northern edge at East Pine Street, even though Capitol Hill claims East Pine as its own.

The southern edge of First Hill is either Yesler Way or South Main Street, which was the commercial center of Nihonmachi (Japantown).

The neighborhood's eastern edge has been variously defined both tightly as Broadway and Boren Avenues, and more broadly as 12th Avenue, and even as far as 14th

RIGHT: First Hill Neighborhood Plan Area map, 1999, prepared by Strategic Planning Office, City of Seattle.

Avenue, to encompass Seattle University's expanding campus. The 1999 First Hill Neighborhood Plan delineated the boundary at Broadway and Boren Avenues, and this stands at present as its defined eastern edge.

Historically, Sixth Avenue was the entry to First Hill from the central business district, although pedestrians trudging up from the waterfront might think otherwise. In the 1960s, the western border of First Hill (as well as Capitol and Beacon Hills) was irrefutably defined by the Washington State Department of Highways with the construction of the Seattle Freeway (Interstate 5).

While our authors have occasionally crossed the line to include a particularly interesting building "on the edge," the boundaries of First Hill discussed in these chapters are East Pike Street, Broadway and Boren Avenues, Yesler Way, and Sixth Avenue.

RIGHT: First Hill map in *An Inventory of Buildings and Urban Design Resources,* commenced in 1975, published 1977. Historic Seattle.

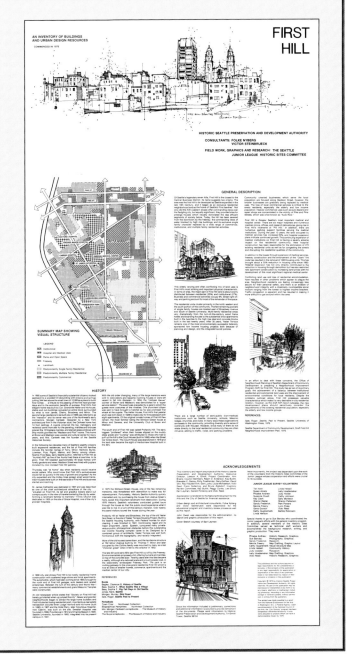

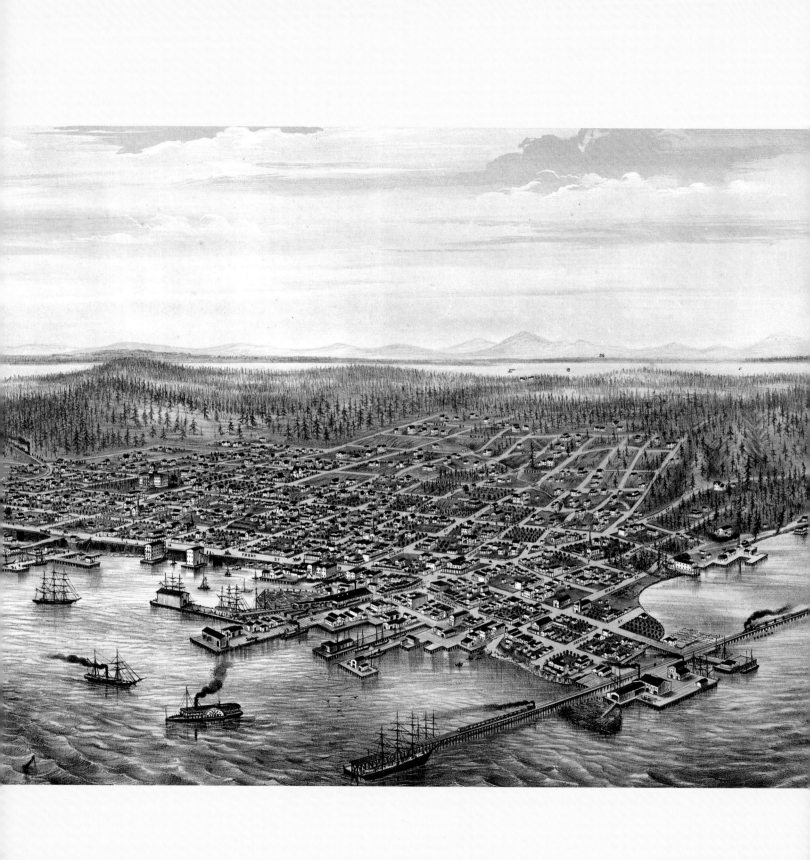

[CHAPTER] 1

PROLOGUE

PAUL DORPAT

THE TOP

ABOVE: Woman with a parasol observes First Hill from her Denny Hill perch, ca. 1880. Courtesy Michael Maslan.

LEFT: Seattle bird's-eye, 1878, makes the terrain seem practically flat from the waterfront to the gradually cleared blocks of First Hill and the forested land reaching east to Lake Washington. Library of Congress.

SEATTLE TOOK A LONG TIME to reach the forested top of its first hill. The crown, the part of the hill that now displays the mix of structures and uses—institutional, residential, commercial—that distinguish First Hill, stood in its own shadows through Seattle's first quarter-century. Below the hill and barely noticing it, the city developed into the second-largest in Washington Territory, after Walla Walla, which slightly surpassed it in the census of 1880. The top of this hill is about 366 feet above Elliott Bay. It was a steep ascent, and early residents must have blessed the coming of cable cars.

Beginning in 1891, a red brick powerhouse with a tall black stack topped the summit at the northeast corner of James Street and Broadway. From there the Union Trunk Line operated a cable car along James Street from Pioneer Square that connected with electric trolleys headed in every direction: north into Capitol Hill, east to Lake Washington, and south to Beacon Hill. These, along with cable cars on Madison Street and Yesler Way, spurred platting and housing development. This

RIGHT: First Hill stagecoach near the summit. Photo by Mrs. Jessie Parker, courtesy Paul Dorpat.

rolling enterprise gave a predictable noise to the hill, a rattling and clanking that was lost to rubber with the conversion of the railways to trackless trolleys and gas-powered buses in 1940.

NAMING

BELOW: Union Trunk Line Power-house at Broadway Avenue between James and Cherry Streets. Courtesy Lawton Gowey.

After reaching the summit of the hill east of the central business district and filing their string of claims, Seattle's ambitious settlers continued to bushwhack through the forest along Indian trails east to the big lake (Lake Washington). The trails covered about two and one-half miles, roughly in line with what became the skid road to Henry Yesler's steam-powered lumber mill. The first hill to climb and to settle became informally known as First Hill. Even much later, when trumpeted by real estate agents with bold type standing tall in the local classifieds, the name First Hill with caps did not take unchallenged hold—not until the 1920s.

Lack of fervent commitment to "First Hill" was revealed by the infrequent use of proper-name formalities like caps. There was also an abiding need felt even among property pitchers to introduce the name with an article, as in "Look to *the* first hill for your answer." This example is pulled from the *Seattle Daily Times* of September 3, 1905. By then First Hill was ordinarily distinguished from Capitol Hill to the north, so named in 1901 by James Moore, Seattle's premier developer of the time. Previous to Moore's Capitol Hill Addition venture, both "first hill" and "the first hill" were repeatedly used for developments far north of Pike Street, the shallow depression and future border between the two snuggling neighborhoods.

SOME BORDERS – NORTH AND SOUTH

Pike Street follows a lucky path. As the first street south of Denny Hill as well as the first street north of the exposed steeper part of First Hill that later became University and Union Streets, Pike became the preferred byway for a narrow-gauge coal railway to the Pike Street Coal Wharf with bunkers—the biggest thing in Seattle in the 1870s—and a graded wagon road to the ridge that quickly developed into a commercial street lined by shops, many of them selling notably bicycles in the 1890s and motor-cars thereafter.

With continued exploring, Seattle's first settlers soon discovered that their first hill was a small part of a long ridge reaching north to Lake Union's Portage Bay and south nearly to what is now Renton. Along the way the ridge had just enough ups-and-downs to be eventually treated as a chain of hills. First Hill is the smallest link in the chain. From Pike Street on the north to Yesler Way on the south, Broadway extends about one block short of one mile. South of First Hill's southern border, the ridge's natural "downs" (graded by the ice age) were deepened when 90 feet of earth was washed away during the 1907-1909 Jackson Street Regrade, followed by the 1909-1912 Dearborn Cut.

YESLER AND PROFANITY

For nearly the first quarter-century of Seattle's run to municipal greatness, the hill directly above the city's commercial heart was left in the forest and hardly noticed even by the factory man most likely to cut into it, Henry Yesler. Instead, Yesler continued to take the easy tidewater timber waiting beside Elliott Bay, and beyond it if need be. The logs could be floated to the mill rather than dragged there. In 1852, Yesler had been lured to join his fate with Seattle's when Carson Boren and David Maynard separated their claims to give him a blockwide strip of land. Like a ribbon, it led up and over the first hill to the hefty reserves of timber waiting for Henry and his wife, Sarah, to claim as far as the homestead laws allowed. This included part of Second Hill. With his improved native trail up Mill Street (Yesler Way), locals—and many of them worked for Yesler—started to think of First Hill as Yesler Hill, a name with flesh, like Beacon, Denny, Queen Anne, and Renton. This last, "Renton," became the preferred name for the "Second Hill" that Arthur Denny, Carson Boren, and William Bell topped on their first hike to the big lake. Like Henry Yesler, William Renton was a resourceful mill man. Both stood for industry and employment.

South of James Street and west of Ninth Avenue, the topography of First Hill swells in the direction of Yesler Way on the south and Pioneer Square to the west. It created a skull-shaped knoll for showing off two oversize Seattle landmarks. First, the King County Courthouse filled the horizon between Seventh and Eighth Avenues from 1891 to 1930. It was followed by Harborview Hospital, built behind the courthouse between Eighth and Ninth Avenues.

From below, this unique knoll is by far the most evident part of First Hill, called "Yesler" by some and "Profanity" by others. The latter name was a folk creation of the 1890s, an appreciation for the naughty words heard from lawyers and litigants climbing the hill to reach the courthouse—and for the muffled cussing heard in its halls.

The city's acrimonious streetcar strike of 1903 was called for higher wages and made for profanity. The *Seattle Daily Times* agreed on March 26 that "Profanity Hill

BELOW: King County Courthouse crowns First Hill in this ca. 1898 view from Beacon Hill. Photo by Wilse, Special Collections, University of Washington Libraries.

richly merited its sobriquet this morning if it never did before. Long before 11 o'clock the sidewalk on James Street, and on the west side of Seventh Ave. were several inches deep with unholy expressions, left there by perspiring, red-faced attorneys, compelled by the exigencies of a street car strike to not only personally climb the mountain . . . but in most cases to carry ponderous law volumes as well. They were an ill tempered lot . . ."

In 1909 the joys of regrading on Denny Hill and Jackson Street inspired the South End improvement clubs to propose removing all of Profanity—or Yesler—Hill as well. The joined clubs denied that the proposal was inspired by any "missionary movement" to clean up the cursing. Proposals for grading away much of Profanity/Yesler Hill seemed to be eternally recurring, and these resurfaced especially when parts of the hill slipped away in landslides of its impermeable blue clay and unstable glacial drift. The *Seattle Daily Times* for July 25, 1928, included an editorial on the name controversy. After reviewing the knoll's profane past, the paper advised that the name Profanity Hill be dropped "in honor of Yesler." The editorial was written in celebration of the news that the old courthouse would soon be razed in favor of a new courthouse off the hill on Fourth Avenue, out of earshot from the curses above.

The name Profanity Hill could not be eradicated, and even stayed appropriate during the 1930s, when the more modest residences at this profane southern end of First Hill evolved into a low-rent and low-maintenance neighborhood for the low-down and almost out. The majority of these structures were later cleared for the construction of Yesler Terrace, one of the rare instances when the elimination of First Hill homes increased the total housing stock. Given that Henry Yesler was one of our pioneers most familiar with profanity, both names might have been kept with a hyphen: Yesler-Profanity Hill. It is an irony we may still enjoy when stuck on the freeway below First Hill.

"SWARMING WITH THRONGS OF INDIANS"

The settlers generally did not like trees, except as a crop for sale to Californians. They preferred gardens and foundations for their homes over the cougars and resentful Yakamas they prudently imagined hiding among the giant, furtive firs. Their caution quickly turned to fear mixed with loathing during and immediately after the war between the Indians and settlers. The first detailed map of Seattle, drawn in 1856 by Navy Lieutenant Phelps at the time of the "Battle of Seattle," captions the forest-hatched hill as "swarming with throngs of Indians." While the Indians—many of them from east of the Cascade Mountains—spattered the village with small-arms fire, Phelps and his sailors hurled exploding cannonballs back at them. More than a century later, intact duds of this artillery were discovered during the digging of the Interstate-5 Expressway, the public work that also resolved any doubt about what counted as First Hill's western border. It is the freeway.

"I LIKE TO HUNT"

Among Seattle's first settlers, Carson Boren was uniquely fond of the forest. While his brother-in-law Arthur Denny wanted to legislate, survey, and sell, Carson liked to hunt, and he had a lot of his own land to do it on. Boren's claims on First Hill were the largest. He soon traded the greater part of his greatest part of the hill to the Alki Point holdout Charles Terry, however. It was the First Hill lots in Charles and Mary Jane Terry's First and Second additions that started attracting mid-1870s buyers for whom city bureaucrats established laws of conduct.

The city's 97th ordinance, passed by its council on March 3, 1876, addressed its concerns about "any violent, riotous or disorderly conduct." In the new law's second section, titled "Hunting," the city's borders of civilized behavior were defined and drawn. It read, in part, "Any person or persons who shall fire any pistol, gun or rifles, or other fire-arms within the following limits: Cedar St. on the north to Judkins Addition on the south and Tenth Street on the east between said limits on the bay shall on conviction thereof before any Justice of the Peace, be subject to a penalty of not less than five nor more than fifty dollars or imprisonment at the [discretion of the] Justice of the Peace before whom he, she or they may be arraigned, not exceeding twenty days." With No. 97's border of concern reaching as far east as Tenth Avenue (Terry Avenue), Seattle's civilized conduct, or the lookout for it, had reached the top of First Hill.

Carson Boren outlived most of his pioneer peers. In spite of his withdrawal from any regular ambition beyond slaying game for the table, farming, and sometimes exploring for gold with his son William, Boren had that enduring advantage that nearly ensured prosperity. He was one of the original settlers, and so by our inflated 21st-century ratings Boren died a millionaire. In spite of his passive economics, with his death in 1912, Carson, or Old Dobbins, as was his nickname, left more than $300,000 to his heirs. Local historian Greg Lange generously speculates that perhaps part of his "closing fortune" came as gifts from members of the Arthur Denny family who made the most from the sale of his land. Boren's funeral was held on the hill, in the stately Denny home at 1220 Boren Avenue, and the procession of his pallbearers was weighted with neither hunters nor salesmen but with what were then Seattle's primary public historians—Clarence Bagley, Thomas Prosch, and Edmond Meany.

A HOLDING TIMBER CURTAIN: 1859-1869

The oldest surviving photograph of Seattle, which is conventionally dated 1859, is also its first recording of First Hill. Another photograph was taken in 1865 from nearly the same Pioneer Square prospect. Both give us a generous glimpse of the same forest curtain that divides the clear-cut community from the hill. Both look due east up James Street, and so directly into First Hill. From the waterfront, the forest-free or cleared blocks reach about as far as Fifth Avenue—at most. The oldest photo,

ABOVE: View of Seattle from Pioneer Place toward First Hill shows the tree line. E. A. Clark, 1859. Seattle Public Library.

BELOW: Pavilion for Fourth of July 1865. E. M. Sammis. Special Collections, University of Washington Libraries.

recorded by E. A. Clark, seems to be taken from a roof, probably Yesler's first sawmill or a shed attached to it. On the left is Sarah and Henry Yesler's home at the northeast corner of First (Front) and James Street. E. M. Sammis, the first itinerant photographer to open a commercial studio here, recorded the 1865 subject with the Independence Day arch. We know the date of his photograph from its description printed in the *Seattle Gazette* for July 6, 1865. It reads, in part, "We have received from E. M. Sammis . . . a view of the S.S.S. Pavilion erected for the Fourth of July celebration." (We can thank Dennis Andersen, another of the contributors to this book, for finding this citation long ago while searching pioneer publications for local news about photography and architecture.)

A third cityscape, from 1869, may be considered the grandest of our pioneer photographs. It wins that distinction with a combination of panoramic reach and clarity. The part of the pan included here, the right side, also looks east up First Hill, this time two blocks south of Pioneer Square from a second-floor window of Snoqualmie Hall, at the southwest corner of First Avenue South (Commercial Street

ABOVE: View from First Avenue South and Main Street. George Robinson, 1869. Washington State Historical Society.

then) and Main Street. Although Henry Yesler built a new sawmill at the foot of Mill Street in 1868, it would seem that a year later his bigger and better blades had had no effect on First Hill. Rather, the Victorian photographer George Robinson's grand panorama shows some of the same forest curtain first revealed in the Clark and Sammis recordings. The point easily made is that there is little evidence in any of the three photographs that any sizable progress had been made in the 1860s toward the clearing of First Hill for development or even for harvesting its timber.

Curiously, 1869 was Seattle's first boom year. According to Thomas Prosch's generally reliable *Chronological History of Seattle* (1901), new construction in 1869 included "one church, 11 store buildings, 37 dwellings and 20 shacks and other structures." There is no sign in Robinson's 1869 panorama that any of these additions were raised high on the hill.

The local excitement of '69 came because of another hill: Snoqualmie Pass. The Northern Pacific Railway was surveying it for a path through the Cascades to a Puget Sound terminus. Elliott Bay partisans assumed that the rails would end up in Seattle: a reward for their long preparation. When the settlers began clearing the forest for their hoped-for community in 1852, they were thinking *railroad*. Their work attracting other settlers to both buy lots and help build a city was also meant to excite a railroad. So grand was their righteous longing for rails that they may have found their other efforts—like developing First Hill—hardly worth much concern. Meanwhile they lived through the anxious Northwest doldrums of two wars, first with the Indians and then with the South, or North, depending. When in 1873 the Northern Pacific chose Stampede Pass and a new but empty creation named New Tacoma instead as a terminus, it was a dispiriting defeat for Seattle.

While the locals could not know it, and it is still hard to figure, within two or three years of the railroad's rejection, the hill would get to hustling and its timber to cutting. Well endowed with knolls, more gentle inclines than cliffs, and plenty of springs, First Hill was ready for building homes once the forest was subdued. For about a quarter-century, the top of the hill had waited behind the curtain in its ancient regime, the old but still growing splendor of big firs, hemlocks, and cedars collaborating with alders. Then it was all cut away.

DENNY'S KNOLL

While the locals did not cut their way up First Hill during the Civil War years, they did begin the 1860s by sawing to the north, preparing Denny's Knoll for their prized Territorial University. This required a great felling of firs to clear the knoll that rose roughly east of Third Avenue and north of Seneca Street. After the school opened in 1861, the cutting continued, and students could help pay their tuition by clearing more forest from the campus, including cords of firewood to help heat the first few buildings on the campus. Once cleared, the knoll was seen from the waterfront as a slight rise on the First Hill horizon. The principal university building, with its classic columns and distinguished belfry, was constructed at the northeast corner of Fourth Avenue and Seneca Street, now footing for the southwest corner of the Fairmont Olympic Hotel. The school and its knoll easily surmounted the horizon. From Yesler Wharf the school would have been described as being on First Hill, or perhaps even on top of it, when in fact this was part of the hill's "lesser horizon." For a few blocks between roughly Cherry and University Streets, it hid the greater horizon that extended between Jefferson and University Streets close to Ninth Avenue. Now Denny's Knoll and the Territorial University of Washington's original campus are no longer considered part of the hill, which, as noted, is first entered after crossing Sixth Avenue to the east.

BOOKEND PANS – CA. 1872-1878

By the evidence of two photographs that behave like "bookends" for the mid 1870s, we can begin to narrow the time allowed for the clear-cutting of the First Hill summit. Both are splendid panoramas of the city and both are recorded from the same Denny Hill prospect. The earlier pan dates from 1872-73 by Moore, and the Peterson brothers' is confidently dated 1878. In the earlier pan, First Hill is still crowded with trees east of Sixth and Seventh Avenues. By 1878, with the exception of a few recalcitrant firs, First Hill has been cleared east across its top at least as far as Broadway. The want of mansions on the horizon of the Petersons' hill confirms what we already know from other sources. The development of the hill as a more or less exclusive neighborhood, as the city's nabobs had hoped, did not begin until the early 1880s, and then with mixed results.

RIGHT: View to Territorial University and First Hill from Denny Hill by Moore, ca. 1872. Special Collections, University of Washington Libraries.

RIGHT: The same view by Henry and Lewis Peterson, 1878, shows clear-cutting that has occurred on First Hill. Courtesy Dan Kurlee.

Midway between the Moore and Peterson pans, Judge York of the probate court confirmed that in the court's most recent term he had given 175 orders confirming sales within the Terry estate, "which embraces one-half of the settled portion of the City of Seattle." With a population well under 3,000, Seattle was growing in 1875. Still, the locals remained in shock over their rejection by the Northern Pacific Railway for the Puget Sound terminus of its transcontinental line. When the rails from Chicago did at last span the West in 1883, Seattle—not the chosen terminus, Tacoma—was the largest town in Washington Territory. By then the hitherto largely empty lots on the summit of First Hill were developing with gardens and, at first, a mix of mostly modest residences. But the top of the hill would soon grow such a crop of elaborately appointed oversized homes that the waiting connotation of "class" in the name "First Hill" would seem both fitting and destined.

VISIONS OF FIRST HILL AND JAMES COLMAN

In 1876 the failing plans for Seattle's own railroad over Snoqualmie Pass to the east— the Seattle and Walla Walla—were revived largely by the brilliance and energy of pioneer James M. Colman. The *Puget Sound Dispatch* described Colman as "the greatest public benefactor in this city; the man who has contributed more to its material wealth than any other." Beriah Brown, the editor, lamented that Colman was "but the lessee of the manufacturing establishment which he operates." Published on April 6, 1876, Brown's sermon on property and its uses was introduced with a vision of First Hill: "From one standpoint, upon the hill east of the business portion of the city, fifty houses can be counted in the course of construction, and this, too, during the most unpropitious season of the year for building."

While Granville and Henrietta Haller were building their mansion on the top of First Hill in 1883, Agnes and James Colman were doing the same nearer the bottom. Had they waited but a year or two they might have joined the move to the top. With its frescoed interior walls otherwise finished in California redwood, four large bedrooms, library, parlor, and servants' quarters in the rear, and a central tower with "tower room" overlooking Elliott Bay, the Italianate mansion would have complemented and extended the affluent reach of the new neighborhood up the hill. Instead

RIGHT: James M. Colman's Italianate mansion at Fourth Avenue and Columbia Street, 1883. Courtesy Michael Maslan.

the Colmans built above the southeast corner of Fourth Avenue, five blocks down Columbia Street from the Coppin water tower. Still, in 1883 the Colman corner was considered "up the hill."

SEATTLE DIRECTORY – 1876

B. L. Northrup and Kirk Ward issued the first Seattle business and residential directory in the fall of 1876. In an introductory remark, Northrup indicated his intention to keep publishing annual directories thereafter. Although it was not to be for these publishing partners, another local printer did manage to assemble a directory in 1879. The 1876 directory's 20-page introduction is an enlightening summary of the community's first quarter-century. The directory provides statistics to support its promotional intentions to make 1876 into a year of exceptional progress and prosperity. The essayist's readiness to reveal the community's difficult journey through its first quarter-century required some worldly-wise candor. In the introduction the partners concluded that 1876 was:

> *…one of the best years for business and growth in the history of the town. There was a considerable influx of new people, as indicated by the large number of votes cast, by the many new business enterprises, by the increased trade, and by numerous other like signs of indisputable character. More than a hundred houses were built, more street work done, more railroad work, more coal mining, more shipping, more manufacturing, more merchandising, more of everything that was required to sustain the increasing number of people. Seattle gained on other towns on the North Pacific coast, and the great anticipation of her most sanguine citizens appeared to be on the point for early realization.*

And Seattle began to move up the hill.

The 1876 directory dutifully counted 1,031 buildings in the city, and 3,700 inhabitants, among whom were five teachers and 379 pupils in the public schools. The directory's alphabetical listing of heads of households—mostly—included 1,014 names. A "pointed-finger" survey of its pages revealed roughly 70 citizens with addresses on the hill, defined as north of Mill Street (Yesler Way), south of Union, and, most important for following the city's expansion up the hill, east of Sixth Avenue. Many of those listed on the hill worked in the useful trades, including several carpenters, brick masons, molders, cabinetmakers, and general laborers. These were all well situated to help with the coming building boom on First Hill. Of the roughly 70 names found living there in 1876, a dozen still kept to their hill addresses 15 years later, as revealed in the 1891 Corbett's city directory. Among them were Thomas R. Emerson, listed on Tenth Avenue (Terry Avenue) three lots south of Seneca Street; the tailor David Kaufman, at the northeast corner of Seventh and Marion; Henry and

Henry Lohse Jr., father-son bricklayers residing at 617 James Street and so next door to the Hotel Kalmar; Erick Ulin, a ship's carpenter residing on Eighth Avenue between Marion and Madison; Lemuel Wilcoe at the corner of Seventh and James; and Charles Coppin.

COPPIN'S WATER

In the 1876 directory, Charles Coppin is listed as a carpenter and joiner living at the corner of Ninth Avenue and Columbia Street. Coppin had climbed the hill in 1875 looking primarily for a place to dig a well. In 1873 the city contracted him to build both its North School House, near Third and Pine, and its South School House, at the southwest corner of Sixth and Main. Perhaps it was from his public works earnings that he purchased the promising lots near the top of First Hill. The hole he dug and walled on his property at the southeast corner of Ninth and Columbia was impressive: six feet wide and 135 feet deep. From the beginning in 1852, the many springs above the east shore of Elliott Bay gave plenty of water, but not so efficiently or forcefully as the carpenter's creation. We may imagine that Coppin's well was an admired fulfillment of one of the primary reasons the Dennys, Bells, and Borens had moved over from Alki Point to the hill a quarter-century earlier. The resulting "fountain" of 900,000 gallons a day was more than anyone could use in 1875. The carpenter's confidence that another stream would spring, that of new neighbors climbing the hill to make new homes, ended up being justified. With a 25-year franchise granted him in 1883—just in time to supply his neighbors, the Phinneys, the Hallers, and many others—Charles Coppin buried pipes across the crown of First Hill and became its principal supplier of good potable water.

RIGHT: Charles Coppin's water tower at Ninth Avenue and Columbia Street. Courtesy Paul Dorpat.

The fanciful three-story tower built in 1883-4 above the well housed a 10,000-gallon tank and an observatory, from which photographer Arthur Churchill Warner recorded his 1891 panorama of First Hill. While it seems incomplete—missing parts to the south, west, and due north—the panorama is still a revelation of the often elegant development applied to the crown of First Hill, with its mix of "regular" homes, a few row houses (precursors of the hill's many apartment houses), and several mansions. When the waterworks was sold to the city in 1899 for $200, the Coppin tap served about 300 customers. The well with its landmark tower became obsolete in 1901, when the Seattle Water Department turned on its gravity system supplied from the Cedar River, filling reservoirs on Beacon, Capitol, and Queen Anne Hills with head or pressure enough to reach the top floors of the tallest anticipated apartment houses.

BELOW: Arthur Churchill Warner's 1891 panorama from Coppin's water tower looks north along Tenth Avenue (later Terry Avenue) to the Ranke house (center). SHS 1018, MOHAI.

Meatpackers and genre art collectors Charles and Emma Frye purchased the Coppin corner, and announced in 1902 that they had hired architects Bebb & Mendel to design their "palatial residence" there.

HIGH HILL CULTURE

The year 1883 marked the beginning of the brief but still splendid era of First Hill as the first retreat for Seattle's upper crust. Escaping from what was rapidly becoming a boomtown of strangers, many of the city's leaders joined to separate their families in often lavish environs of mansion-sized homes and clubs. The old Indian-fighter Colonel Granville Haller and his wife, Henrietta, were among the leaders of this elevation. Morgan and Emily Carkeek soon followed the Hallers. While the English stonemason and contractor built many of the region's most substantial buildings, including the Dexter Horton Bank and the Federal Post Office, his wife became the grande dame of First Hill culture and their towering home at the southeast corner of Madison Street and Boren Avenue its center. A salon for concerts, dress dinners, and card parties, here Emily Carkeek also founded the enduring Seattle Historical Society, which is now the Museum of History & Industry.

ABOVE: The Haller house, 606 Minor Avenue, witnesses the arrival of electricity and awaits street paving in the 1880s. Courtesy Ron Edge.

Other higher-culture institutions settled on the hill as well. The Seattle Tennis Club built courts behind the Stacy Mansion across Madison Street from the Carkeeks. The club held its first invitational tournaments in what is now the parking lot for a McDonald's restaurant. Eventually, the sprawling Stacy mansion at the northeast corner of Madison and Boren was purchased for the University Men's Club. Three blocks north on Boren at University Street, the Sunset Club built its Georgian Revival-style clubhouse. Both clubs still operate in their First Hill quarters. Among those joining the Hallers and Carkeeks were the Lowmans, Hanfords, Burkes, Rankes, Agens, Collinses, Minors, Stimsons, Blethens (briefly before moving to Queen Anne), and many Dennys. "Aunties' Hill" is what Arthur and Mary Denny's granddaughter Sophie Frye Bass called it in her memoir, *When Seattle Was a Village*. Five of the author's aunts lived on the hill at one time, on lots that were part of A. A. Denny's Broadway Addition.

RIGHT: A costume ball at the home of Emily Carkeek, 1914. Special Collections, University of Washington Libraries.

STREET RAILWAYS

Between 1888 and 1891, three street railways were built to cross First Hill (and every other hill or ridge between it and the amusement and recreational parks that were developed on the west shore of Lake Washington). The cable railway along Mill Street (Yesler Way) to Leschi Park was the first. Soon cable cars climbed James and Madison Streets to Broadway. Beyond Broadway they headed east through a patchwork of forests and stump fields, the latter surmounted by real estate signs promoting the convenience of cleared lots placed so close to the tracks. A fourth electric line ran north and south along Broadway connecting the three hills—Capitol, First, and Beacon—topographically three sisters in the same ice-age ridge.

The street railways made First Hill more convenient to everyone. The mix of this new convenience with Seattle's booming growth signaled the end of the Hill's residential exclusivity even as the majority of the 40 or so mansions that defined it were still being planned or constructed. The reality of nearly every other burgeoning American city was fulfilled on First Hill. Its highbrow culture steadily slipped to mid-brow. Business districts prefer modest workers' residences and services near downtown, and First Hill got its share. Madison Street quickly developed as the hill's commercial strip, offering services such as shoe repair, cigars, and confections. In time the diversity of this middle-class culture would itself shrink when hill space, including that facing Madison Street, was increasingly taken over by hospitals and clinics and an ever-stretching Seattle University campus along the hill's eastern border.

FROM HIGH HOMES TO HIGH HOTELS AND PILL HILL

The symbolic first surrender of First Hill's high culture to high-rises came with the sale of Judge Cornelius Hanford's home at the southwest corner of Boren Avenue and Madison Street, at the heart of the hill and facing the Carkeeks. The big Hanford home was razed in 1907 and replaced with the multistory Perry Hotel. Nearby St. James Cathedral was also dedicated that year. The following year the plush Sorrento Hotel was preparing to open to tourists one block west on Madison Street.

The most fortuitous development of 1908 was the founding of Swedish Hospital. Soon another of First Hill's hospitals (eventually there were six) found its place at the old Hanford home site when the Perry Hotel was itself converted into the Columbus/Cabrini Hospital. Whether as hotel or hospital, the Perry was the first

RIGHT: A colored postcard of the Perry (misspelled "Parry") Apartments. Dodge/Kreisman Collection.

of the multistory buildings that now cover much of First Hill real estate. Today, three hospitals—Virginia Mason, Swedish, and Harborview—steer the institutional life of First Hill. In the early 1970s, not counting clinics, there were three more hospitals operating on the hill as well. They were Doctor's, Seattle General, and St. Frances Xavier Cabrini, a presence sufficient to lend the hill its nickname, Pill Hill.

HENRY YESLER'S COUSIN – JAMES LOWMAN: A SURVIVOR

BELOW: The Lowmans, dressed in kimonos, enjoy a tea ceremony with a Japanese screen as backdrop in their First Hill home. Courtesy Michael Maslan.

Of First Hill's homes and their homeowners, Henry Yesler's cousin James Lowman and his 1891 residence at the southeast corner of Boren Avenue and Marion Street may be noted for faithful perseverance, although ultimately not for preservation. The sportsman entrepreneur held on in his home until 1947, when the then 91-year-old pillar of First Hill club life and worldly travels died. James Lowman had lived at his First Hill corner for 56 years. Like much else on First Hill, including the Haller and Carkeek home lots, the Lowman corner is now incorporated into Swedish Medical Center.

The few important remnants of First Hill high culture that survive add enormously to the neighborhood's sometimes tense companionship of commercial, institutional, and residential structures. There are four key residences: the Stacy mansion (University Club); the Hofius house (Connolly House, the Roman Catholic archbishop's residence); the Henry H. Dearborn house (Historic Seattle); and the Stimson-Green mansion (Washington Trust for Historic Preservation). Significant pre-Depression apartment buildings include the San Marco, Gainsborough, Marlborough, and 1223 Spring Street. The Sorrento Hotel and Piedmont Hotel (now Tuscany Apartments) reflect tourist and residential options close to downtown. St. James Cathedral, Trinity Episcopal, and First Baptist churches, Summit School (now The Northwest School), and O'Dea High School reveal the breadth of religious and educational opportunities on the hill.

THERE GOES THE NEIGHBORHOOD

A comparison of the 1912 *Baist's Real Estate Atlas* for First Hill with Google Earth satellite images from the summer of 2013 tells an interesting story. An informal accounting of residential homes (not including apartments or hotels) within somewhat limited parameters reveals the Baist footprints for 1912 to have more than 800 such front room to front yard (or sidewalk) residences on our truncated hill. For the same blocks, Google Earth of 2013 had about 60 such residences. And so went the neighborhood for the most part to institutions and apartments, and with the many tall ones mixed in with the latter, we have more First Hillers now than then.

A SLIPPING HILL

We conclude our Prologue with a confession. We have failed to understand and so explain the role of Skid Road in the development of our book's subject. Rather, we have become skeptics about the early conversion of that Indian path, also known as Mill Street and Yesler Way, into a highway of greased logs for skidding the big timber of First Hill down to Henry and Sarah Yesler's waterfront mill. If this popular story eventually gets its brakes and/or corrections, it will probably be based at least in part on the steadfast work of Greg Lange, the Seattle historian impassioned by Skid Road history. But for now we leave it behind.

The best-known skidding on this hill was of the hill itself: large saturated parts of its blue clay. In 1902 the city put a chain gang to work digging a drainage ditch up Alder Street that was 30 feet deep in places. The *Seattle Daily Times* complimented the gangs of 12, on average, for making "a very good showing for men compelled to work against their will." Ten years later 14 buildings were wrecked on the large knoll above Fifth Avenue when it gave way, slipping toward the bay. During the most manic years of the city's street regrading—from 1903 to 1912—proposals to be rid of the sliding problem by cutting away the crown of Yesler Hill were widely considered. One public work popular in the City Council described cuts as much as 80 feet deep on the "court house district." The proposal also described lowering the steepest 25 percent grades on Yesler Way to a maximum of 10 percent. The forward crown of Yesler Hill was not cut away, of course, although it continued to slide. For instance, considerably more fortification than planned was required for the construction of the Seattle Freeway through the fluid dynamics of the Yesler aka Profanity Hill knoll between James and Main Streets.

Finally we returned to the top of First Hill to raze its Castlemount, that first of the oversized mansions built on the hill in 1883. With the owners' passing, Colonel Haller first in 1897 and his wife, Henrietta, in 1910, the grand home was left in the hands of their son Theodore, then a businessman in his mid-forties preoccupied with the frugal management of his sizable inheritance. In 1917 Theodore, by then a 53-year-old capitalist, married Constance, who was 30 years his junior. Eleven years later the couple was in divorce court. Constance complained that she had to drive a second-hand automobile, wear clothes inferior to her station, and live in a great "ghost house." Judge Ronald concluded, "It was not pleasant for a young woman to be alone in that house day after day with nothing to look forward to but a game of dominoes in the evening. The mansion was once the finest in Seattle, its gingerbread scrollwork highly regarded and its furnishings considered the last word in luxury. But the windows did rattle, its floors were warped and cold. Naturally, Haller didn't notice it—he was used to the house. Mrs. Haller was not." The divorce was granted and the inconstant Constance was awarded a $30,000 settlement. Within two years Theodore was dead. Castlemount was eventually razed, and during World War II, its lot was outfitted with temporary apartments for 40 families, not one unhappy couple.

Sources:
Clarence B. Bagley, *History of Seattle* (Chicago: S. J. Clarke Publishing Co., 1916); Sophie Frye Bass, *When Seattle Was a Village*; Murray Morgan, *Skid Road* (New York: The Viking Press, 1951); Sophie Frye Bass, *Pig-Tail Days in Old Seattle* (Portland, Oregon: Binfords & Mort, Publishers, 1937); Paul Dorpat, *Seattle Now and Then,* Vols. 1, 2, and 3 (Seattle: Tartu Publications); Roger Sale, *Seattle Past to Present* (Seattle: University of Washington Press, 1976); *First Hill: An Inventory of Buildings and Urban Design Resources,* Consultants Folke Nyberg & Victor Steinbrueck (Seattle: Historic Seattle Preservation and Development Authority); Paul Dorpat interviews with Patsy Collins, March 14, 2001, Seattle; Greg Lange, 2013; Stephen Lundgren, 2013; Biographical Pamphlets, University of Washington, Pacific Northwest Collection.

Vanessa
Helder

[C H A P T E R]

THE RESIDENTIAL GOLDEN AGE: 1885-1910

LAWRENCE KREISMAN

IMAGINE YOURSELF AS AN OUT-OF-TOWNER transported back to 1909 Seattle at the time of the Alaska-Yukon-Pacific Exposition. You are comfortably settled in for a week at the newly completed Sorrento Hotel. First Hill is at its peak as the most exclusive neighborhood and home to Seattle's most prominent citizens, among them the contractor Morgan Carkeek, timber man and real estate investor C. D. Stimson, Judge Cornelius Hanford, and successful meatpacker turned art collector Charles Frye.

Tree-lined streets on the crown of First Hill frame homes of distinction in wide-ranging styles, reflecting the architectural evolution fostered by the newfound wealth of its business community. Most sit on quarter-block lots with detached carriage houses and manicured grounds. Closer to Pike Street to the north, Yesler Way to the south, west of Terry Avenue (originally Tenth Avenue), and east of Summit Avenue, more modest single-family housing and multifamily workers' flats have sprung up.

French Empire, Queen Anne, and Eastlake Victorian homes built in the 1880s are interspersed with understated shingled homes that reflect Arts and Crafts ideology and Classical and Colonial Revival homes built with locally harvested Douglas fir and characterized by their low, broad proportions and symmetrical facades. Brick and

ABOVE: Captain and Mrs. S. P. Randolph and daughter Edith enjoy the porch of their home, Rosedale, at 1018 Columbia Street, June 16, 1888. Theodore E. Peiser. 12604, Special Collections, University of Washington Libraries.

BELOW: Horseback riding, First Hill, ca. 1896. Casper Clarke Collection.

RIGHT: The J. B. MacDougall living room (1109 Terry Avenue) show-cases furniture and Oriental carpets reflecting Victorian "good taste." Many of the goods likely came from his MacDougall & Southwick department store. Curtis 5518, Washington State Historical Society.

half-timbered English medieval and Tudor Revival residences join the neighborhood's architectural mix. By the first years of the 20th century, cement stucco homes emulating the increasingly popular Mediterranean and Spanish Mission Revival start to make their appearance as well.

Some of these residences, such as Morgan Carkeek's towered Victorian, are the work of East Coast designers whose plan and pattern books were heavily promoted nationally. Others are by architects from other parts of the country who find Seattle a lucrative place to practice. Spokane's Kirtland Cutter makes valuable contacts in his work for lumberman C. D. Stimson that lead to commissions for the Rainier Club, the Seattle Golf Club in The Highlands, and numerous homes for the well-to-do, including the shingled Arts and Crafts Manson Backus residence.

Charles Bebb, Cutter's local representative for the Stimson residence, finds his success once he sets out in partnership with Louis Mendel. Their residential work on First Hill includes an Elizabethan Revival for O. O. Denny, Classical Revival designs for Dr. George Horton and Clarence Hanford, an American Foursquare for William Perkins, and a substantial home for art collectors Charles and Emma Frye. Henry Dozier designs Henry H. Dearborn's atypical stucco Classical Revival home and several more modest homes and apartments before leaving town.

While the exteriors of these homes vary stylistically, they all participate in some way with the social and cultural life of a community where "going out" is not highly evolved. Domestic life on the hill means carriage houses and chauffeurs, servants, and an "at home" day for visiting, socializing, and planning charitable and cultural works in the community (see Chapter 3).

Theaters and restaurants are still developing down-town, making home life the center for entertainment—teas, lavish dinners, and after-dinner fun. While few can compete with Emily Carkeek's costumed Founders Day parties, the C. D. Stimsons manage to seat 18 guests at their dining table and have a large multipur-pose living room/library/music room/stage where house guests, many of them celebrities from the music world, perform informal con-certs, and friends and family members put on plays. In the basement, the gaming/smoking room and billiard room provide a retreat for the men of First Hill.

This chapter offers a glimpse of the upper crust of First Hill through some of its distinguished buildings and the occupants who resided there from 1880 to 1910.[1] They are generally listed in the order in which they were constructed. With few exceptions (Ward, Stacy, Hofius, Stimson, and Dearborn houses), all have been demolished.

GEORGE W. WARD RESIDENCE, 1025 PIKE STREET/1431 BOREN AVENUE | 1882

George W. Ward, a building contractor who later made money in the real estate, insurance, and loan businesses, built a modest wood-frame Italianate-style residence on Pike Street at Boren Avenue in 1882. The house combined square bay windows,

RIGHT: Ward residence, 1431 Boren Avenue (no date). Lenggenhager, shp_20088, Seattle Public Library.

decorative shingles, brackets, and ornamented window caps in a pleasing asymmetric composition. The focal point was a three-story tower and a wraparound porch with spindle work and brackets below the eaves. Ward resided there until the financial crash of 1893. In 1905, a developer turned the house 90 degrees on the lot and built a hotel next to it. A fire damaged the hotel in 1974, and the property was later donated to Historic Seattle by Dr. and Mrs. Michael Buckley. Historic Seattle helped attorneys David Leen and Bradford Moore relocate their historic structure to its present location on the corner of East Denny Way and Belmont Avenue in order to save it from certain demolition for a new apartment development in 1986.

GUY CARLETON PHINNEY HOUSE, SOUTHEAST CORNER OF MINOR AVENUE AND JAMES STREET | 1883

RIGHT: Elevation view of Guy Phinney residence by Donald MacKay, 1883. Washington State Historical Society.

Entrepreneur Guy Phinney achieved immediate success in property development shortly after his arrival in Seattle in the late 1870s. He commissioned architect Donald MacKay to design a Gothic Revival home called at the time "Carleton Cottage," one of the earliest pretentious residences on the hill. Phinney later purchased and developed Woodland Park as his own country estate and extended a streetcar line to promote its fledgling zoo and gardens. He died before he could begin construction on a much more lavish mansion there.[2] Carleton Cottage was razed to accommodate the Minor & James clinic.

BELOW: Granville Haller residence at 606 Minor Avenue. MOHAI.

COLONEL GRANVILLE HALLER HOUSE, 606 MINOR AVENUE AT JAMES STREET | 1883-85

After his retirement from Army service throughout the West, Colonel Granville Haller and his wife, Henrietta, moved to Seattle, where their eldest son, attorney

Granville Morris Haller, had already established himself in business as one of the organizers of the Seattle, Lake Shore and Eastern Railroad Company. The Colonel's estate, which he called "Castlemount," encompassed the entire block on the northeast corner of James Street and Minor Avenue, approached by a winding drive and sheltered by the surrounding woods. The three-story mansion with a central tower boasted unobstructed views of the city and the Sound, and served as a social gathering place for Seattle's elite. After Haller's son died in 1930, the property was sold, the house razed, and a government housing project was erected in its place.

MORGAN AND EMILY CARKEEK HOUSE, 918 BOREN AVENUE AT MADISON STREET | 1884-85

RIGHT: Guendolen and Theodor Plestcheeff in period dress (including his handlebar moustache) for a "Gay Nineties" party at the Carkeek residence, February 1934, shortly before it was razed. PEMCO Webster & Stevens Collection 1995.71.201, MOHAI.

Contractor Morgan James Carkeek and his wife, Emily, built a mansion on the southeast corner of Madison Street and Boren Avenue soon after the Hallers' arrival. Completed in 1885, the cupola-crowned Victorian contained six bedrooms, with a large fireplace in each; 14-foot-high ceilings; stained glass windows; and a reception hall with a balcony finished in imported mahogany and redwood. Palliser, Palliser & Co., New York, the preeminent publishers of residential plan books in the country at the time, had prepared the plans. *Homes and Gardens of the Pacific Coast 1913* rhapsodized about the residence: "In the early days when a craftsman built his home, he selected the finest of native materials, and hewed and shaped them by hand into a home which for workmanship and durability are seldom equaled in these modern days."

Due largely to Emily's dynamism, her home became the principal social center on First Hill. She instituted such traditions as the Wednesday night Card Club in 1893, Renaissance parties, "At Home Night," and the annual Founders Day celebration, inaugurated in November 1911 to celebrate the 60th anniversary of the 1851 landing at Alki. She was the founder and president of the Seattle Historical Society, which later became the Museum of History & Industry. The last social event, a costume party, was held there in February 1934. The mansion was demolished that year to make way for a "super-service station." The original wrought iron gate was saved and can be seen today guarding the University Club across Madison Street. The Carkeeks' daughter, Guendolen Plestcheeff, took over her mother's interest in the historical society.

BELOW: Morgan and Emily Carkeek residence, 918 Boren Avenue at Madison Street. 1020, MOHAI.

ROME EXPRESS

First Hill neighbor Bertrand Collins penned a novel, *Rome Express*, published by Harper & Brothers in 1928. It revolves around the family of Arthur and Editha Pendrick and their daughter, Gretta Pendrick. There is no doubt that Morgan and Emily Carkeek and their daughter, Guendolen, are the subjects. Collins painted a most unappealing picture of what life in early Seattle must have been like for an educated British woman accustomed to London life:

Editha hated Chinook, hated everything about it—the sag fires of the droning sawmills; the wharves; the whitewashed cottages, meandering dirt streets and wooden sidewalks; the frontier stores— Schwabacher's Hardware Emporium, Baillargeon's Lace House; The Golden Rule Bazaar; The Deadline, and its women with rouged cheeks, and flavor patchouli and Jockey Club; hated the China-men in blue denim, baskets of vegetables swung across their shoulders on wooden yokes; and the Indians in bowler hats and bedroom slippers, or lace pantalettes and Hudson Bay blankets, who would wander into town from their shanties on the tide flats at the south end of the Bay. Hated it all, especially the people, but survived it.

Her first winter in Chinook there was a lynching. She never forgot it, nor the Chinese Riots that followed on its heels. It made no difference to Editha Pendrick that Chinook grew, that gas and water-works were built, that a morning and evening paper appeared, or that horse cars crept up Front Street. To her Chinook was always the last frontier, the place where anything might happen. She saw it reduced to ruins in two hours, the Big Fire that started in Jim McGough's paint shop up on Humptulips Street, and like a phoenix rise out of the ashes. The year after she persuaded her husband to buy a block of land on top of the First Hill.

They built a grand new house—a flamboyant wooden efflorescence with glass, two bathrooms, many porches, and an almost English garden with a lily pond and tennis court. From that stronghold she watched Chinook with more security, and managed to create an illusion of English country life, faint as the projection of an old-fashioned magic lantern, but colorful to satisfy eyes which had never seen but wharves and mills and forests. Her tennis tournaments succeeded the strawberry festivals and buggy-riding of the pre-fire era. Young men in white-duck pants and blazers flirted with young ladies in leg-o'mutton sleeves about her lily pool. Editha Pendrick in those days was the last criterion of what should be . . . and when . . . from Victoria to Portland, Oregon.

T. T. MINOR/JOHN COLLINS RESIDENCE, 702 MINOR AVENUE | 1885

ABOVE: Mrs. John Collins (Angela). Casper Clarke Collection.

RIGHT AND BELOW: Dr. T. T. Minor residence exterior and library engravings were published in *Northwest Magazine* (St. Paul and Minneapolis, May 1886, Vol. IV, no. 5). Courtesy Dennis Andersen.

Thomas T. Minor, a Yale-trained physician, moved to Seattle with his wife, Sarah, from Port Townsend in 1882. He was elected mayor in 1887 and, along with Judge Thomas Burke, established the Seattle, Lake Shore and Eastern Railway. Following the lead of the Hallers and Carkeeks, he built a commodious home in 1885 according to plans by Portland architect John Nestor, with a prominent two-story bay window defining the front parlor and second-floor bedroom. The house was illustrated in souvenir booklets of Seattle. The May 1886 issue of *Northwest Magazine* (St. Paul, MN) included both exterior and interior views of the Minor house—the first published interior view of any Seattle residence.[3] Minor died in a canoe accident in 1889. After the Great Fire of that year, the home was purchased by John and Angela Collins, who had decided to develop their residential property on Second Avenue for the Collins Block, an office building.

John Collins became the city's fourth mayor in 1873, and as a successful businessman, real estate developer, and active participant in the Democratic party, used their home as a social center for a long line of visitors. Angela played hostess, and after her husband's death in 1903, continued to entertain in high style in her famous blue drawing room while raising four children—Edana, John Francis, Edward Bertrand (Bertie), and Catherine.

INTERIOR VIEWS IN DR. T. T. MINOR'S RESIDENCE.

Recollections of her step-granddaughter, Virginia Clarke Younger, paint a fascinating picture of a strong, imposing, brilliant woman who asserted herself, a woman who expected her family and acquaintances to give her the respect and admiration she most assuredly had earned through her good works in the community. By the time of her death in 1947, she had made a significant impact upon Seattle's social scene.[4]

Her son Bertrand—an author whose *Rome Express* (1928) gained notoriety for its thinly disguised fictionalized account of Guendolen Carkeek Plestcheeff and life on First Hill—maintained the house, with its Continental and American antique furniture and crystal chandeliers, filling it with his own collection of Asian antiques.

As Elise Kelleher wrote in the Women's News-Amusement section of the *Seattle Sunday Times* on November 1951, "Seattlites didn't give up their old homes and ways of living without one last sentimental tribute to the past. Just this year, Bertrand Collins gave a farewell party at the home of his late parents, Mr. and Mrs. John Collins, before the fine old Minor Avenue residence was broken up." He died in 1964.

SEATTLE.—RESIDENCE OF DR. T. T. MINOR.

STACY MANSION (MEN'S UNIVERSITY CLUB), 1004 BOREN AVENUE | 1889

For all their wealth, the Stacys never seemed to find a place to nest for very long—at least not together. Lumber and real estate man Martin Van Buren Stacy and his wife, Elizabeth, saw to the construction of an ornate French-styled mansion on Third Avenue and Marion Street in 1885, but they continued to occupy quarters at Second Avenue and Columbia Street for several years before moving in, and they never completely furnished it. Instead, they built another house at the urging of Elizabeth to be closer to her dear friend Emily Carkeek. In 1889, they moved into their new Queen Anne style residence directly across Madison Street from the Carkeeks. To be more precise, Elizabeth moved in. The couple appear to have had an estranged relationship from the beginning and rarely occupied the same premises. Two years later, in 1891, Mr. Stacy began living by himself in a series of downtown hotels.

By 1891, even Elizabeth had moved—she had built a house for herself at 1016 Boren Avenue and another at 1111 Spring Street for her best friend, Mrs. Addie Burns, the wife of Captain Burns. In 1901, the Stacy Mansion, which had been rented for several years, was sold to Lyman Colt, who in turn sold it to the Seattle Men's University Club. By 1902, the club had nearly doubled the size of the house with a major expansion extending to the property edge on Madison Street (see Chapter 3).

BELOW: Stacy house (left) and Carkeek house (right) face each other across Madison Street. Special Collections, University of Washington Libraries.

OTTO AND DORA RANKE HOUSE, 916 TERRY AVENUE | 1890-91

Otto Ranke was one of the leading contractors in Seattle, maintaining a brickyard south of town. He was also well known as a tenor who performed in local productions of Gilbert and Sullivan, while his wife, Dora, danced. Their first home was a simple two-story Italianate on the northwest corner of Fifth Avenue and Pike Street. With their financial success—and what better way than to be a contractor and brickyard owner after the Great Seattle Fire of 1889—and Dora's burgeoning social outreach, they decided that a larger house was called for. Ranke commissioned local architect Elmer Fisher for plans.

Fisher was best known for designing some of Seattle's most distinguished late-19th-century commercial blocks, such as the Austin Bell Building, Pioneer Building, and Burke Building, the architectural vocabulary of which bridged Victorian and Romanesque stylistic elements into unified compositions with great street presence. He did very few private residences; the Ranke mansion would be his largest and most

ABOVE: Ranke residence, 916 Terry Avenue, during Moritz Thomsen ownership. Curtis 2828, Washington State Historical Society.

imposing residential work—a Queen Anne–style Victorian with a slate roof (reputed to be the first in the city). It featured gabled bays, a two-story covered entrance porch, and a three-story tower at the corner of Madison Street and Tenth Avenue (later Terry). And he did it using the materials he knew best—brick and stone—instead of wood and sawn millwork. Huge stone slabs were laid under each window, and enormous stones were placed in a semicircle above the stained glass window on the left of the porch.

The interior reflected prevailing taste—Oriental carpets, a moose head hung on a wall, a library filled with bookcases and wrought-iron hinges, stained glass windows, and rockers and upholstered chairs, statues, and oil paintings in the living room. The home had a circular conservatory on the first landing, seven bedrooms on the second floor, three on the third floor, and a billiard room.

Ranke died in 1892 and the family remained in the house until 1901, when it was sold to Moritz Thomsen, who resided there for the next 24 years.[5] Thomsen came to Seattle in 1897 and formed the Centennial Mill Co., of which he was president. He also served as president of the Seattle Grain Co. and the Denny-Renton Clay & Coal Co. and was a member of the Masonic Fraternity.[6] Thomsen sold the Ranke house to the Missionary Sisters of the Sacred Heart in 1925. Later, it housed student nurses training at Columbus Hospital, which was run by the sisters.

RIGHT: Beautifully carved and paneled woodwork and bold wallpapers greet visitors to the Ranke residence stair hall. SHS 9418, MOHAI.

LOWMAN HOUSE, 820 BOREN AVENUE AT MARION STREET | 1891

Mary and James D. Lowman built their house one block south of the Carkeeks. Lowman came to Seattle in 1877, at the age of 20, and began his career as assistant wharf master on Yesler's wharf. Four years later, he purchased one-half interest in a bookstore of W. H. Pumphrey, and over the years, he broadened and incorporated the business as the Lowman & Hanford Stationery and Printing Company. Lowman served as its president and principal stockholder.[7]

RIGHT: Lowman residence at Marion Street and Boren Avenue, July 1894. Courtesy Michael Maslan.

James and Mary planned their home themselves and had it built by day labor, thus saving $4,000 on its cost. The three-story frame and shingled home in the English style was understated on the outside, in marked contrast to some of the more palatial homes that started filling the hill. By 1913, *Homes and Gardens* referred to its aged state, covered with trailing vines, and managed to grudgingly muster, "While the architecture is different to that of homes of later date, the house is cosy [*sic*], comfortable and homelike."

BELOW: Lowman family members enjoy a musical moment in the stair hall, with its ornate carved newel posts. Courtesy Michael Maslan.

In the *Seattle Daily Times* in 1944, Margaret Pitcairn Strachan provided a glimpse of the interior, with its massive doorway, a vestibule with carved paneled doors designed by Mary Lowman, and woodwork throughout of polished cedar, inviting fireplaces—seven of them—and oil paintings by Mary. Large windows in the dining room look upon the garden and lawn.

According to Paul Dorpat, "Long after the Carkeeks, Rankes, Stacys and most other First Hill families had moved on and surrendered this neighborhood to apartments and hospitals, the Lowmans held on. Mary died in 1939, and James in 1947."[8] (See Chapter 4).

JUDGE THOMAS BURKE HOUSE, 1004 BOYLSTON AVENUE AT MADISON STREET | 1892

Thomas Burke's home was designed by architects William Boone and William Willcox in 1891 and built for Judge Julius A. Stratton, who came to Seattle in 1888 and moved to First Hill in 1892. It was described in the *Seattle Daily Times* as "Italian in style, quite a new departure in Seattle architecture, which has rather given itself over to the Queen Anne craze."[9]

RIGHT: Mrs. Burke in her carriage, with residence behind her. Curtis 2847, Washington State Historical Society.

Thomas Burke—attorney, judge, transportation promoter, and businessman—was responsible for establishing the city's horse-drawn and later electric streetcar lines and for bringing the Great Northern Railway to Seattle. He married Caroline E. McGilvra, who shared his civic and cultural interests. Both of them had concerns about the decline of the Native American population and collected and displayed Native American art in their Lake Washington home, Illahee, and in the home he purchased from Judge Stratton in the mid 1890s. (The Burke collection of Native American art later became the heart of a collection housed in the Burke Museum on the University of Washington campus.)

Homes and Gardens of the Pacific Coast concluded that the Burkes' First Hill home was "somewhat along the lines of the mission style, the interior being more after the colonial in effect." In truth, it was a house that freely combined elements of various building styles. The two-story house was roofed in tile and framed by three-story-high tiled wings with open loggias at the top floors and Palladian window treatments on the second floor. An enclosed porch with a band of windows extended above the entrance. Inside, the stair hall had white enameled paneled woodwork and a colonial stairway, and the living room had Ionic capitals framing the fireplace and as room dividers.

BELOW: Kirtland Cutter designed a gallery wing for the Burkes' Native American collections. Curtis 8956, Washington State Historical Society.

Kirtland Cutter designed a north museum wing for the Burkes' expanding collection of Native American objects. It was rustic, about 25 feet in height with timber trusses, a balcony, a large fireplace at one end, a copper teepee hooded fireplace on the opposite brick end wall, and ledges for display of baskets.

Burke died in 1925 and his wife in 1932. In 1940, Charles Olmstead purchased the property and replaced the house with a streamlined modern office building for the Opticians' Guild, which did prescription work for the doctors in the expanding medical center.

ALFRED H. AND AGNES (HEALY) ANDERSON RESIDENCE, 718 MINOR AVENUE | 1897

ABOVE: Mrs. Anderson is helped into her carriage at the Frederick & Nelson department store. Courtesy Paul Dorpat.

Lumber baron Alfred H. Anderson built his home on Minor Avenue at Columbia Street in 1897. The wood-frame house, designed by James Stephen, who later became the architect for the Seattle School District, featured decorative woodwork. A large carriage house at the rear of the property, facing Summit Avenue, housed Agnes Anderson's horses and carriages. The coachman and family resided in the carriage house's second floor. In 1935, when the City of Seattle decreed that horse-drawn vehicles would not be permitted on downtown streets, Mrs. Anderson was reluctantly forced to give up a way of life she had enjoyed long after her neighbors had done so. She replaced her team with a Rolls-Royce automobile. The British manufacturer had a policy against delivering its luxury cars to any area that did not have a factory-trained Rolls-Royce mechanic nearby. Not to be discouraged, Mrs. Anderson ordered a mechanic too and guaranteed to provide him with a home and complete auto-repair shop.

JOHN B. AGEN RESIDENCE, 1321 SENECA STREET AT BOYLSTON AVENUE | CA. 1900

John Agen arrived in Seattle days after the 1889 fire and established a wholesale dairy business. He started the Mount Vernon Milk Company and owned properties in Mt. Vernon and Ferndale that supported production of butter, cheese, and eggs. Soon he began exporting condensed milk to the Far East and Alaska, his business profiting from the 1897 Klondike Gold Rush, which enabled him to open branch stores in Alaska. His warehouse on Railroad Avenue connected directly to Pier 6 (now Pier 57) at the foot of University Street. Later he sold his milk business to the Carnation Company. About 1900, he moved his wife, Frances Ryan, and family into a First Hill home that was the epitome of Victorian Queen Anne-style taste, with a conical corner tower and wrap-around veranda. Three children grew up here.

BELOW: The southwest corner of Boylston Avenue and Seneca Street showcased the Agen residence's conical tower with decorative shingles and arched turret windows. Courtesy Patricia Baillargeon.

By 1915, the Agens had hired architect Carl Gould to design a new home on 10 acres just south of The Highlands. They sold the adjoining 10 acres to longtime friend Arthur Dunn (another First Hill neighbor), and they hired the Olmsted Brothers to design gardens for both. First Hill connections also led to nuptials. In 1923 their daughter Katherine married Cebert Baillargeon, the son of J. A. Baillargeon, a prosperous dry-goods merchant, and Abby Collins Baillargeon, daughter of John Collins. The Collins family lived on First Hill, and the Baillargeons and the Agens had been integral to the construction of St. James Cathedral. In fact, the building committee held its first meeting in the dining room of the Agen home. Katherine played an important role in many social and civic causes, including the founding of the Seattle Art Museum and support for the Seattle Symphony, and as a trustee of Seattle General Hospital. During World War II she was active in French war relief.

For a time, the Agen house fared better than some of its neighbors, razed or turned into rooming houses. It was sold to a car dealership for their Motor Car Dealership Club in 1919.

C. D. STIMSON RESIDENCE, 1204 MINOR AVENUE | 1899-1901

Lumberman C. D. Stimson had lived at First Avenue North and Ward Street, on lower Queen Anne Hill north of the downtown area, since 1888. While not modest, this house probably seemed crowded with the birth of a daughter, Dorothy Frances, in 1892. More important, by 1898, Stimson had done quite well with the mill business. He had been helped by the 1889 fire, the Yukon Gold Rush, the influx of many new families to the area, and the resulting platting and sale of home lots throughout the city. The substantial homes of Seattle's first families could not have escaped his eye, nor would he have wanted anything less than he could afford for his wife and children. He saw First Hill as a suitable site for the new family home.

For C. D. Stimson—as he had for Spokane's A. B. Campbell and other notable clients—Kirtland Cutter chose a half-timbered style that harkened back to medieval England. His house design incorporated hand-adzed timbers, sawn decorative barge-boards, and mock rafter ends. Cutter's English design, while gaining considerable popularity elsewhere in the country by 1898, was just beginning to make its appearance on the West Coast.

Cutter was also responsible for the complete decoration of the 10,000-square-foot interior, from wall colors, fabrics, and furniture down to the most minute finish

BELOW: The C. D. Stimson residence and carriage house on Minor Avenue, 1901. Dodge/Kreisman Collection.

ABOVE: The C. D. Stimson residence dining room features sycamore panels and box beams, blue tile fireplace surround, and painted frieze. Dodge/Kreisman Collection.

details. Rooms took inspiration from British, French, Middle Eastern, and Native American sources. Visitors entered the pointed arched doorway into the Romanesque hall. Columnettes with carved capitals supported a Roman barrel vault decorated with hand-painted red and gold canvas. Stairs led into the main hall and dining room. Furnishings were all in Flemish Gothic carved oak.

The main living room functioned as a library and a performance stage. It bore the characteristic dark oak and Gothic carvings of an English manor house, and was dominated by a huge hearth supported with hand-carved lions. With its magnificent copper and steel dragon andirons, it was truly a room with the qualities of a private men's club.

By contrast, to the left of the entry was a light-colored, delicately plastered Neoclassical parlor with Empire period–style fireplace and furniture where Mrs. Stimson could receive her friends and serve tea on Thursday afternoons, when she was "at home" to callers.

In the English Tudor dining room with sycamore paneling, scenes of medieval court life were painted on corduroy above the wainscoting. A blue glass tiled fireplace with carved leaf and vine mantel and handsome brass sconces was the focal point of the room.

While the principal entertaining rooms were drawn from Western European traditions, the Middle East did not go unnoticed. The most exotic space in the house was the den in the basement. It had been inspired by the predilection during that era for Moorish smoking rooms where the men could retreat after dinner to play cards, drink brandy, and discuss the latest business deal. Its brass-filigree mosque lanterns, teakwood taboret, Oriental carpets, and the choice of saturated colors and patterns for fabrics and wall coverings captured the flavor of the "casbah." Adjoining the gaming room was the one room that acknowledged American heritage—a billiard room with American Indian motif wallpapers.[10]

With the development of the Seattle Golf Club in The Highlands, Stimson had Kirtland Cutter design a much larger estate on bluff property overlooking Puget Sound, and the family moved there in 1914. Joshua Green purchased the First Hill mansion in 1915. He was a significant force in Puget Sound shipping who later took charge of Peoples Savings Bank. When the Greens passed away, the house was purchased by Historic Seattle and resold with protective covenants. Priscilla Bullitt Collins, granddaughter of C. D. Stimson, purchased the home in 1986 and gifted it to the Washington Trust for Historic Preservation in 2001.

KELLEHER HOUSE, 1116 SPRING STREET | 1900

The Kelleher house was built at the turn of the century across Spring Street from the Seattle Tennis Club courts. The understated shingle residence designed by Charles Bebb was featured in the February 1902 issue of *The House Beautiful* magazine.

Daniel J. Kelleher was born in 1864 in Middleboro, Massachusetts, and graduated from Harvard in 1885. In March 1890, he moved to Seattle and entered into a law partnership with Judge George Meade Emory under the firm name Kelleher & Emory. Several years later, in 1894, he married Elise C. Meem, the only daughter of Gilbert S. Meem of Seattle, who had been an officer in the Confederate army, a member of the Virginia House of Delegates, and a state senator.

For several years, Kelleher divided his time between banking and law. In September 1914, he retired from the law practice to devote his time to the Seattle National Bank as chairman of the board of directors. During his tenure, it grew to become the largest bank in the state (later renamed SeaFirst Bank). He was also president of the Riverside Timber Co., which had large timberland holdings throughout the state.[11] Daniel Kelleher passed away in 1929.

RIGHT: Mrs. Daniel (Elise) Kelleher and her dog in the reception room of her home on Minor Avenue and Spring Street. Courtesy Raleigh Watts.

In later years, the residence housed medical offices and then became a rooming house. By the 1970s, it had fallen into disrepair and was considered an eyesore by many of the area's residents. By 1978, the five tenants were evicted to make way for the construction of Kelleher House Condominums.

JOSIAH COLLINS HOUSE, MINOR AVENUE AT UNIVERSITY STREET | 1901

RIGHT: Josiah Collins's residence was one of the most purposely modest Bebb & Mendel–designed homes in the neighborhood. From *Seattle Architecturally, 1902*, a thinly disguised advertising piece for the architectural firm.

The dawn of a new century saw the introduction of a new kind of house to the Pacific Northwest. Surrounded by its older, elaborately decorated Queen Anne Victorian and Classical Revival neighbors on First Hill, the shake-and-shingle home of Josiah Collins by the newly formed partnership of Bebb & Mendel stirred discussion. It was an early instance of the entry of the Arts and Crafts into Seattle society. The *Real Estate and Building Review* of the *Seattle Daily Times* considered it worthy of coverage on July 20, 1901:

> *One of the most artistic residences in Seattle is that of Josiah Collins . . . The general design of the house, which is almost perfect on its detail, is greatly strengthened by its color scheme. The shingle roof is stained a moss green, while the walls are a silver gray giving the whole the appearance of an old house that had been beaten into harmony by the nature artist with the strong tools of sun and storm. A goodly porch eight feet wide which runs the full length of the house looks as if it were made to be enjoyed. The chimney of cobble stones serves to clinch the rusticity which of course is the key to the whole design.*

W. D. HOFIUS HOUSE, 1104 SPRING STREET | 1902

ABOVE: Red Roman brick, cream terra-cotta, and copper fittings make a colorful statement on its prominent corner. Historic Seattle.

RIGHT: Interior of Hofius House. A colonnade with spiral columns separates the living room from the stair hall and entrance foyer. Curtis 5519, Washington State Historical Society.

ABOVE: Art Nouveau stained-glass windows add pattern and color to the Hofius residence entrance, stairway, and bathrooms. Historic Seattle.

William D. Hofius was an owner-operator of various steel-making operations in New York, Pennsylvania, and Ohio before coming to Seattle in the late 1880s. He formed a partnership with William Pigott and in 1893 organized the firm W. D. Hofius &

Co., which handled railroad equipment and supplies. This was the predecessor to the Hofius Steel and Equipment Co., furnishing the steel for many Seattle buildings. He remained at the head of this business until his death in 1912. Hofius was also president of Seattle Dock Company, director of the Superior Portland Cement Company, and director of the First National Bank of Seattle.

He commissioned architect A. Walter Spalding to design his First Hill residence, prominently sited on the corner of Boren Avenue and Spring Street. The exterior featured finely laid brickwork, copper roof and dormers, and Venetian Gothic terra-cotta entrance porch and veranda. Corinthian columns terminating in curvilinear pointed (ogee) arches supported the flat-roofed portico. The ornamental elements of the exterior were restated as decorative themes throughout the interior, which illustrated a stylistic mix of Greco-Roman, Moorish/Venetian Gothic, and Art Nouveau.

The entrance vestibule featured a mosaic tile floor and Art Nouveau stained glass windows. The main hall was finished in Honduran mahogany woodwork and dominated by a Moorish-inspired ogee-arched fireplace of variegated green Italian onyx. The Moorish influence was carried through in the heavily carved cornices and ceiling panels.

Carved mahogany Gothic-style screens separated the large reception room from the window bay rear parlor. The mahogany stair leading to the second floor was illuminated with stained and leaded Art Nouveau windows.

After Hofius's death, the house was sold to Thomas Green, who in turn sold it to Moses Prager. The Corporation of the Catholic Diocese of Seattle acquired the property from Prager and his wife, Fannie, in September 1920, and presented it to Bishop Edward O'Dea upon his return from Rome. It has served as residence for four Seattle Ordinaries. Renamed "Connolly House" after Seattle's first archbishop, it retains some of its original building features.[12]

DR. GEORGE HORTON HOUSE, 1107 SENECA STREET | 1902

ABOVE: Dr. George Horton's residence at Boren Avenue and Seneca Street shares a similar form and architectural aesthetic to Bebb & Mendel's house for Charles and Emma Frye at Ninth Avenue and Columbia Street. Curtis 5481, Washington State Historical Society.

Born in Illinois in 1865, George Horton received his medical training at Bellevue Hospital Medical College in New York City in 1890. He settled in Seattle, eventually setting up his practice at the newly built Cobb Building, which opened in 1910 to provide space for the medical and dental professions.

His First Hill residence was a two-and-a-half-story frame Classical Revival designed by Bebb & Mendel, featuring a spacious walled terrace set back and above the sidewalk. The American Foursquare home was symmetrical, the central staircase leading to a generous covered porch supported by multiple grouped columns. Ionic capital pilasters formed the corners of the house, and the Ionic order was repeated in the front top floor pedimented windows. A balustrade wrapped around the parapet, and there was a well-balanced porte cochere.

In later years, the Horton property became a rooming house. Seattle University alumni recalled it as the location of some raucous parties that raised the ire of the archbishop living in the former Hofius home to the south. The Horton house was razed for a streamlined modern medical office building, which was later replaced by the Parkview Plaza condominium tower.

CLARENCE HANFORD HOUSE, 1103 SUMMIT AVENUE | 1902

The substantial home of Clarence Hanford presented a palatial face to the street, with a monumental two-story portico supported with Corinthian columns and pilasters framing the entranceway and a balcony at the second floor. A one-story side entrance echoed the front treatment. The building was crowned with a wrap-around balustrade that partially blocked views of the gabled third floor. In their frequently ambiguous language, seeming to say much when in fact revealing very little, *Homes and Gardens of the Pacific Coast* praised the work of Bebb & Mendel for its appropriate style:

There is no type of architecture which the American people more admire and none that is more appropriate for them to use than the colonial, for while many of its details are of classic mould, the result in the main is distinctly American. Mr. Hanford's home follows the true letter and spirit of the colonial builders, and an attention to appropriate completeness is apparent throughout.

M. F. BACKUS HOUSE, 1110 UNIVERSITY STREET | 1907-8

BELOW: The Manson Backus residence is as new as the streets and sidewalks themselves. Curtis 5913, Washington State Historical Society.

Carl Nuese, one of Kirtland Cutter's most talented draftsmen, responded to Manson Franklin Backus's commission with a non-symmetrical Arts and Crafts home with varied gables that took advantage of its location and view, having several bay windows facing the west, and a semi-round arched loggia to provide protected upstairs porch space. By 1926 the Backuses had moved to The Highlands.

DEARBORN HOUSE, 1117 MINOR AVENUE | 1907

The residence at the southwest corner of Minor Avenue and Seneca Street was built for Henry H. Dearborn in 1907 at a cost of $15,000. An East Coast banker, Henry moved to Seattle to join his brothers George and Leonard in H.H. Dearborn & Co., a real estate development firm established in 1886-1887. He played an instrumental role in the city's early growth as a promoter of the Northern Pacific Railway. He invested heavily in tidelands on the southern waterfront, which earned him the title "tideland king." It is said that he and his brothers suggested the angle at which the Seattle piers were built.

Dearborn chose architect Henry Dozier to design a modified Classical-style residence. The well-proportioned building had a cement stucco exterior and metal roof with upturned ends. Its design was so unusual at the time in Seattle that the local press called it "Spanish Japanese" in their attempts to find some architectural precedent. In fact, what they surmised were pagoda-like edge flourishes were Greco-Roman palmettes. And the stucco had nothing to do with the Spanish Colonial style and more to do with making the house look as though it was built with more expensive sandstone. There were front and south side porches supported by fluted Doric columns, dentil courses, beveled glass, and scrolled wood brackets. The Classical elements were used inside as well, in the white oak fireplace surround in the living room, the Ionic order mahogany columns framing pocket doors, and the dentil molding and trim in the dining room. Floral and geometric colored and leaded glass windows in the then popular Prairie style embellished the curved north bay staircase and four sets of French doors that led to terraces above the first-floor porches.

ABOVE: H. H. Dearborn House (1907).

Henry Dearborn died in 1909, and his daughter sold the home in 1912 to Mrs. Ranke, who was downsizing to this house from her Elmer Fisher–designed residence nearby. She had the porches enclosed with glass and added a corner wrap-around as well to create usable sunrooms all year round. She also relocated the central stair to

RIGHT: The Barber Asphalt Paving Company promoted its work by showing off First Hill streets, such as the corner of Seneca Street and Minor Avenue.

provide for more entertainment space on the main floor and divided the top-floor dance room into additional bedroom space.

A private home into the 1950s, the house was purchased by opthalmologist Robert Laughlin, who hired J. Lister Holmes to modify the house for his office—steps that removed oak paneling and hearth in the living room in order to make it Colonial Revival. In 1985, a cosmetic surgeon converted the carriage house at the rear into a surgery, removing original windows and doors. Historic Seattle purchased the building in 1997 for its offices and has undertaken restoration and system upgrades.

FREDERICK STRUVE RESIDENCE, 1221 MINOR AVENUE | 1907

BELOW: The Struve drawing room was lavishly furnished in the French style for entertaining in the height of fashion, as featured in *Homes and Gardens of the Pacific Coast*, 1913.

Two Views of Drawing-Room in the Residence of Mr. and Mrs. Frederick Karl Struve

"Few homes on the continent where a thousand years of culture and art have made elegance among the wealthy imperative, are better in design and artistic effect than the rooms in the home of Mr. and Mrs. Struve in Seattle," raved the author of *Homes and Gardens of the Pacific Coast*, in 1913.

The drawing room has been carried out completely in the style of Louis the XV and is probably as perfect an example of this period as any to be found in the country. The furniture, as well as some of the wall decorations, are from [an] old chateau near Paris, secured from the descendents of old Bourbon families. The rugs are Aubusson made especially for these rooms and match in coloring and symbolism the other furnishings. The dining room is finished completely with old Italian pieces brought from Florence. The library is done entirely in old English. Nothing in the rooms anywhere but has the mark of individual design, and an artistic execution.

The author gave the Colonial Revival residence a double spread showing the dining room and library, with two views of the drawing room. No doubt it was the Struves who were trendsetters, demonstrating by the interior design of their First Hill home what was appropriate to aspire to as one made one's mark on high society. The home was demolished in 1958 for Sutton Place, a tile-faced apartment building that quickly earned the nickname "the purple palace."

END OF THE GOLDEN AGE

First Hill's "Golden Age" was short-lived. As the crest of First Hill began its shift from an exclusive residential enclave to denser apartment buildings and medical services, many of its first families sold their homes and moved to less congested, more desirable neighborhoods developing outside the city's center—north Capitol Hill, Washington Park, Mt. Baker, Broadmoor, Medina across Lake Washington, or The Highlands—which offered more land for gardening and entertaining.

RIGHT: Photographer James Lee recorded this two-story residence at the northwest corner of Eighth Avenue and Marion Street in 1911, with a new four-story apartment building behind it. Lee 642, Special Collections, University of Washington Libraries.

ABOVE: By 1911, when this picture was taken, the simple 1890-era residence at 906 Seventh Avenue was already being overshadowed by apartment buildings. James Lee 630, Special Collections, University of Washington Libraries.

Older apartment buildings and construction activity along the hill's periphery brought an influx of middle- and working-class residents from other parts of the country and abroad. They also provided affordable housing and studio space for artists, writers, and performers who appeared in the many live entertainment venues downtown.

Leonard Saari arrived in Seattle with his mother in 1931, during the Great Depression. They lived in a one-room unit with toilet down the hall on Spruce Street (the Amon Apartments) until he graduated from Broadway High School in 1939. His memory of First Hill was bittersweet:

I was not aware of our poverty until I reached adulthood. Somehow the lack of money or even physical comforts never really penetrated my small world. My friends on First Hill were as poor as I, so there was no basis for comparison. Besides, we were too occupied with being boys to concern ourselves about life outside our circle. My friends were a mixture of kids from Finnish, English, Japanese, Chinese, and African-American and Filipino families. Our pleasures were the usual ones boys pursue. Playing softball with a really ragged ball on an empty basketball lot just west of Harborview Hospital . . . a real source of fun was roller-skate hockey on a one-block stretch of smoothly paved street just east of Harborview.

An ancient building with a meeting hall on the second floor occupied a lot near the intersection of Broadway and Yesler, with Ninth Avenue emerging close by. The Finnish Veljesseura [Finnish Society] met there. We saw plays written in Finnish and cast with amateurs. On Saturday night the place rocked to the stomping feet of schottische and polka dancers. Waltzes provided quieter interludes. Little people like me ran around laughing and playing tag. I think that's where my mother met Charlie. (Historic Seattle interview, 1999.)

While some of the large houses were razed in the 1930s and 1940s, others continued to serve different populations. Some owners kept income flowing in by operating rooming houses or boarding establishments or by selling to doctors and medical services for use as offices. However, as property value increasingly lay in the land as opposed to the structure, owners were less interested in maintaining these "white elephants" because of their costly upkeep. They had outlived their usefulness.

GREENWICH VILLAGE OF SEATTLE

Noted photographer Imogen Cunningham and her husband, Roi Partridge, lived on First Hill in a boarding house on Terry Avenue in the 1910s. Residents of the house were later evicted and the property was razed for the Virginia Mason clinic. "In Art Circles" by Madge Bailey, a *Seattle Post-Intelligencer* article from the early 1920s, referred to this small enclave of First Hill as Seattle's Greenwich Village.[13]

Seattle has its own "Greenwich Village"—just a tiny spot at present, shadowed on either side by modern buildings proudly dominating scenic sites on the First Hill. It occupies less than a half block, with frontage on Seneca Street and Terry Avenue. Ambrose Patterson's studio is at the corner and the former home of Roy [sic] Partridge and Immogene [sic] Cunningham snuggles picturesquely among the trees at the side. The place recalls to our memory the names of John Butler and the Tanakas now following

successful art careers in Paris. It was here that the creative talent of Mrs. Singerman, whose miniatures have won repeated honors throughout the country, was encouraged through the instructions of Tanaka, and where Mabel Lisle, whose hand-wrought jewelry is a distinctive feature of the Arts and Crafts exhibit, posed for "The Black Lily," a canvas insured at a valuation of three figures. But it is particularly interesting to us today because a water color painting of the old garden as seen through his studio door has won honors for Ambrose Patterson at the international Exhibition of Water Colors at the Chicago Art institute. This picture is called "My Garden" and will be sent with the touring exhibit through the United States this summer.

LEFT: Imogen Cunningham evokes the rural nature of her small residence on Terry Avenue, ca. 1910. The title is alternately referred to as "In Moonlight" and "In Sunlight." The Imogen Cunningham Trust.

[CHAPTER]

SOCIAL AND CULTURAL LIFE

LUCI J. BAKER JOHNSON

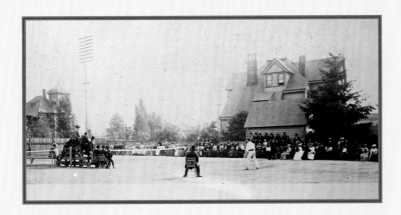

SOCIETY LIFE ON FIRST HILL

IN THE 1890S AND EARLY 1900S, Seattle society life was on an upward swing. In 1888, six Seattle civic leaders had organized The Rainier Club, an exclusive private gentlemen's club in the James McNaught mansion on Fourth Avenue. It offered members "a place away from the office and public rooms of restaurants and hotels where political and business leaders could breakfast or lunch, play cards or billiards, and discuss new ideas, opportunities, or collaborations."[14] From the days of pioneer settlement, Washington women had defied the Victorian dictum that "woman's place is in the home" and formed their own clubs. Suffragist Carrie Chapman Catt and several others founded the Woman's Century Club in 1891. Their 1893 club history explained, "Its need was felt in the sordid atmosphere of a rapidly developing western city."[15]

The first *Social Blue Book of Seattle*, published in 1894, listed acceptable guests whom the "old guard" and "new elite" could invite to social functions: the perfect mix of family, friends, and society members for an afternoon tea, card party, birthday celebration, dance, musical performance, or lecture. The 1904 *Blue Book* listed 1,030

society members and 24 clubs, with each club's date of organization and roster of officers and members.

Newspaper society pages described club and association meetings, as well as events about town. Indeed, ceremonies of Society garnered more space than the proceedings of Congress. Daily papers included *The Seattle Daily Times*, the *Seattle Post-Intelligencer*, *The Seattle Star* (Scripps-Howard tabloid), and the *Seattle Mail & Herald*. Weeklies included *The Town Crier*, devoted largely to social doings, *The Argus*, published on Saturdays by H. A. Chadwick, and *The Week-End*, launched in 1906. Society sections boosted upcoming parties and provided lavish descriptions of weddings, cotillions, and celebrations: the decorations, dresses worn by guests, and tidbits of society news. An October 1905 *Seattle Sunday Times* article with the head-line "Women's Clubs Are Beginning Work for This Year" featured portraits of 14 society women, followed by each club's detailed plans for the coming year.

The *Social Register of Seattle* listed "full names and addresses of members of prominent families grouped together, the clubs to which they belong, and the marriage and death of each person as it may occur." By 1912, the annual list had expanded to include the spouse's first name, names of adult children, and the household's phone number. The *Register* listed 125 families living on First Hill, both in personal residences and in residential hotels such as the Hotel Terry, Sorrento Hotel, and University Club.

ENTERTAINING GUESTS AT HOME

ABOVE: Stained glass window from demolished Carkeek residence. First Hill display, 1101 Madison Street.

The *Social Register* and the *Blue Book* also revealed customs that influenced First Hill residents' social lives. In the 1917-18 *Blue Book*, in small type under a woman's name was the day of the week she stayed home to receive friends. The phrase "at home" was viewed as a noun. Typically each neighborhood (Queen Anne, Capitol Hill, West Seattle, etc.) selected a different day of the week. For residents of First Hill, that day was Thursday.

"At home" references also carried over into the newspapers. The *Seattle Daily Times* of January 24, 1915, reported that "Mrs. William Biglow has issued invitation for an at home to be given Thursday afternoon at her residence on Summit Avenue." A few days later, on January 29, the newspaper reported the event:

> One of the largest and most attractive affairs of the week was the "at home" given yesterday afternoon by Mrs. William Biglow at her residence on Summit Ave. It was in the nature of a farewell, for Mr. and Mrs. Biglow leave soon for an extended trip east and south. The rooms were fragrant and beautiful with quantities of pink roses, freesias and spring flowers, jonquils predominating. The tea table and dining room were exquisite with baskets of orchids and prim-roses . . . During the afternoon several delightful solos were given by Mr. Theo Karl Johnson. About 250 invitations were issued for the affair.

RIGHT: Mrs. John Collins, in black dress (center), hosts a garden party at her Minor Avenue residence. Guests included Italian ambassador Prince Gelasio Caetani, Mrs. George Donworth, University of Washington President Henry Suzzallo, and Judge George Donworth. Casper Clarke Collection.

Not all "at homes" were so lavish, and the custom could be suspended. In February 1916, the *Seattle Daily Times* reported, "At Home Discontinued: Madam Bogolavlensky [a First Hill resident], wife of the Russian Consul-General, announces she will discontinue her evenings at home until after the Lenten season."

SEATTLE SOCIETY LIFE AFTER WORLD WAR I

At-home entertaining continued until about the time of World War I. The outbreak of war had a significant impact on all Seattle residents. Social and club activities shifted to support the war effort, especially soldiers and their families.

On August 8, 1918, a *Seattle Sunday Times* column quoted Mrs. F. K. Struve as saying Seattle women could never go back to the old ways. "Judging by my own feelings," she said, "they will want to do good, in some way. There will be lots of Red Cross work to finish, charitable organizations to assist and many other necessary occupations . . . There is an exhilaration about work that fascinates me. When the war is over I would like a day or so to myself, just to look after my home. Otherwise, I would like to continue with some needful occupation."

Social life on First Hill would never be the same again.

CLUBS AND ASSOCIATIONS

The high life on First Hill began about 1890, and continued through about 1915. Many prominent clubs and associations that took up residence on First Hill had their beginnings during this era. Some took over First Hill mansions for their own use, as the University Club did; others, like the Sunset Club, built new facilities. Some groups were for men only, others women only, and still others had an ethnic basis or an athletic focus. Some maintained an exclusive membership; others, like the

Dreamland Pavilion at Seventh Avenue and Union Street, were open to all who walked through the front door. They had one thing in common: each was a place where people gathered to express or share a mutual interest.

OLYMPIC TENNIS CLUB | SEATTLE TENNIS CLUB

Northwest corner of Madison Street and Minor Avenue: 1890-1897; south block of Madison Street between Summit Avenue and Boylston Avenue: 1897-1919

The Seattle Tennis Club was launched on First Hill in 1890. Many of its early male tennis players later rose to prominence in Seattle society. "To think of Josiah Collins, Daniel Kelleher, Judge Robert B. Albertson, W. A. Peters, Bernard Pelly, Harry M. Hoyt, George H. Preston, David Baxter, Dr. G. H. Sparling, or W. W. Bush, today prancing around a tennis court after an elusive India rubber ball, might cause a smile," said an August 25, 1912, article in the *Seattle Sunday Times*. "But they were among the first to play the game of tennis in Seattle."

In 1888, these ambitious young men often gathered on a small clay tennis court that Captain George D. Hill had built on land next to his home at Sixth Avenue and Spring Street. The new game of tennis was certainly an attraction, but so were the young ladies who gathered there for tea and cookies served by Captain Hill's Chinese servant Sing.[16]

The sport's growing popularity in Seattle soon demanded more courts, and these were built on a nearby vacant lot that the First Presbyterian Church would eventually occupy (in 1907), in back of "the old Osgood home" at Seventh Avenue and Spring Street. The players organized the Olympic Tennis Club in 1890, and established clay tennis courts on a 120-by-120-foot open lot on the northwest corner of Madison and Minor.[17] On Sunday, August 3, 1890, the *Seattle Post-Intelligencer* reported:

> *Lawn tennis is one of this summer's favorite diversions. In the city there are several large courts, and courts on private residences' grounds are quite numerous . . . The Olympic Tennis Club, the only large club in Seattle, was organized this year by the tennis enthusiasts of this town, and at this early period already contains thirty or forty names. They have secured grounds at the corner of Twelfth [now Minor][18] and Madison streets, directly behind Mrs. Stacy's house, and have two magnificent clay courts in running order . . .*

RIGHT: First Hill ladies compete at an Olympic Tennis Club match. Stacy residence is in the background. Courtesy Michael Maslan.

More than half of the 39 founding members were employed at banks and in other white-collar professions, such as law, real estate, and architecture. The women, whose most strenuous sports up to that time had included bicycling and croquet, persuaded the men to let them use the courts. However, the men would not play tennis with the women. The women wanted a little masculine competition on the courts, so they bribed boys (with ice cream sodas) to play tennis with them.

Watching tennis matches was as popular as playing in them, so the women banded together and had a small shack built; this became the tennis club's first clubhouse. The total cost for this "tea house"—or "the shed," as spectators and players called it—was $79.80. The first president of the ladies' branch established in 1894-95, Mrs. E. A. Strout Sr., hosted a tea here every Wednesday afternoon. At an old-timers' tea in 1947, Mrs. James D. Hodge (Ethel Hanna) recalled the days when she lived a "tennis ball's throw away from the first club near the present site of The Gainsborough." As one of the women who grew tired of sitting on the sidelines, she was the youngest of the charter members in the ladies' branch.[19]

RIGHT: Seattle Tennis Club spectators riveted to the match. MOHAI.

In 1896, the club changed its name to Seattle Tennis Club and joined the National Tennis Association. By 1897, it had absorbed several other tennis clubs: Marion Street Club, Seattle Field Club, and University Tennis Club.

As the area built up, the location grew less convenient. By 1910, the tennis courts were surrounded by First Hill mansions. Membership had continued to grow, and had outgrown the facilities. The club incorporated in 1913 and began seeking a new home. They found it soon after the Great War ended. At the 1919 annual meeting, Mr. Crawford Anderson reported that the Seattle Athletic Club had sold the old Firloch Canoe Club grounds. Investigating, the board of trustees learned that this property could be purchased for $22,500. A flurry of activity followed, and "as the Roaring Twenties arrived, the Seattle Tennis Club found itself on the western shore of Lake Washington."[20] It has been there ever since.

PROSCH'S HALL - ASSAY OFFICE - GERMAN HOUSE - OFFICERS' CLUB

613 Ninth Avenue

Designed by Seattle architect John Parkinson and built in 1893 for mixed retail and social event use, this building represents Parkinson's more classicizing tendencies, moving away from earlier Romanesque Revival and Queen Anne styles. It has served in turn as the Seattle Assay Office, German House, and wartime officers' club.[21]

Turning his interests to buying and selling property, retired *Seattle Post-Intelligencer* publisher Thomas W. Prosch built this cast-iron and masonry commercial structure next door to his home at 619 Ninth Avenue. The two-story building had 11 rooms and a basement. Retail stores occupied the street level, including a bakery.[22] The upper level featured a ballroom. Its tall-windowed classical facade had two traditional brick storefronts with large windows and transoms. Columns and a pediment surrounded the arched entrance. Five narrow rectangular windows flanked centrally located arched windows on the second floor. A wooden cornice and brackets decorated the protruding central portion of the parapet wall. The front of the building faced east, while the back had a superior view of Puget Sound and the busy harbor.

PROSCH'S HALL | 1893-1898

Prosch's Hall's first years were lively, renting out the ballroom for dances, meetings, and social events. In 1895 the Montefiore Literary Society held monthly entertainments here, each finishing with a "social hop" on the "spring" floor.[23] Westminster Church members met here in July 1896 to discuss calling a minister and constructing a church for their Presbyterian congregation.

Thomas Prosch and fellow Seattle Chamber of Commerce member Erastus Brainerd were on hand when the steamship *Portland* arrived at Seattle's Schwabacher Dock on July 17, 1897, with "a ton of gold" from the Klondike. The U.S. Government was soon persuaded to open an assay office in Seattle, and Prosch had the perfect location for it. The government leased his hall for $175 per month, and the assay office opened on July 15, 1898, to a long line of gold-laden miners. It operated at this First Hill location for over 30 years, until 1932 (see Chapter 5).

BELOW: German House.
Luci J. Baker Johnson.

German House, 1934-1941, 1946-present

After the assay office moved to the new U.S. Immigration Station in 1932, a group of German clubs purchased the hall. As Thomas Prosch himself had written in his *Chronological History of Seattle, from 1850-1897*, German-Americans had been established in Seattle since the 1880s. The heritage societies that underwrote this venture included the

Vaults That Once Held Gold
Will Glow with Golden Brew

Sons of Hermann, the Plattdeutscher Ladies' Society, and the Arion Singing Society.

The "old assay office" was remodeled into a clubhouse, and renamed *Deutsches Haus* (German House). Theodore Buchinger, a native of Vienna and builder of many churches and theaters in Europe and the United States, provided the design. Now the hall had a clubroom, two large rooms, a bar room, a kitchen, a banquet hall, and managers' apartments. A newspaper commented, "The gold vaults will now be used to store the German national beverage."[24] In December 1935, the club celebrated the project's completion with a festive New Year's Eve party.

Not all neighbors welcomed the German House to First Hill. Richard G. Lewis, who ran a boarding house next door, complained about parking issues and noise in a letter to the City Council in October 1935. "It is impossible to get scarcely a good night sleep in the week . . . It was a great mistake for them to come up here at all, the way they carry on they should be on the tide flats." The city investigated, and the club was found to be in compliance with city and state ordinances. Similar complaints and meetings hosted on controversial topics kept the German House in the news in the 1930s.

United States entry into World War II effectively ended mention of German House activities in Seattle newspapers. The building was turned over to a new wartime use as an officers' club in May 1943.

Seattle Officers' Club, July 25, 1943-1947

"A place for Officers to hang your hat, sleep, play cards or badminton, leisurely read and smoke, and most importantly, to have someone to talk to."[25]

BELOW: German Choir, 2013. Manfred Bolender.

Seattle's growing role as a base of war operations brought military officers to the area, and several women's organizations banded together to operate an officers' club in this hall. The Colonial Dames converted the high-ceilinged ballroom into a dormitory: sleeping quarters for 32 men. The Sunset Club furnished the main-floor lounge, which included a library, table tennis, and a piano. The Seattle Garden Club built a badminton court and planted trees and shrubs around the terrace. The Junior League provided downstairs grill equipment and furnishings, and ran the club.[26]

By February 1944, over 4,100 officers had been overnight guests at the club, which employed at least 12 people, from cooks to errand boys. The social program included entertainment by local musicians, Saturday night dances, and Sunday morning horseback rides followed by a late brunch. In January 1945 a Women Officers' Annex was opened across the street at 704 Ninth Avenue, with a dormitory, powder room, showers, living room, writing room, and access to all the amenities at the Officers' Club. Sometime in the winter of 1946-47, the wartime Officers' Club was returned to the German Club's leadership. It continues to host social gatherings today.

UNIVERSITY CLUB/STACY HOUSE | FOUNDED 1900 - PRESENT

Birds of a feather flock together.

1004 Boren Avenue, northwest corner of Boren Avenue and Madison Street

"Kindred spirits to foregather for mutual pleasure and edification."[27]

In the early 1860s, a small group of young Yale University graduates who worked and lived in New York City gathered for dinner and conversation. During these discussions, they formed the concept of a "gathering place for fellow graduates and other esteemed men who were alumni of similar institutions." In 1865, they formed The University Club of New York, which inspired similar clubs throughout the United States, including Seattle.

During the 1880s and 1890s, Seattle attracted a number of graduates of eastern universities, and these men eventually established an exclusive club of their own. When the University Club was incorporated in December 1900, with a waiting list and membership limited to 200 white men, the 23 charter members included Bernard Pelly, Erastus Brainerd, O. H. P. LaFarge, Daniel Kelleher, Thomas Burke, and Charles H. Bebb.[28]

Lumber and real estate mogul Martin Van Buren Stacy had had a First Hill residence built in 1889 at the request of his wife, Elizabeth (see Chapter 2). Owner-occupied for only a few months, the 15-room, three-story Queen Anne–style mansion at Madison Street and Boren Avenue was rented as a private residence until February 1901, when *The Seattle Daily Times* reported that Lyman R. Colt had just purchased it and the University Club planned to lease it from Mr. Colt. At this time, Mrs. Stacy's elegant furnishings still filled the house. Mr. Colt tried persuading her to remove them; finally she took her silver and nothing else. The article speculated that bachelors might rent some of the mansion's eight bedrooms. When 60 members inspected their new clubhouse in April 1901, the club's officers were banker and *bon vivant* E. W. Andrews [Yale], president; Erastus Brainerd [Harvard], vice president; C. M. Austin [British Consul], secretary;

BELOW: University Club, ca. 1910, at the corner of Boren Avenue and Madison Street, shows the 1906 addition that nearly doubled the size of the former Stacy residence. PEMCO Webster & Stevens Collection 1983.10.6721, MOHAI.

UNIVERSITY CLUB DEBUT

On June 1, 1901, *The Seattle Star* carried word of the University Club's debut:

The new clubhouse of the University Club of Seattle, at the corner of Madison Street and Boren Avenue, was formally opened last night by a banquet, at which nearly 50 persons were present. Topics of the day were chosen as toasts, and some of the most representative citizens of Seattle responded to them.

• *Judge C. H. Hanford, the only honorary member, responded to "Higher Education on the Frontier."*
• *Judge Burke spoke on "The Value of the Law."*
• *President Graves, University of Washington, responded to the toast, "The Upbuilding of a University."*
• *E. L. Smith spoke on "The Clergy as an Educated and Educating Class."*
• *Joseph Gilpin Pyle spoke on "The Influence of Educated Men Through Journalism."*
• *Hon. John B. Allen could not be present to speak upon "University Men in Public Life." Which, subject had been assigned to him, and in his stead Hon. John Barrett, ex-minister to Siam, was called upon and spoke extemporaneously.*

The evening was one of much pleasure and learning, and it is freely predicted that the club will be a great success.

Bernard Pelly [British Vice Consul], treasurer; and a house committee made up of O. H. P. LaFarge, Edgar Ames, and George A. Hurd.

Within a year, architect W. D. Kimball had plans prepared for an annex as large as the original clubhouse, with five bedrooms on its third floor, an entrance on Madison Street, and a ladies' clubroom designed especially for dinners.[29] Constructed in 1906, the annex featured the latest amenities: shower baths, electric lights, and steam heating. Cold-storage facilities on the annex's main floor connected with the kitchen in the original residence, and a stairway led to the second floor, a billiard room, a reading room, and four bedrooms.

Several members of the "U-Club" made this address their permanent residence. The 1910 federal census lists 12 single men (ranging in age from 23 to 42) living at the residence, plus seven servants of Japanese descent. In 1918 the club purchased the building from Mr. Colt.

University Club members were seen as persons of position, substance, and achievement: "You are suspected of certain things—of being a good bridge player, an excellent host, an interesting sort of person."[30] Members often contributed large numbers of books to the club library, which was founded shortly after the annex was built.

ABOVE: The University Club baseball team poses in 1903 on the club lawn. Dr. Ivan A. Parry is on the lower righthand side. The Carkeek mansion is in the background. Dr. Parry came to Seattle in 1902 and took over the Ballard Hospital in 1907. Courtesy of the Parry Family.

The University Club was a men's club, but quickly recognized the value of being able to entertain wives and other female guests at lunch or dinner. When the annex was completed in 1906, the first floor had a combined cocktail lounge and dining room for mixed parties. This space was expanded in 1953 to accommodate about 50 people. The rest of the clubhouse was forbidden to women except at the annual New Year's Day Tea, which generally welcomed between 400 and 500 people. Other gatherings included the annual Christmas show that began in 1910, member-hosted celebrations, and similar activities planned by and for the membership.[31]

"The University Club has neither fine athletic facilities nor elegant furnishings. It is simply a place where a select group of men meet to enjoy each other's company, away from people of differing race, religion, sex, or social class. As it is, the organization's selectivity and secrecy give it a certain glamour," reported one female journalist.

The University Club continues today as a gathering place for men only. It sits quietly on the very busy northeast corner of Boren Avenue and Madison Street, tucked behind large foliage with no obvious signage indicating its significance. Many pass by the mansion without suspecting that this exclusive men's club even exists.

THE MONKS CLUB | FOUNDED MAY 1, 1904; DISBANDED IN 1962

1108 Terry Avenue (Crescent Club)
321 Boren Avenue (1½ years, 1904-1905)
514 Terry Avenue (9½ years, 1905-1915)
1334 Terry Avenue (47 years, 1915-1962) - residence demolished

"An exclusive residential club for young men at a reasonable cost. A home away from home, for young unmarried businessmen getting established in Seattle . . . where bachelors hide out while weighing the merits and responsibilities of marriage and rearing a family."

— John Reddin reminisces about the Monks Club in
"Alums Sing Farewell to Monks Club," *Seattle Times,* May 16, 1962, p. 2

The 1897 Alaska-Yukon Gold Rush spurred much of Seattle's growth in the early 20th century. Each day men—and some women—arrived with dreams of going to the Yukon and finding gold. The city's growing economy also attracted young professional men, who filled such white-collar positions as bank teller, office clerk, insurance agent, real estate broker, contractor, salesman, accountant, or attorney. Often they arrived without the means to live on their own in an apartment. Alternatives included hotels and boarding houses.

In the fall of 1901 a group of young professional men formed the Crescent Social Club, pooling their resources to rent a house at 1108 Terry Avenue (at Spring Street).[32] An advertisement in the June 17, 1902, *The Seattle Daily Times* lists it as a "modern 8-room furnished first hill home." Later ads describe its rooms as "suitable for one or two gentlemen, use of parlor, piano, telephone, close in, and very reasonable." A shared room cost about $5 a week (about $135 in today's dollars). In March 1903 the Crescent Club was described as "running on the co-operative plan," with "men who hold clerical positions in different lines of business" as members.[33] Arguments arose over its operation, however, and in the spring of 1904, nine members left to establish a new club.

On April 18, 1904, they organized the Monks Club. Dexter Horton & Co. employee Charles L. LeSourd was elected president, a position he held until 1907. They found a suitable house at 321 Boren Avenue (at East Alder and Broadway). It came partially furnished, the rent was reasonable, and it was within walking distance of downtown. They employed a housekeeper/cook and a maid.

A description of the grand opening social at the Monks Club, September 1904, appeared in *The Seattle Daily Times*:

> *The veranda of the house was enclosed with evergreens and made cozy with rugs and couches and decorated with large palms and varied-colored lights. Ferns, summer flowers and palms were used to decorate the club house. An orchestra rendered selections from a canopy of cedar branches, mingled with sweet peas and gladiolas. The club flower was the white carnation, worn by all of the men at the social.*

In September 1905 they moved to 514 Terry Avenue, between James and Jefferson Streets, their home for almost 10 years. They organized social gatherings for members and guests, including frequent Sunday evening dinners with entertainment by touring concert musicians, and dances where the young single men could bring a date or meet a nice girl. There were New Year's parties at the residence, and Fourth of July picnics at Agate Pass (Bainbridge Island). During the Alaska-Yukon-Pacific Exposition (AYPE) of 1909, they hosted a number of out-of-town guests. Unusual for the time was the fact that neither smoking nor liquor was allowed in the house. Monks Club life also included good-natured shenanigans. If a member was about to marry or spoke out of turn, he was ducked in a cold bath; his clothes might be thrown in after him.

After 10 years, members sought to put the Monks Club on a more solid financial basis, noting that it took all the money coming in to run the house, and hard times could force them to disband. They incorporated as a nonprofit organization, and all *new* members were obliged to buy stock. Shares were $10 each, but only had value as evidence of membership. All Monks—stockholders or not—were welcome at the December stockholder meetings.

As funds accumulated from the sale of stock, the Monks Club looked into purchasing its own house. A committee established in 1915 soon found a three-story house that the Sunset Club had used at 1334 Terry Avenue. The house was old (1887) but well built, and a relic of past grandeur. The owner agreed to rent it to the Monks Club and consider selling it to the club at some future date, so they moved in. In 1920 they purchased the property for $35,000, financing it with bonds that were paid off by 1945.

RIGHT: The Monks Club at 1334 Terry Avenue served bachelors from 1915 until 1962. PEMCO Webster & Stevens Collection 1983.10.3667, MOHAI.

Frances Backus, who lived with her husband, Manson Backus II, at the Adrian Court, reminisced:

> *I have a number of friends who met their husbands on Terry Avenue, just where it comes to a very steep hill . . . there was a lovely old house that was made over into a men's club. It was called the Monk's Club. There were just loads of attractive young men who lived there, worked in the offices and so on downtown. We used to go to parties that they had . . . There were probably 20 or so living in there, and they had a wonderful fireplace.*

The Monks Club held its 50th-anniversary banquet at the Rainier Club on April 26, 1954. By then the club roster contained 502 names; 372 were still on the mailing list, and 95 former members had died. Nevertheless, it was the venerable club's swan song. Efforts to attract new residents included a June 18, 1961, *The Seattle Sunday Times* classified ad: "Everything provided including traditional hospitality in this famed mansion located within walking distance of city center. All at surprisingly low cost."

In May 1962, just after the Seattle World's Fair opened, members met one last time to dispose of old trophies, liquidate assets, and disband the 58-year-old club. As a *Seattle Times* article reported, "The average member lived at the club two to three years. And there usually were about 30 men in residence. William M. Allen, president of The Boeing Co.; John Cartano, attorney and president of the Seattle Chamber of Commerce; and Justice of the Peace William Hoar once called the Monks Club home."[34]

In 1963 the residence was sold to Eighth Avenue Apartments, Inc., for a reported $100,000. The proceeds were distributed among approximately 800 holders of 13,800 Monks Club shares. The building was demolished and replaced by a four-story convalescent-and-nursing home operated by Hillhaven, Inc. of Tacoma. Ownership changed hands several times over the years. In 2008 the interior was demolished and rebuilt to convert it into an 80-bed hospital, currently owned and operated by Kindred Hospital, Seattle-First Hill.

SUNSET CLUB | FOUNDED JUNE 1913 - PRESENT

1021 University Street, southwest corner of University Street and Boren Avenue

"Women Organize Club Exclusively for Sex: Membership Will Include Writers, Musicians and Others Prominent in Intellectual Life of Seattle."[35]

This inadvertently scandalous headline appeared in *The Seattle Daily Times* on July 7, 1913. In March, Mrs. Winfield R. Smith (Susie Wegg Smith) had hosted a tea at her First Hill home at 912 Minor Avenue. At this tea, 15 women discussed starting a new invitational social club run *by* and *for* women, to meet for luncheon and dinner, lectures, recitals, private parties, and receptions.

At the first official Sunset Club meeting, on Friday, June 27, 1913, 22 women signed the incorporation documents, "establishing the Club with the purpose of ensuring the social and intellectual welfare of its membership."

The Sunset Club's first bylaws were taken almost verbatim from those of the Colony Club, a New York City women's club established in 1903.[36] The initial bylaws set a membership ceiling of 300, the number believed sufficient to ensure financial success. They also called for "the Club House to be open at 9AM every day and for members to sign vouchers for all expenses and to be billed for them monthly. No cash would be exchanged at the Club."

RIGHT: The Sunset Club funded a distinctive Georgian Revival clubhouse at Boren Avenue and University Street. PEMCO Webster & Stevens Collection 1983.10.9418, MOHAI.

In September 1913, the Sunset Club formally opened its doors in a furnished First Hill apartment sublet by Mrs. John L. Wilson at 911 Summit Avenue at Madison Street—the elegant Adrian Court apartments—for $150 a month (see Chapter 4). In 1966, charter member Willye A. White recalled that "linen, silver, kitchen ware, magazines and stationery and casual furniture was purchased" for the club's use, despite the temporary location.

BELOW: A costumed affair at the Sunset Club, ca. 1940. Sunset Club Archives.

Nearly every Friday afternoon the temporary clubhouse was busy with business meetings, a "Sunset Tea," entertainments, literary gatherings, or musical performances.

At the first annual meeting, in April 1914, club secretary Christobel Eden reported on events hosted at the fledgling club's First Hill apartment. "The Sunset Club's speakers during the first year revealed the members' interest in becoming informed about public affairs: Judge Burke, who lectured on 'Conditions of Government'; Rev. Dr. Herbert Gowen, rector of Trinity Episcopal Church [and] an Asian scholar involved in missionary work with the city's largest racial minority, Japanese immigrants; and others." It had been an exhilarating year since the Rainier Clubmen downtown had said no to more events involving females.[37]

By March 1914 the club had established a committee to purchase a lot and develop a plan for financing a permanent clubhouse. They chose a property away from

ABOVE: Sunset Club Song, written by request and dedicated to the club. Sunset Club Archives.

BELOW: Wicker furniture in the parlor, Sunset Club, ca.1920. Sunset Club Archives.

RIGHT: Ladies in the library, Sunset Club, ca. 1920. Sunset Club Archives.

the city's commercial and business center, but in an affluent neighborhood that was home to many club members. The southwest corner of Boren Avenue and University Street was within walking distance of both the (men's) University Club and the Seattle Tennis Club. Agnes Healy (Alfred H.) Anderson, of 718 Minor Avenue, and Jeannette Whittmore (David) Skinner advanced the $20,000 for the land purchase.

The members hired 40-year-old French-Canadian architect Joseph Simon Coté to design their new club building, the first in the West planned specifically to house a women's club. Coté had arrived in Seattle in 1904 to help manage design and construction of St. James Cathedral. He formed a firm with W. M. Somervell and they worked together until 1910, after which Mr. Coté was on his own (see Chapter 7).

Construction of this Georgian Revival–style building began in 1914 and was completed the following year. Although the outbreak of World War I raised the cost of materials and made them increasingly scarce, members sold bonds, donated furnishings, and oversaw the construction despite the greater difficulty. They celebrated completion of the club building with a 116-member meeting on June 23, 1915, followed by a luncheon and a formal dedication ceremony. That evening, 750 members, spouses, and guests attended a gala reception and ball.

Contemporary descriptions of the clubhouse referred to woodwork with ivory finish, marble benches covered in red brocade, stairs and railings of mahogany, and walls painted a shade described as "champagne." South American mahogany was used as flooring throughout, and the floors were designed to provide resilience for dancing. The donated furnishings included a Persian rug in the entry hall, plus Chippendale chairs, Hepplewhite tables, and Duncan Phyfe sofas in the drawing room. A small space at the south end of the drawing room, which served as a stage for plays and musicals, was equipped with a proscenium curtain decorated with the club's signature peacock symbol. The second floor featured a sitting room, a library, and three bedrooms for visiting speakers. During the 1930s, the club benefited from the involvement of Mrs. Donald Frederick, wife of the cofounder of Frederick & Nelson department store, in commissioning designs for interiors and furniture from Mrs. Elsie Cobb Wilson, an important New York interior designer.

In a commemorative book on the club published in 1998, author Barbara Stenson Spaeth wrote that "despite the city's female population being in the minority, its women exercised a degree of power and influence that members of that sex living elsewhere could only envy."[38]

In 2013 the Sunset Club celebrated 100 years of women gathering together on First Hill to seek respite from household responsibilities and routine, in a place where women could be graciously served, entertained, educated, and informed while surrounded by friends and family members encompassing two, three, or even more generations. They had weathered many changes in those years: two world wars, the Great Depression, women's suffrage, and women's changing role in the family. Many members lived on First Hill again, but their homes were in high-rises with underground parking, instead of formal mansions with coach houses. Still an important center for Seattle women, the Sunset Club enters its second century.

DREAMLAND PAVILION | EAGLES AUDITORIUM

1402 Seventh Avenue - Northeast Corner of Seventh Avenue and Union Street

Motorists take the Union Street exit off I-5 and zip by the corner of Seventh Avenue and Union Street with little knowledge of its history. Today it is generally seen as set apart from First Hill, but until Interstate 5 "took a slice out of the hill and the neighborhood," it was seen as First Hill's northwest corner. In the late 1880s and 1890s, Mrs. J. C. Haines hosted socials and tea parties for Seattle's elite in her home on this site. In the 20th century's first two decades, thousands gathered here at Dreamland Pavilion to skate, dance, and even attend church services. Eagles Auditorium was built here in the Roaring 1920s, and has dominated the corner ever since. ACT Theatre ensemble actors have entertained Seattleites in the auditorium since 1996.

This was originally part of Arthur A. Denny's land claim. He deeded it to Mary R. Denny in 1874. Seven years later, in July 1881, she and John W. Denny deeded it to Frederick A. Gasch.[39] It is not clear who built the house, but Colonel and Mrs. J. C. Haines leased it in January 1885, and two years later they purchased the home for $8,500. Mrs. Haines hosted parties for Seattle's elite here for several years. A few years after Col. Haines's untimely death in 1892, the Haines home was foreclosed and sold, then used as a multifamily dwelling for several years.[40]

DREAMLAND PAVILION | 1906-1921

"Dreamland Stands for Amusement," says proprietor Mique Fisher.

In June 1906, real estate developer and idea man Bert Farrar announced plans to build a huge auditorium on the site of the Haines residence with its main entrance facing Seventh Avenue. The building was expected to cost about $10,000.

ABOVE: Dreamland Pavilion, color postcard, postmarked June 21, 1912. 2002.48.670, MOHAI.

Roller Skating in Seattle – It will soon be just as unfortunate to say "I don't skate" as "I don't dance."

RIGHT: The Dreamland roller skating rink had a wood truss supported barrel-vaulted roof. It was later converted to a dance hall. UW21029z, Special Collections, University of Washington.

Indoor roller-skating was first introduced in Brussels in 1877. By the 1880s roller skates were being mass-produced in the United States, but the first Seattleites who journeyed east to "get their skates on" found no skating rinks to exercise the sport when they returned to the West Coast. Three skating rinks were operating by 1906, and Bert Farrar's Dreamland became the fourth.

James Schack's architecture firm drew plans for the auditorium, which boasted maple hardwood floors, balconies lining three sides of the pavilion to accommodate as many as 1,500 spectators, and a series of dressing rooms, cloakrooms, and kitchens to support the hall's multiple uses: roller-skating, dancing, conventions. *The Seattle Sunday Times* displayed an architectural rendering of the building on June 24, 1906, noting that its 70-by-150-foot floor could accommodate 500 skaters.[41]

By September 1906, *The Seattle Daily Times* was reporting, "At the rink on First Hill there are morning classes for ladies who are learning, and many well-known people are found there twice a week . . . It's the same jolly, healthful, captivating sport as it was then [20 years ago]. Different fashions, different tunes, different skates—but the same good old fun."

The rink's opening generated excitement, but some saw it as yet another gateway to Sin City. The October 21, 1906 *The Seattle Daily Times* carried a story on page 12 with the banner "New Rink Opens Monday – Big Amusement Enterprise to Be Launched by Invitation Party under Auspices of Monday Night Club." But page 15 of the same issue carried another story, with the headline "Condemn Skating Rinks: Workers in Young Women's Christian Association Declare Places of Amusement Have Baneful Influence, Plan Systematic Campaign of Protest for Sake of Young Girls Who, Seeking Pleasure, Fall into Evil Ways."

Dreamland Pavilion would have a strong 10-year lock on the corner of Seventh Avenue and Union Street. Hundreds of thousands of people passed through its massive doors,

but not all came to skate. The auditorium was also rented out for special events. In early 1907, the Seattle Police held a dance at the rink. In October 1907, the rink hosted a performance by Madame Maconda, America's foremost soprano soloist. In June 1909, the Hon. David S. Rose, mayor of Milwaukee, Wisconsin, delivered a lecture titled "The Other Side of Prohibition." In March 1910, the Rev. Frank E. Hertum, pastor of the Georgetown Union Church, preached to 1,500 at Dreamland on the "saving grace of brotherly love.[42]

February 1910 found the Dreamland Pavilion embroiled in legal controversy. Mique Fisher, proprietor, and J. L. Wood, manager, of the Dreamland "dancing pavilion" were accused of selling liquor, cigars, and cigarettes to females and minors at cafés and other unlicensed places. The two were arrested and immediately released on bail.[43]

The auditorium continued to host events. In September 1910, a Miss Coralyn Piere and Laird A. Wray were married at Dreamland in the presence of 1,000 dancers; Dreamland proprietor Mique Fisher was the best man. The following April, Colonel (and former United States President) Theodore Roosevelt addressed the faculty and students of the University of Washington in the afternoon, then spoke to the public at Dreamland Rink in the evening. In March 1911, the Seattle Commercial Club sponsored a "Famine Dance" to raise money for a famine-affected district in China. Mique Fisher donated the space for the dance. Mayoral debates, Santa Claus visits, and even boxing matches were held at the pavilion.[44] The auditorium was also a popular gathering place for labor unions.

Interest in Dreamland began to dwindle after U.S. entry into World War I. The very real practicalities of supporting the war effort were perhaps difficult to reconcile with the lightheartedness of Dreamland. It was seldom mentioned in the society pages after early 1918. The Pavilion had served its purpose, and a new venue soon arose on the corner to take its place. On May 15, 1921, the headline on page 36 of *The Seattle Daily Times* read, "Dreamland Rink Sold."

EAGLES AUDITORIUM | 1921-1981

The Brotherhood of Good Things

The Fraternal Order of Eagles' Aerie #1 purchased Dreamland Pavilion for approximately $75,000 in May 1921. The lodge's 6,000 members had outgrown its previous location at Seventh Avenue and Pine Street.

The Eagles were founded in Seattle in 1898 as a fraternal benevolent society, and Aerie #1 is called the organization's Mother Chapter. It was launched by six men, owners and managers of some of Seattle's leading theaters, who had gathered to discuss a way to settle a local musicians' strike. They got to musing about democracy and brotherhood, and decided to start the "Seattle Order of Good Things" to carry out the spirit of their ideas. They called on their members to "make human life more desirable by lessening its ills and promoting peace, prosperity, gladness, and hope."[45] Early membership was made up largely of theater people—actors, stagehands, and playwrights.

Early growth was spectacular. Within a year, Seattle and Spokane were joined by 18 more aeries in the Northwest, northern California, and British Columbia. Within 10 years there were 1,800 aeries in the U.S., Canada, and Mexico, with 350,000 members. This phenomenal growth can partially be explained by the social conditions of the time. The Eagles sought to serve the common man, and became a champion for his cause.

Having purchased the Dreamland property, the Eagles launched a program to raise funds for building the six-story Eagles Auditorium. By the summer of 1924 a church located on adjacent property (see Chapter 6) was being razed, and demolition of the Dreamland Pavilion was set for one week later.

BELOW: The Eagles Auditorium showcases Henry Bittman's penchant for terra-cotta-clad facades. PEMCO Webster & Stevens Collection 1983.10.3141, MOHAI.

The Eagles Auditorium Building was designed by local architect Henry W. Bittman (1882-1953). Constructed of steel and reinforced concrete, the Renaissance Revival–style terra-cotta building measured 120 by 175 feet, with about 21,000 square feet on each floor. The south elevation (facing Union Street) was divided into five bays, and the west side (facing Seventh Avenue) was divided into nine. The monumental base of the structure was clad with granite base blocks and terra-cotta facing. Above the base, giant fluted pilasters rose four stories to a terra-cotta cornice that separated the fifth and sixth floors. Stylized composite capitals displaying an eagle motif adorned these pilasters.[46] The building's interior provided office space, a gymnasium, apartments, a nightclub, and ceremonial halls. The large ballroom took up most of the space on the second, third, fourth, and fifth floors. One end of the hall featured an elevated stage.

On February 22, 1925, approximately 12,000 Eagles gathered for the cornerstone ceremony. Speeches were made, crowds cheered, and a copper box was placed in a niche as a time capsule.

A full-page spread in *The Seattle Daily Times* on July 14, 1925, heralded the opening of the new building, which had both commercial and fraternal aspects. The top four floors held 81 two- and three-bedroom apartments, served by elevators near the Union Street entrance. The mezzanine level had parlors for members' wives, a lounge and library for the men, and restrooms and checkrooms.

Eagles Auditorium was a popular dance venue from the start, and it continued to play an important role as a performance space well into the 1980s. It was also rented for rock concerts in the 1960s and 1970s.

However, by the 1990s the Eagles found it impractical to maintain their headquarters. Most members had moved to the suburbs and joined Eagles aeries closer to their homes. The Mother Aerie #1 also moved (it is on Lake City Way now), and Eagles Auditorium was sold. The building was sound, but it needed a facelift. In August 1993, the Seattle City Council pledged $3 million in city funds toward preservation of Eagles Auditorium and the Paramount Theatre. A Contemporary Theatre (ACT), founded in 1965, moved into Eagles Auditorium following a $30 million update to the designated landmark, which preserved the terra-cotta exterior and constructed a stage and seating within the ballroom that did not damage significant architectural features.

SCOTTISH RITE TEMPLE | 1910 (DEMOLISHED)

1115 Broadway, at the intersection of Harvard Avenue and Broadway

Seattle has many "triangles": irregularly shaped pieces of land created where early developers' street grids meet at odd angles, as at Pioneer Square, or where an early thoroughfare still crosses a grid that came later. The Polyclinic currently owns one

RIGHT: Scottish Rite Masonic Temple at Harvard Avenue and Broadway, ca. 1915. 2002.48.723, MOHAI.

such triangle, formed by the intersection of Harvard Avenue and Broadway just a few yards north of Madison Street, fronting at 1121 Broadway today. If you peek through the eight-foot-high privacy fence, you'll see a concrete stairway with a railing: a stairway to nowhere, with no building to go with it.[47]

One hundred years ago, an imposing Scottish Rite Masonic Temple stood on this narrow piece of land. The lodge purchased land from the city in August 1910, and hired builder Frank Allen to design and build the frame building, with a south-facing entrance that fronted at the intersection of Harvard Avenue and Broadway. The cornerstone was laid on December 14, 1910.[48]

In the early days, lodge members rode the Madison Street Cable Railway to get to the Temple, but the need for parking grew as the century progressed and automobiles became more prevalent. By 1957, lodge members were planning a new lodge hall near East Highland Drive between Harvard Avenue and Broadway, with extensive off-street parking. The new temple was completed and occupied in the fall of 1961.[49]

Today, there is a vacant lot where the original Scottish Rite Temple once stood.

KNIGHTS OF COLUMBUS HALL | 1912 - PRESENT

722 East Union Street, on the northwest corner of Union and Harvard Avenue

Charity • Unity • Fraternity • Patriotism

"Seventy of Seattle's peaceful citizens will be decorated with the helmet and spurs of valiant knights . . ."[50]

The Knights of Columbus, one of the world's largest Catholic fraternal service organizations, began in Connecticut in 1882 under the leadership of Reverend Michael J.

ABOVE: Russian orphans in front of the Knights of Columbus Hall, ca. 1920. The Russian Revolution caused many Russians to flee their country in search of a safe haven. Seattle took in many of them. PEMCO Webster & Stevens Collection 1983.10.2157.2, MOHAI.

McGivney, whose initial goal was to provide a measure of security for widows and orphans in his parish. The Seattle Council was established in June 1902. Seattle so impressed national organizer James J. Gorman (a steamship agent from Fall River, Massachusetts, who had been sent to organize councils in the Pacific Northwest's larger cities) that he ultimately made it his home.[51]

By 1909 there were about 350 members, who gathered for meetings, events, and banquets at the Elks Hall, the St. Francis Hall (at Sixth and Spring), the Renton Hill Club House, and the Hotel Washington. It wasn't until 1912 that the association established a formal presence on First Hill.

In 1912, Mrs. Elizabeth Foss donated a 74-by-128-foot lot on the corner of East Union Street and Harvard Avenue to the Knights of Columbus. Ferdinand W. Bohne was hired as the architect, and Ryan & Co. Materials as the contractor. An early estimate of the four-story steel-and-brick building's cost was $60,000. Its Colonial Revival design featured a main entrance with a marquee of wrought iron and decorative glass that fronted on East Union Street. Inside, a vestibule lobby connected all of the principal rooms on the first floor. Included were a 70-by-54-foot ballroom, a ladies' parlor, a men's smoking room, and a kitchen. The basement was to have a 24-by-42-foot swimming pool, surrounded by a 23-lap running track. As *The Seattle Daily Times* reported, "There will be a standard double bowling alley, lockers, shower baths and everything that goes to make modern athletic equipment."[52] The mezzanine floor housed administrative offices, a billiard room, a lounging room, and a library.

The clubhouse opened in April 1913 with a band-led procession from St. James Cathedral to Harvard and Union. Bishop O'Dea and Mrs. Elizabeth Foss were prominent participants in the parade, and the ceremony concluded with a singing of "The Star-Spangled Banner."

Through the years, the clubhouse has hosted dances, weddings, funerals, and club events. Its first annual Gridiron Banquet was held here in 1937, honoring the O'Dea High School and Seattle Prep football teams. In later years, the Blanchet, Kennedy, and Eastside Catholic high school football teams were also recognized at these annual banquets. The building also hosted night-school and free evening classes offering a

ABOVE: Knights of Columbus free evening school automotive class for demobilized servicemen, January 1920. PEMCO Webster & Stevens Collection 1983.10.1791.8, MOHAI.

variety of practical skills, including automobile repair, typing, and bookkeeping.

Before the advent of community field houses and school gyms, the Knights' basement gymnasium facility was probably the best known and most used in the city. The U.S. Coast Guard used the swimming pool during World War II. The pool is obsolete now, and has been cemented over.

By the mid 1960s, membership was declining, and the building was being referred to as "the old K of C Hall." "Most of the members live in suburbia and no longer spend their evenings at the club, playing bridge, billiards or whatever members do at their clubs," wrote *Seattle Times* columnist John J. Reddin on May 21, 1967. "Instead, they head for home at the end of the day, or for an afternoon of golf, yachting or other recreation."

Plans announced in 1968 to replace the clubhouse with a high-rise, multiuse building did not go forward, and the original building was saved from the wrecking ball. An elevator was installed in 1998, providing access to all floors. New security safeguards and disabled access were added when its Harvard entrance was remodeled, and major plumbing upgrades throughout the building helped prepare the third floor for tenants.

Today the Knights of Columbus Hall at the corner of Harvard and Union continues to be a prominent part of the First Hill community. Much of it is available for rental, and Seattleites continue to gather there to celebrate with family and friends. The legacy continues.

RIGHT: Knights of Columbus Hall, 2014. Historic Seattle.

TWELVE TWENTY THREE
SPRING STREET
·EARL W. MORRISON· ARCHITECT·

[C H A P T E R]

APARTMENT LIVING ON FIRST HILL

JACQUELINE B. WILLIAMS

ABOVE: The residential Hotel Lee, 909 Eighth Avenue, offered $3-and-up rates for its furnished rooms. A two-story frame residence from the 1890s is dwarfed by its new neighbor in this 1911 photograph. 22210 Curtis, Washington State Historical Society.

LEFT: Architect Earl Morrison's presentation rendering of 1223 Spring Street, ca. 1929. Courtesy 1223 Spring Street Condominium Owners Association.

IN THE LATE 19TH CENTURY, First Hill's spectacular views of the Olympic Mountains and Puget Sound, proximity to Seattle's downtown, and a functioning street railway system attracted wealthy homeowners. Hidden behind hedges and shrubs, their well-appointed houses resplendent with spacious rooms displayed the accoutrements of wealth, such as silver, crystal, paintings, and sculpture.

Unfortunately or fortunately, depending on your viewpoint, the millionaires soon left for the suburbs and their stylish mansions became rooming houses or medical offices. Eventually most were torn down.

Karen Harris and Barbara Olsen, whose mother operated a boarding house from 1949 to 1951 in the James and Mary Lowman home at 820 Boren Avenue, remembered its faded grandeur. "It was a large house with a large entryway that also had a fireplace in the main entryway . . . some of [the rooms] had large sliding wood doors . . . the bells for the servants were still there. It was very grand." When their family moved in, it also needed major repairs and remodeling such as painting and wallpapering.[53]

By 1904 homeowners lamented the coming of apartment houses. It was "The Tragedy on the Hill," said a reporter for the *Seattle News-Letter* on October 22, 1904:

> *In a greater or lesser degree many homes on the First Hill have been destroyed ... There is nothing so pitiless—so merciless—as contrast and when the First Hill of today is mentally placed alongside the First Hill of a year ago ... This was prior to the invasion of the "dollar doublers," as the sponsors of flat buildings are termed by some of the disgruntled home owners. Since the advent of the dollar doublers (who, by the way were the first to realize that the very exclusiveness of The Hill was a most valuable asset, and factor in renting small apartments) there have been something like a score of flats, apartment houses and hotels.*

By the early 1900s soaring land prices and increases in the price of building materials made home-building costly for the many newcomers who had migrated to Seattle. "[T]hose who think they possess but sufficient capital for a modest home find their little money is not even sufficient ... The result is they abandon the idea of owning a home and decide to live in a flat building," wrote the *Seattle Daily Bulletin*, September 6, 1902.

Multifamily buildings, such as boarding houses, residential hotels, and apartment houses, appealed to the many ambitious men and women, immigrant and native born, laborers and professionals, skilled and unskilled, who swarmed in to take advantage of Seattle's strong economy. Like others before them, these newcomers wanted to live close to work and keep house with a minimum of trouble. Single women who began coming to Seattle as nurses, teachers, and sales clerks found these residences especially desirable. Some lived there for many years; others viewed apartments as a way station until funds for a home became available.

Most renters on First Hill were white. People of color were not welcome. "Discriminatory housing patterns upheld by restrictive covenants forced virtually all Asians, Native Americans, and about 65 percent of the Central District's blacks to reside on the Southside (also known as lower Jackson Street)," according to historian Quintard Taylor. Although the 1948 U.S. Supreme Court ruling in *Shelley v. Kraemer* outlawed restrictive covenants, most Seattle real estate agents and homeowners set up "voluntary agreements" and continued to refuse to sell or rent to people of color. As late as 1961, "apartment house operators and real estate spokesmen" opposed any Fair Housing Laws, saying they "would infringe on constitutional property rights, were dictatorial, confiscatory and would lead to evasion and disrespect for the law." Discrimination in housing remained legal until 1968.[54]

BOARDING/ROOMING HOUSES

With the rapid growth of cities in the late 19th century, both blue- and white-collar workers lived in boarding and rooming houses. Boarding houses were places where "tenants rent rooms" and the proprietor provided family-style meals in a common dining room. Rooming houses were places where tenants slept but purchased meals elsewhere. Although in many such houses a group of strangers might share the walls and sit down together for meals, frequently residents chose and/or were forced to live with members of their own ethnic and racial populations. The boarding/lodging house arrangement might not have been ideal, but it could provide like-minded companions and a sense of community. Also it could provide a private room, steam heat, hot and cold water, and either a private or shared bathroom. Many came furnished.

Early Polk directories for Seattle reveal that women managed many of the boarding and lodging houses. It was a respectable occupation for a woman, and it made sense economically. If she was single, the job could provide free rent and possibly a salary. If she was married or widowed, the rent added to the family income.[55]

Contemporary classified advertisements appearing in Seattle newspapers pointed out that investing in boarding/lodging houses gave one a good financial return. "These close in locations are being rapidly picked up for flats, apartment houses or business blocks," announced a classified advertisement in the February 3, 1900, *Seattle Daily Times*. The "NEW MANAGEMENT" note at the beginning of many of the advertisements suggests that ownership and function frequently changed. For example, in 1908, 1424 Belmont Avenue rented as a house, then offered board and room, and finally changed management and stressed good cooking, boarding house style.

PICKWICK | 1409 BOREN AVENUE (DEMOLISHED)

The Pickwick was a typical example of this kind of housing arrangement. In 1903, this two-story frame building, called the Puritan, advertised "single or in suite rooms, furnished or unfurnished with or without board." In 1905, when the owner decided to sell, it claimed to have 40 rooms, 7 bathrooms, and hot and cold water. "One of the greatest bargains on the hill; a few thousands cash will handle this property and the balance on easy terms." By 1907, when the new owner changed the name to the Hotel Pickwick, it boasted of a large veranda and excellent dining room.[56]

RIGHT: Pickwick Hotel, at 1409 Boren Avenue, offered "meals served to transients," ca. 1926. PEMCO Webster & Stevens Collection 1983.10.3364.2, MOHAI.

BELMONT/BOYLSTON (BEL-BOY PROJECT) | 1410, 1420, 1424 BELMONT AVENUE; 1411, 1417, 1423 BOYLSTON AVENUE

Six buildings, constructed between 1893 and 1902 on Belmont and Boylston just south of Pike Street, shared a similar late Queen Anne and Colonial Revival architectural vocabulary that included columns, turned posts, and balusters, dentil

molding, and Palladian windows. The three houses on Belmont were built and used as single-family homes, while those on Boylston were large middle-class multiple residences made to appear like single-family residences. They are "double houses" or duplexes; one had four entrance doors leading to four units.[57]

Like so many First Hill buildings, these once elegant homes had become boarding/rooming houses, and were considered derelict properties when Historic Seattle acquired them. Restoration, which was managed by David Fergus of Stickney & Murphy, project architects, included adding fresh paint that matched the original colors,

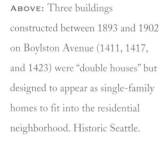

ABOVE: Three buildings constructed between 1893 and 1902 on Boylston Avenue (1411, 1417, and 1423) were "double houses" but designed to appear as single-family homes to fit into the residential neighborhood. Historic Seattle.

installing new carpets and kitchen cabinets, keeping the high ceilings and dark, aged woodwork, and in some rooms retaining the original fireplaces, even though they were no longer usable. The new units became one-bedroom, studio, and single-room-occupancy low-income apartments. The project received numerous awards for successfully combining historic preservation and affordable housing. Five of the six buildings are now owner-occupied housing.

RIGHT: 1423 Boylston Avenue is painted its original color. Historic Seattle.

HOTELS

In 1907 Seattle defined a hotel as a building—or part of one—intended, designed, or used for lodging purposes and having more than 20 sleeping rooms for guests. Many were very similar to large boarding/rooming houses. A construction boom that began in the 1870s had boosted the number of Seattle hotels, to appeal to both temporary and permanent residents.

ELEGANT HOTELS

Seattle had several "grand" or first-class residential hotels, such as the Lincoln, Sorrento, Perry, and Stander. Many people listed in the *Social Blue Book of Seattle*, a yearly compilation of prominent Seattle citizens, gave these hotels as their place of residence. All offered well-appointed suites, elegant dining rooms, trained staff, personal service, and social prominence. All promoted easy access to streetcar lines

going to and from downtown theaters, social clubs, restaurants, and shopping. To the upper-middle class, who wanted the luxury and elegance of stately homes without the hassle of upkeep and struggle to find servants, grand residential hotels were especially appealing.

PERRY HOTEL, 1019 MADISON STREET | 1906-7 (DEMOLISHED)

"PERRY FLATS UNDER WAY . . . New York Apartment house transplanted in Seattle," announced the *Seattle Post-Intelligencer*, October 21, 1906. Joseph S. Coté and W. Marbury Somervell, who had been sent to Seattle by the New York firm Heins & LaFarge to supervise the construction of St. James Catholic Cathedral, designed this splendid building on the southwest corner of Boren and Madison at a cost of $275,000.[58] The site, close to the cathedral, had been occupied by Judge Cornelius Hanford's former home. Although it was an elegant building resembling apartment houses in New York, it was a hotel.

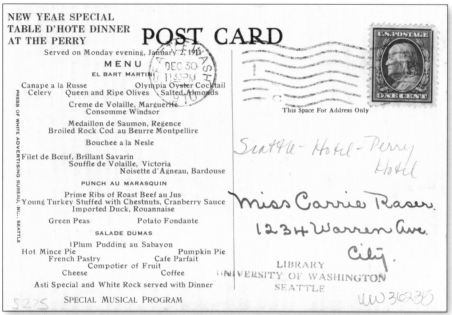

ABOVE: A colored postcard of the Perry Hotel promoted a New Year special table d'hôte dinner served on Monday, January 2, 1911. UW36235, Special Collections, University of Washington Libraries.

The eight-story brick building featured 83 units, ranging from one to eight rooms, each with an outside room. The front page of *The Week-End* heralded its opening in glowing terms. According to the newspaper, the rooms had been arranged to accommodate each distinctive guest, "from the bachelor who wants one room and a bath to the family that requires a housekeeping suite of eight rooms, a dressing room and two baths."[59] The larger suites had 15-by-23-foot living rooms with fireplaces, kitchens, dining rooms, three bedrooms, and a maid's room. The smaller ones had two bedrooms but no maid's room.

The Perry management considered the hotel's splendid cuisine a notable feature. The spacious dining room seated 250 with small tables. Guests could order à la carte meals throughout the day and evening, along with a table d'hôte dinner beginning at six o'clock. Additionally, two rooms on the main floor were set aside as tea rooms. The two men in charge of the restaurant had previously worked at New York's Waldorf-Astoria Hotel. An article in *The Week-End* from December 1907 described the management and trained staff as providing "such service as has not before been known in Seattle."

The Perry's popularity had declined by 1910, due to completion of the nearby Sorrento Hotel. Advertisements now emphasized that the Perry would be especially good for "TRANSIENT VISITORS away from the noise, congestion and discomforts of the business center."[60] In an early example of adaptive reuse, Mother Frances Xavier Cabrini purchased the Perry in 1916. The following year, she founded Columbus Sanitarium, which became Columbus Hospital and later was renamed Cabrini Hospital in honor of its founder [61](see Chapter 7).

SORRENTO HOTEL, 900 MADISON STREET | 1909

Businessman Samuel Rosenberg, proprietor of Kline and Rosenberg Clothiers, hired architect Harlan Thomas to design an elegant hotel on the northwest corner of Madison Street and Terry Avenue. The as yet unnamed building was simply called a "modern family and tourist hotel" by the *Post-Intelligencer* on April 10, 1908. But its presence had far greater import. Many years later, in a 1940 newsletter article, Leslie Jackson said, "The building of The Sorrento epitomized a change in the life of the city from the pioneer era, the time when men and women lived close to the soil was over and the building of a luxurious residential hotel was one of the first steps toward 'The New York of the West.' "[62]

The seven-story Italianate-style hotel accommodated a sloping site and took advantage of the then-panoramic westerly views of Elliott Bay, Puget Sound, and the Olympic Peninsula. Two perpendicular wings are separated by a courtyard, which operates as a barrier between the hotel and busy Madison Street. The hotel entry is

RIGHT: The Sorrento Hotel was an impressive addition to First Hill, with its wings framing a formally landscaped courtyard. PEMCO Webster & Stevens Collection 1983.10.9468.1, MOHAI.

ABOVE: Sorrento Hotel's mahogany-paneled lobby with Mission rockers, ca. 1909. PEMCO Webster & Stevens Collection 1983.10.2195.2, MOHAI.

through the courtyard area, via a porte cochere. The courtyard facades and the other principal elevations are primarily clad with Flemish bond maroon brick, highlighted with gray-white brick. The facade is distinguished by a classically derived terra-cotta ornament comprising a sixth-floor oculus (circular opening), with an elaborate terra-cotta surround and gable pediments. In designing the Sorrento, Thomas "bespoke some willingness to explore innovatively rather than accept routinely the conventions of the day."[63]

Amenities included a ladies' parlor and reception rooms, and a billiard and grill room on the first floor. The Fireside Room, adjacent to the main lobby, is octagonal in shape, with dark Honduran mahogany paneling and trim. A distinctive feature of this room is the 12-foot-wide inglenook fireplace, decorated and faced with a variety of glazed tiles commissioned from the Rookwood Pottery and installed by the Kellogg Company of Seattle[64] Tiles over the mantel are hand-painted, illustrating an Italian garden complete with blue skies and cypress trees.

To enable visitors to enjoy the view of Puget Sound and the Olympics, Thomas placed the sunroom, tearooms, roof garden, kitchen, and 3,000-square-foot main dining room on the top floor. A trussed roof covered the dining room and kitchen. A Mission design was first used for the dining room furniture, but in a 1925 remodel the management replaced it with Colonial Revival. This, they believed, would evoke a homelike atmosphere.[65]

The hotel opened in 1909, just in time for the Alaska-Yukon-Pacific Exposition. Some people checked in for a few days and ended up making the Sorrento their home for years. During World War I, the Red Cross set up headquarters in the dining room, and "long tables were spread out for the purpose of making bandages. Tea dances were frequently given in the lobby in honor of

RIGHT: The Sorrento Hotel top floor dining room, ca. 1921. For years the Top O' the Town was a popular gathering place. PEMCO Webster & Stevens Collection 1983.10.2195.3, MOHAI.

RIGHT: A specially commissioned Rookwood tile fireplace depicts an Italian garden. Courtesy Sorrento Hotel.

the officers."[66] In spite of the war, those who lived at the Sorrento had a grand time.

The Sorrento sold in 1937 for approximately $100,000 to the Hotel Sorrento Operating Company.[67] As a result of remodels and renovations through the years, today's guests enjoy modern conveniences in a historic building. In recent years, with oversight by local owners, it has become one of the city's most charming boutique hotels.

RESIDENTIAL/FAMILY HOTELS

Residential or family hotels had a broad appeal for those who came to work in the myriad service businesses and industries. None of these establishments described kitchens or cooking facilities in the rooms, but they did stress the service of a community dining room. "Superior table service and cuisine will be features carefully looked after," claimed The Hawthorne, a family hotel at 614 Madison Street.[68] Schoolteachers especially enjoyed living in family hotels, as they "provided social opportunities and friendships" in a casual and congenial atmosphere. "Managers often knew the residents by name and knew 'their individual needs and peculiarities' . . . A young woman accustomed to middle-class standards in her parents' home could replicate them more affordably in a hotel than she could in furnishing a separate household," wrote Doris Pieroth, author of *Seattle's Women Teachers of the Interwar Years*.[69] Though Pieroth was referring to teachers, the same could be said about professionals such as doctors and lawyers, salespeople, office workers, and clerks. In fact, hotels such as the Akronhurst announced that businessmen and professionals would find the hotel a "delightful retreat."[70] Having someone else prepare the meals, wash the dishes, change the sheets, and make the beds had enormous appeal, especially for men and women who worked all day. "Oh it was fun! Living in those small residential hotels was fun," recalled Doris Chargois, a Seattle teacher.[71]

OTIS FAMILY HOTEL, 804 SUMMIT AVENUE | 1900 (DEMOLISHED)

RIGHT: The Otis Hotel, at Summit Avenue between Columbia and Marion Streets, ca. 1905, comprised the original building and additions, and a more palatial classically inspired three-story building to its north. SHS 5334, MOHAI.

The Otis House began as a boarding house, but in 1902 owner C. R. Otis hired architect E. W. Houghton to design a three-story brick addition.[72] Thereafter the Otis, occupying the entire block between Marion and Columbia on Summit Avenue, began billing itself as a family hotel. It emphasized a large veranda, lawns, flowers, and homelike atmosphere. At the Otis, lodgers had their choice of single rooms or suites with private bath. The Otis also offered long-distance telephones in every room, and advertised a "cuisine of the highest order" in a community dining room. The Otis preferred to receive applications "in person only." "No smoke, no noise, and no mosquitoes," said a 1907 advertisement.[73]

GREYSTONE, 1200-12 MARION STREET AND 912 MINOR AVENUE | 1892 (DEMOLISHED)

Teachers and others desiring comfortable lodging also chose the Greystone, first called the Greystone Terrace, at the corner of Marion and Minor. It was a block from the Madison Street streetcar, and offered fine cuisine in a "richly furnished" dining room. It also provided a music room, call bells, hot and cold running water, telephones, large rooms and suites in a fireproof building, and "well kept lawns." The Greystone occupied Seattle's only stone row buildings. It was built of Tenino bluestone in 1892 by architect John Parkinson. "Each will cover a space 20 feet by 70 feet, will be three stories high and contain twelve rooms," announced the *Seattle Post-Intelligencer*.[74] The Greystone was demolished in 1970.

MANCHESTER ARMS/ACIREMA, 1412 SUMMIT AVENUE | 1908

In July 1907 a notice in the *Seattle Daily Times* announced that Charles Donaldson had a building permit for a new five-story elevator hotel at 1412 Summit Avenue. It would have 29 tubs and 29 toilets distributed among 105 rooms.

Throughout the years it seemed to straddle the line between boarding/lodging house, hotel, and apartments. For example, an August 1911 advertisement boasted rented furnished two-room apartments and single rooms and was listed under apartments; a November 1911 advertisement appearing under the Board and Room category said furnished and unfurnished apartments as well as furnished rooms with or without board; and finally in July 1912, the Acirema, the new name, viewed itself as a "strictly first-class family hotel. Rooms and board by the day, week or month."[75]

APARTMENTS

With an increase in the popularity of multifamily dwellings as well as more stringent fire-prevention ordinances, builders and architects replaced the earlier-built frame flats with brick and concrete fireproof apartment buildings.[76] "A feature of the realty development of Seattle is the apartment house invasion of the first hill . . . the city grew and is growing beyond the expectations of the early residents," commented the *Seattle Post-Intelligencer*, December 16, 1906. By 1910, single-family homes had ceased to be built on First Hill, as its location made commercial enterprises—such as apartments, hospitals, hotels, banks, and businesses—lucrative investments.

What is more, Seattle apartments made their appearance just when Americans had begun to spend more to achieve an easier lifestyle. No longer content with self-denial, consumers challenged the moralistic approach to spending and began a debate on how to "economize in a world where yesterday's luxuries seemed to become today's necessities."[77] By the first decades of the 20th century, Americans had "more money and more time to purchase more goods . . . Society's task was, therefore, no longer how to make do with less, as it always had been, but instead how to live with much more," said historian Thomas Schlereth.[78]

Seattle's introduction of home services such as clean water, gas, and electricity had made it possible for apartment builders to offer these up-to-date amenities. Coinciding with the rise in industrialization that began in the early 1880s and Seattle's growth, these functioning utilities, abetted by the switch from privately owned utilities to those municipally owned, facilitated the city's acceptance of apartment houses as a way to accommodate its burgeoning population. They were essential for turning Seattle into a metropolitan area, and as indispensable as lumberyards and seaports.

Tenants in many of First Hill's apartments were among those who desired the accoutrements of a good life. Apartment building owners recognized the advantages of having a building with no vacancies and filled them with distinctive furnishings, such as electric ranges, built-in cabinets, Hide-A-Beds, tubs with showers, telephones, and rooms wired for radio aerials. Aware of the importance of appealing to the middle class, some apartment buildings hired decorators to choose specially designed wallpaper and select fabric for lobby furniture.

BELOW: "The Herrick Refrigerators Are the Best." 29472z, Special Collections, University of Washington Libraries.

On First Hill the apartment buildings ranged from three- to four-story rectangular-shaped brick structures with simply painted rooms to lavishly decorated penthouses in eight- to nine-story terra-cotta ornamented buildings. Many retained the bay windows so popular in Victorian houses because they provided additional light and increased the square footage.[79]

Residents frequently moved between buildings. Margaret Reed recalled the time when her family lived in First Hill apartments:

> *There was one more move in that time, too, always looking for more room. The next move was in 1934 to the Lawton apartments on Union Street. Then in 1936 we moved to the Cassel Crag Apartments, between Seneca and University on Terry Avenue. It is a U-shaped building of light brick. You could do the washing there, and they had mangles for ironing. The apartment didn't have a bedroom, but it did have a living room, a dining room and bathroom and a very small kitchen. There was a bed, like a Murphy bed, that swiveled around and folded into the closet. My parents moved again in 1938, when I was a sophomore in high school, this time to the Knickerbocker Apartments at 1022 Union between Terry and Boren. Each move represented a step up to a more spacious apartment. Now, we had a bedroom! We also had a large kitchen with space. I lived there from 1938 until I got married, in 1944.[80]*

Presented here are short descriptions of some of these well-constructed buildings, built in the first three decades of the 20th century, which have been standing amidst the comings and goings of trolleys, cars, and people for more than 100 years.

1900-1910 APARTMENTS

ST. PAUL, 1206 SUMMIT AVENUE AND 1302-1308 SENECA STREET | 1901

The St. Paul has the distinction of being Seattle's first purpose-built apartment house. Edwin C. Burke, a builder, owned the property, which he named to honor St. Paul, Minnesota, the city of his birth. The Tacoma firm Spalding & Russell designed the three-story L-shaped building in a style they termed "modern colonial."[81]

RIGHT: St. Paul Apartments at Seneca Street and Summit Avenue had three entrances, and its quoins, bay windows, columned loggias, and shallow balconies provided visual interest (ca. 1920). PEMCO Webster & Stevens Collection 1983.10.2601, MOHAI.

"Cement plaster [stucco] applied to sheet steel lath" covered the exterior walls. Each of the entrances opened onto a lobby, once elegantly furnished with rugs and pier-glass mirrors. From each of three entrances, there were two apartments per floor for a total of 18,

divided among five-, six-, seven-, and eight-room units. This configuration eliminated a long corridor, one of the least liked features of apartments, and assured the tenants of more privacy.

Before many of the facade's architectural details—such as loggias on the second and third floors just above the Seneca entrances, decorative finials, and brick quoins—were removed to "modernize," the St. Paul was considered a showplace and was home to distinguished Seattle families. Some of its former elegance can still be seen in individual apartments, which have retained the 10-foot ceilings and some of the kitchen and bathroom fixtures.

Nearly all of its distinctive facade features disappeared during later remodeling.

SAN MARCO, 1205-09 SPRING STREET | 1905

Just a block away, the San Marco is another reminder of an earlier era. To distinguish this three-story plus daylight basement building, the architects, Charles Saunders and George Lawton, and the builder/developer, Bert Farrar, chose a stucco exterior and Mission style. Within a few months it became investment property for Senator Cyrus F. Clapp, who purchased it for $70,000.[82]

Gabled dormers with curvilinear parapets, typical of the Spanish Mission style, are centered on the San Marco's central section and symmetrical wings. Three recessed arched marble-faced entrances, each with broken pediments topped with an ornamental medallion, invite residents inside. All entrances are accessed from the courtyard, once "brilliantly lighted at night."[83] Inside, large living rooms let in an abundance of natural light and once had butler's pantries. Crossed by more than a century of footsteps, the courtyard provides a protective green space amidst the somber facades of First Hill's many new condominiums.

Other extant apartment buildings from the first decade of the 20th century include: the four-story, 132-room Westminster (1906), designed by architect Andrew McBean at 903-05 Ninth Avenue; and the 84-room Russell Apartments (1906), designed by Charles Saunders and George Lawton, at 909 Ninth Avenue; the two-and-a-half-story Buckingham/Shannon (1905) at 1220 Boylston Avenue; and the Old Colony (1910), at 615 Boren Avenue, credited to the Frank P. Allen firm of architects.

ABOVE: One of the three entrances to San Marco Apartments, 2014. Historic Seattle.

RIGHT: San Marco Apartments on Spring Street at Minor Avenue, ca. 1905. Its stucco walls, Mission dormers, and decorative mullion upper lights were distinctive features. 36240, Special Collections, University of Washington Libraries.

Nearby a group of early-20th-century apartment buildings have all been demolished due to the expansion of the hospitals. The three-story Adrian Court (1903-4) at 911-913 Summit Avenue boasted four- and six-room apartments, with a maid's room in the larger apartments. It was designed by S. A. Jennings and advertised as "the first solid concrete building to be erected in the Pacific Northwest."[84]

RIGHT: Old Colony apartments were elegant and spacious, with high ceilings and large windows (ca. 1910). PEMCO Webster & Stevens Collection 1983.10.8720, MOHAI.

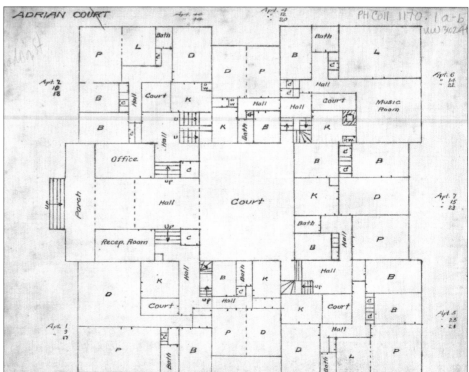

RIGHT: Ground floor plan, Adrian Court, shows orientation of apartments and stair access. PH Collection 170. 1a-b (36244), Special Collections, University of Washington Libraries.

RIGHT: Adrian Court Apartments on Summit Avenue and Madison Street, ca. 1906, was elegant enough to attract the fledgling Sunset Club for its initial location (see Chapter 3). UW36241, Special Collections, University of Washington Libraries.

FRANCES BACKUS REMEMBERED THE ADRIAN COURT

It was built by a man who had a crush, you might say, on the Emperor Hadrian of Rome . . . This man had the court built in a Roman domestic architecture mode. It was really a very beautiful building although by the time we arrived in 1938 it was quite run down. We had an apartment that was half of one of the ground floor apartments, which were very commodious and elegant. We had a 24-foot living room with plate glass windows, hard wood floors and two gas-log fireplaces with elegant over-mantles . . . The building was built around an interior courtyard, or atrium, which had a glass roof. It was a three-story building and the roof was reinforced with chicken wire. On the floor of the atrium, made of tiny mosaics, lovingly installed by hand, there were little carts with plants on them, which the manager pushed around everyday to get some sunshine on each of the plants. Our kitchen looked out into this courtyard, and our bedroom looked out on the cable car, which came to an end while we were living there. We watched them tear up the tracks and they were sent off to Japan and returned a few years later as bombs. Our rent was $50 a month and we thought that was very high and so did our friends, but we managed it.

And it had maid's bells, the maids lived in dreadful little rooms down in the basement of the building. There were bars on all the windows of course. The original inhabitants used to ring these bells, but by the time we arrived, they'd all been painted over so many times you couldn't possibly summon anyone from the bowels of the basement. [Adrian Court] was a very beautiful place. It had a great deal of style and it was like an old dowager who was declining into poverty, but it was very beautiful. I often wondered how they got it down, it had very thick cement walls.[85]

1911-1919 APARTMENTS

ARCADIA APARTMENTS, 1222 SUMMIT AVENUE | 1916

ABOVE: Arcadia terra-cotta entrance, 2014. Historic Seattle.

North of the St. Paul, the four-story Arcadia Apartments has weathered the years and retained its earlier architectural style. Builder Isham B. Johnson, employed by the property's owners, Simon and Max Kreilsheimer, in 1915, used dark red brick, interspersed with contrasting Gothic Revival ivory-colored terra-cotta, on the exterior walls of this U-shaped building. Two entrances, with oak doors and beveled glass inserts, are located opposite one another on either side of an irregular-shaped courtyard. Light from the original glass ceiling fixtures brightens both lobbies. Green marble wainscoting decorates the lobby walls and the stairway walls to the first floor.

The building has exceptionally large one- and two-bedroom apartments, with an average space of 1,044 square feet.[86] The units are entered from wide corridors, and each apartment has two entrances, each with its own doorbell. One door opens into the kitchen, another into an entrance hallway. All apartments have a living room, dining room, bedroom, kitchen, bathroom, linen closets, and large walk-in closets. The kitchens have built-in wood cabinets that extend to the ceiling. Wood pocket doors separate the living and dining areas.

In 1936, Mary Bard Jensen, sister of Betty MacDonald, author of the popular memoir *The Egg and I,* lived in the Arcadia. "They had not chosen the apartments because they were light and sunny and had two bedrooms. They [Mary and husband Clyde, a physician] had chosen them because they were across the street from Maternity [Maynard] Hospital and would be so convenient for night calls," wrote Mary in *The Doctor Wears Three Faces.*[87]

MAXMILLIAN, 1414 SENECA STREET | 1918

Architect Victor Wilbur (V.W.) Voorhees, who designed Maynard Hospital on First Hill, designed the Gothic Revival three-story plus basement, 27-unit Maxmillian Apartments. It replaced a boarding house. His judicious use of cream-colored terra-cotta on the facade makes a striking contrast to the dark red pressed-brick walls. The recessed entry has a Tudor arched terra-cotta surround with the name MAXMILLIAN incised in it. A straight flight of marble stairs leads through the recessed entry to the front door, with beveled glass side windows, still intact on the right side, and a beveled glass transom. Inside the small lobby, Gothic crosses are incised in the newel posts of the wood stairway leading to the upper floors.

Studio apartments featured kitchens in alcoves off the large living rooms. Cooler boxes, which kept foods cold before refrigerators became common appliances, were installed in the dining areas of some apartments. Double doors in the living rooms hid wall beds. Advertisements indicate that the Maxmillian did not accept families with children and required "references for prospective tenants."[88]

THE 1920S

Apartment-building construction continued into the 1920s and "converted the First Hill into one of Seattle's best apartment house districts," noted the *Seattle Daily Times* on March 24, 1929. Local investors found that apartments provided lucrative opportunities. As permits for new structures continued to increase, returns on investment in real estate soared. A writer for the *Times* touted apartment houses as "the safest and surest investments in the City of Seattle." Furthermore, those with $10,000 to $25,000 could safely invest in good apartments and be assured of a very good income.[89]

RIGHT: A typical apartment kitchen in a building designed by Stuart & Wheatley. UW 36239, Special Collections, University of Washington Libraries.

Representing a smaller increase than in previous decades, it was still enough to buoy the building, buying, and selling of apartment houses, which peaked in 1925 and continued strongly until 1929-30. They were built with brick, usually had recessed openings on the floors above the front entrances, varied in height from three to 12 stories, and had all of the modern conveniences, such as electric ranges, telephones, and radios.

As the effects of the Great Depression began to be felt in Seattle, construction of new apartments almost ceased, and the heyday of the entrepreneurs was over.

PAUL REVERE, 1018 NINTH AVENUE, AND JOHN ALDEN, 1019 TERRY AVENUE | 1924

One prominent architect, Harry E. Hudson, left his signature on many of the First Hill apartments built during the 1920s. They are easily recognized, as Hudson named his buildings after figures of New England history and literature—John Alden, Paul Revere, Ralph Waldo Emerson, and James Russell Lowell. His contractor, the Colonial Investment Company, reinforced Hudson's history bent.

Hudson and his brother John, a licensed architect who preferred building, created the plans for the Paul Revere and the John Alden, two buildings almost identical in plan and located back-to-back on adjacent sites. Favoring colonial motifs, the brothers incorporated "the spirit of Colonial America in both structures," reported the *Seattle Daily Times* on July 20, 1924. The Paul Revere windows portrayed the story of his midnight ride, and a brick pedestal holding a relief of Revere on his horse was centered on the steps.

The four-story, U-shaped John Alden is notable for its brick detailing with brighter colored brick as ornamentation, forming quoins, string courses, lintels, and a

water table above the concrete foundation. Cream-colored terra-cotta is used for cornice and coping and arched panels between windows in the center bay. The entry bay is more ornate, with a narrow portico supported by four columns, window surrounds and pilasters, and a shield design on the parapet. The spandrels have a parquet pattern in varying shades of red brick. The doorway is elaborate, with oak doors and sidelights with leaded art glass medallions of ships, pilgrims, and Indians on the shore. Art glass windows in the lobby depict the *Mayflower* leaving England and arriving at Plymouth. The leaded-glass windows in the stair hall on each floor incorporate unique medallion designs of Indians and pilgrims at work in the fields, at spinning wheels, and hunting and fishing.[90]

The two- and three-room apartments featured such conveniences as breakfast alcoves, Murphy beds, tile baths, refrigeration, and ample laundry facilities. The breakfast alcove had ivory-painted gate leg tables and chairs. Solid oak was used for flooring. Both buildings rented furnished or unfurnished. Just a month after the opening, the Paul Revere was sold. It "is regarded among real estate agents as one of the most desirable apartment properties in the city," said the *Seattle Daily Times*, August 24, 1924.

LOWELL, 1102 EIGHTH AVENUE, AND EMERSON, 1110 EIGHTH AVENUE | 1928

Harry E. Hudson also designed the Lowell and Emerson apartment houses. The two buildings, constructed in 1928, are clad with "faced brick" and trimmed in terra-cotta. When the L-shaped Lowell conjoined the rectangular-shaped Emerson, they had "more suites than any other apartment house on the Pacific coast north of San Francisco," reported the *Seattle Daily Times*, December 16, 1928.

The Lowell contained 158 two-room apartments on the first 10 floors, while the 11th, the top floor, contained four five-room bungalow suites. The smaller Emerson had 37 units. A courtyard, formed by the two joined buildings, was enhanced by a fountain and shrubbery. Both the lobby and dining room, which occupied a separate one-story wing, were furnished with Adam Period furniture. The Neo-Classical decor included plaster moldings, fabric-paneled walls, crystal chandeliers, and white linen table-cloths. It was a popular gathering place managed by Herb and Cathie Pryor. Regular guests included Royal Brougham, sports editor of the *Seattle Post-Intelligencer*, and Dewey Soriano, manager of the Rainiers baseball

team. Because every unit had a kitchen, and tenants and their guests had access to a dining room, these buildings were classified as Apartment Hotels.

Amenities included kitchens with electric ranges and refrigeration, telephone and radio service, and a French-style telephone connected with the central switchboard. The woodwork and picture moldings were ivory colored. The bungalow suites had inlaid parquet floors; the dining room had blue and gold carpeting.[91]

A short poem in a short-lived but popular 1920s tabloid, *Seattlite: News and Notes of People and Places*, praised the decor, location, and dining room's cuisine:

THERE's an apartment known as the Lowell,
Perched on quite a respectable knoll,
The view is immense
For such reasonable rents,
Perfection is held as its goal.
Its dining room ranks with the best,
Their lamb chops could stand any test,
The location indeed
Is just what you need
For comfort and Service and rest.

By the 1950s its popularity had declined and it catered to lesser-known persons. It also replaced the Adam decor with a lavender makeover.

PIEDMONT RESIDENTIAL HOTEL, 1109 SUMMIT AVENUE | 1926
PIEDMONT APARTMENT HOTEL, 1215 SENECA STREET | 1928

It took little time before the stucco-faced Italianate Piedmont residential hotel of 1926 required expansion to accommodate more tenants. Architect Daniel Huntington

RIGHT: The clean geometric stucco facade of the Piedmont Hotel is countered by Italianate ornament and colorful Malibu tile. PEMCO Webster & Stevens Collection 1983.10.3578, MOHAI.

ABOVE: One of the largest Malibu tile installations in the Northwest frames the arched windows and entrance doors of the lobby and the ground-floor residences, as well as the capitals of the lobby columns inside. Historic Seattle.

had a long-standing love of the Italianate style. In 1927, following his interest in the handiwork and crafts movements in California, he decided to face his Piedmont Hotel addition in a colorful skirt of Malibu tile—one of the largest installations of this tile in the region. It comprised arched surrounds for the lobby windows and the entrances to the lobby and the restaurant, as well as the geometric-patterned column capitals in the two-story lobby. For the dining room, he incorporated Claycraft tile inset in the stucco plaster walls, choosing appropriate scenes and buildings reminiscent of the Southwest.

In addition to the dining room, the apartment hotel had a music room, a lending library, and "an especially fine radio installation, providing unit control in every apartment." The apartments had kitchens and dinettes, electric ranges, automatic refrigerators, all-night telephone and elevator service, and use of a large garage staffed with attendants. The Piedmont offered 112 hotel rooms and 30 two- and three-room apartments.

In 1963, when freeway plans forced the Salvation Army to relocate its Evangeline Home from Sixth Avenue and Madison Street, it purchased The Piedmont. The building was converted to apartments in 1987 and renamed the Tuscany.

BOREN AVENUE APARTMENTS

Boren Avenue, named for Seattle founder Carson D. Boren, became especially desirable for apartment houses during the 1920s. Buildings with distinct architectural designs, materials, and features, such as the Marlborough and Sovereign, extended

RIGHT: North of the Gothic Marlborough on Boren Avenue, the Sovereign Apartments embraced an earlier Romanesque style for its brick and terra-cotta facade. PEMCO Webster & Stevens Collection 1983.10.3117, MOHAI.

northward along Boren Avenue to form a continuous street facade. Despite the loss of the Hungerford and Northcliffe apartments between Spring and Seneca Streets (both razed for Virginia Mason Medical Center expansion), these buildings preserve the successes of that era in high-density vertical development.

Before the city widened the street in 1946, residents enjoyed a pleasant scene of landscaped parking areas.[92] "Oh, the boys used to skate on Boren. There was no traffic of course," recalled Frances Backus.[93]

NORTHCLIFFE, 1119 BOREN AVENUE | 1925 (DEMOLISHED)

Daniel Huntington drew the plans; John S. Hudson owned the property and constructed the Northcliffe, which was originally an apartment hotel.[94] Sited at the northeast corner of Boren and Seneca Street, this L-shaped five-story reinforced concrete building was clad in varied-color brown brick with cast-stone elements. Several half-timbered gable dormers enhanced the roof. Granite steps led to the Boren Street entrance, which had a cast-stone and brick surround.

The 1925 reviews in the Real Estate section of the *Seattle Daily Times* emphasized that the Northcliffe's large living rooms had specially designed carpets "heavily felt padded so that the surface of the carpets is flush with the terrazzo and marble floors," which made for "noiseless halls." Additionally, the units featured an "electrically equipped kitchenette with electric refrigeration in which you can make your own ice with power supplied by us."[95]

A public dining room capable of serving the occupants of the entire building and neighborhood guests was expected to be a popular feature. When the building contractors did not have the kitchen completed by the Northcliffe's opening, the management arranged for the tenants to eat in the Sorrento dining room. In the 1920s the Northcliffe offered complete hotel service—meals, maids, bellboys, and elevator boys. Tenants, whether temporary or permanent, could choose meals from several dining rooms or request room service. They also had the option of asking the resident cooks to prepare the meals in their own kitchenette.

The Northcliffe had 51 apartment units, which ranged from one-rooms to five-rooms. Shirley Fuller, who managed and lived at the Northcliffe between 1939 and 1948, said that during World War II the Northcliffe eliminated its hotel services and became a "full-time occupancy because people were really standing in line to apply for apartments." At that time apartments were hard to find and the owners judged prospective tenants by appearance: "whether they bothered to dress up for the occasion . . . what their backgrounds were . . . There was some racial discrimination. In other words we could have Black—as it is called now—maids, but we couldn't have tenants that were Black. That was true for Asians and Hispanics as well, and Jews too. However, we did have Jewish people occupying one of the apartments when I came there, and they stayed a long time."[96]

MARLBOROUGH HOUSE, 1220 BOREN AVENUE | 1928

The Marlborough replaced the Chateau, a popular boarding house that originally had been the home of Margaret Denny, daughter of Seattle founders Arthur and Mary Ann Boren Denny. Construction for the 13-story luxury-class apartment building began in 1927, and it opened the following year. Built of steel and reinforced concrete, faced with brick in varying shades of ochre and brown, and trimmed with ochre-colored terra-cotta, the Marlborough represented quality. Architect Earl W. Morrison drew the plans after making a study of the finest apartment buildings in New York.[97]

The imposing entrance has a terra-cotta surround made up of "flat triple-arched porches crowned with a blind arch balustrade." Four projecting bays on the facade extend to the 12th floor. At this level the bay piers are elaborately ornamented with terra-cotta. Both the cornice and parapet wall also have decorated terra-cotta, some with English Perpendicular-style motifs.

BELOW: The Marlborough, tallest of the Boren Avenue apartment buildings, used vertical piers and Gothic terra-cotta crowns to emphasize its height, ca. 1928. PEMCO Webster & Stevens Collection 1983.10.3572, MOHAI.

The 12th-floor penthouse, advertised as an eight-room maisonette, boasted a large living and dining room, both of which had floors suitable for dancing. Each of the three bedrooms had a private bath, large closets, and dressing rooms. There was a butler's pantry off the roomy kitchen. Individual apartments in the Marlborough had tile baths with showers, mahogany woodwork, and walls painted or wallpapered in colors made popular by Louis Comfort Tiffany. The services of maids, butlers, and valets, as well as a commissary, laundry, and garage, made it easy to live at Marlborough House. Advertisements boldly announced that here "you will find an outstanding combination of exclusiveness, distinction of address, convenience of location and extreme 'livability.'"[98]

1223 SPRING STREET | 1929

On January 6, 1929, the *Seattle Daily Times* chronicled the construction of a $580,000 apartment house at 1223 Spring Street that "will be built with a direct appeal to persons of means who are dissatisfied with maintaining large residences in the suburban districts." Using only street and number for the name, the building conveyed a certain cachet and eliminated the possibility of others copying the name.

RIGHT: A 1929 brochure promotes exclusivity by comparing 1223 Spring Street to the luxury apartment buildings along New York's Park Avenue, but "with surroundings much superior." Historic Seattle.

TWELVE Twenty-Three Spring Street is truly a 1929 model of Apartment Home—the finest north of San Francisco and west of Chicago. The apartments embody the same beauty and luxury to be found on Park Avenue, New York, with surroundings much superior.

Reinforced concrete makes up the structural frame of the building. The exterior walls of the first and second stories are surfaced in cut stone, the third through 11th floors have a tawny-colored brick veneer, and the 12th is brick, generously adorned with terra-cotta. Design elements such as ornamented terra-cotta stringcourses to mark a transition from stone to brick and from plain brick to diamond-pattern are characteristic of the architect, Earl Morrison.

The combination of Morrison's plans and specifications, and builder L. H. Hoffman's skills and expertise, produced a magnificent building. Realtors would not have to exaggerate when describing this apartment house. Seattle had not seen such a luxurious building since the days when grand mansions and residential hotels, such as the Perry, lined First Hill streets. Plans for the 12-story building called for one palatial apartment occupying the entire top floor, and two apartments—one three-bedroom, one two-bedroom—on each of the remaining floors. These well-appointed apartments had a foyer, reception room, living room, dining room, tile kitchen, pantry, tile bathrooms with enclosed glass showers, and a maid's room, complete with its own bathroom.[99] An integral garage at the rear of the building housed the residents' cars. Resplendent views of the lakes and mountains surrounding Seattle could be seen from the windows of the upper floors. Formal gardens on the garage roof provided a place for outdoor relaxation for those not fortunate enough to have the penthouse, with its east and west terraces.

Many prominent and notable Seattle citizens have chosen it for their homes, among them David W. Bowen, president of Puget Sound Sheet Metal Works; Alfred Shemanski, owner of Eastern Outfitting Company; Henry Isaacson of Isaacson Steel; Prentice Bloedel, owner of MacMillan Bloedel Ltd., a lumber company; Joseph A. Swalwell, president of Seattle First National Bank; and Anne Gould Hauberg, daughter of architect Carl Gould and a founder of Pilchuck Glass School. It is ironic that within a year or two of the opening of this most grand apartment building, Seattle's golden age of apartment building came to a halt.

THE BARONESS APARTMENT HOTEL, 1005 SPRING STREET | 1930-31

RIGHT: The last tourist and residential hotel to rise on First Hill, the Baroness was completed in 1930-31 by the firm Schack, Young & Myers. Its design showcases cast-stone Art Deco embellishments. Historic Seattle.

BELOW: Gothic-style terra-cotta trim banding, along with window spandrels and surrounds, visually reduces the mass of the Exeter House facade. Curtis 54260, Washington State Historical Society.

John H. Armin and L. Stark, working with the Mackintosh-Truman Lumber Co., pioneer Seattle hotel and apartment developers, brought in James Hansen Schack, architect, and Arrigo M. Young, engineer, to design the Baroness. John C. Owsley supervised the construction of the six-story Baroness Apartment Hotel.

Buff-colored brick veneer over reinforced concrete faces the second through sixth floors. The vertical full-height corner bays, rising from the first to the sixth floor, are faced with faux stone. The stylized floral design in the spandrels between the metal casement windows and the three-dimensional zigzag brickwork in the parapet are characteristic Art Deco design. The Baroness opened with 30 apartments and 30 hotel rooms.

The first floor provided a reception lobby, with an elevator, stair, and secondary entry on its south side. An adjacent lounge was built to the west of the lobby. This lounge featured a marble-clad fireplace on its west wall, and accessed a raised platform on the south that once featured low curvilinear walls. Early advertisements called this the Music Room, as it was used for musical performances. Local lore says that visiting opera stars stayed at the Baroness and used the stage when practicing. The stage is now behind one lobby wall.[100]

Early advertisements stressed "the utmost in convenience and luxury." Amenities included spacious closets, a basement laundry with electric washer, dryer, and mangle, electric refrigeration, and an exclusive feature of twin beds in the three-room apartments.

"A CASTLE OF COMFORT IN THE HEART OF SEATTLE"

ABOVE: Sorrento Hotel promotional brochure reprint (no date). Courtesy Sorrento Hotel.

The promotional brochures for First Hill hotels and apartment buildings in the 1920s featured picturesque, romantic images to attract tourists and tenants alike. The Sorrento Hotel, making efforts to entice clientele that had faded since its heyday during the Alaska-Yukon-Pacific Exposition of 1909, extolled its location "majestically crowning the crest of First Hill, a gem in the skyline of the Queen City of our great Northwest, with the most wonderful panoramic view of any hotel in the world, of city, lakes, sound, and mountains in every direction; a view which is always beautiful, presenting an ever changing vista of eternal charm." Of the hotel's distance from the commercial district, the hotel made it a positive, "near enough to be convenient, but away from the noise and confusion of the busy streets." Its most attractive drawing cards were its Fireside Lounge and its view restaurant, Top O' the Town.

The 14-story Exeter Apartment-Hotel, opened in 1928, did nearly identical advertising. "The Exeter, a delightfully quiet place to stop for a night or to live permanently. Near every downtown point of advantage, and overlooking city, Puget Sound, lakes, and Olympic Mountains." And it had a distinct advantage over the Sorrento in its location on Eighth Avenue and Seneca Street, saving its visitors several extremely steep uphill blocks required of Sorrento guests returning from shopping expeditions in the central business district.

Like the investment company that took the name, the Exeter was tied to the ancient British city, and the name was meant to associate the company with old English "stability and integrity," according to D. H. Yates, secretary and treasurer. The architectural firm B. Dudley Stuart & Arthur Wheatley would have no challenges considering the appropriate style for such a building—it called out for the medieval touch of Gothic Revival. Its brick sheathed facades were punctuated with glazed terra-cotta window bays, door frames, and lion shield embellishments.

While this was not a luxury hotel, the Exeter Investment Company promised the not-so-rich that there would be no sacrifices in comfort, claiming that "the rates will attract those of moderate means who insist upon refinements, exceptional comforts and the convenience of being close to the theatres and shopping centers."

ABOVE: Exeter House promotional brochure (no date). Courtesy Exeter House.

A NEW ERA

Apartment building on First Hill and elsewhere in Seattle ceased during the Great Depression and World War II. When construction began again in the late 1940s, apartments had a new look. Almost all facades lacked decorative ornamentation, front doors and windows gave up their beveled and leaded glass, and interiors no longer had coved ceilings or ornate lighting fixtures. In their place, tenants would find TV antennas instead of wiring for radios and more modern kitchen appliances such as dishwashers. Only advertisements remained the same. They were always written in glowing terms.

1000 EIGHTH AVENUE APARTMENTS/NETTLETON, 1000 EIGHTH AVENUE | 1949

The Nettleton, the first elevator apartment structure to be built on First Hill in 20 years, opened in December 1949. Seattle architect Earl W. Morrison designed it, and the building firm Nettleton-Baldwin-Anderson supervised the construction. The twin fireproof 14-story buildings were of reinforced concrete "built under the rigid requirements of Seattle's new earthquake code."[101] Early advertisements proclaimed that "privacy and quiet are assured by acoustic and sound-deadening plaster on walls dividing apartments." The 360 units were to be rented unfurnished, except for refrigerator and range.

Roland and Dorothy Brennan, who moved into the Nettleton in 1955, recalled that time. "Each building had a doorman and any time we received packages that were mailed . . . they brought them right up to us . . . We had an engineer . . . we had the electrician, we had the painters . . . and [if] anything went wrong they knew exactly how to fix it. You never had any worries . . . If something went wrong you'd call the office."[102]

There were also laundries, complete with self-service washers, dryers, and mangles, in each building, as well as a dry-cleaning unit. The residents were assigned times according to their schedule, usually two hours. "It was a very, very nice place," said the Brennans. Early advertisements also mention a nursery for preschool children.

A swimming pool replaced the front lawn in 1958 because so many people, both residents and nonresidents, had been using the front lawn for parking. "We had a beautiful lawn there—this is kind of funny you know—people couldn't find a place to park on the street. They'd come up and park on that beautiful lawn . . . When the pool was built we had lifeguards from the time the pool was opened in the morning. It was only open during the season."[103]

Today, the newly remodeled kitchens have a breakfast bar and a dishwasher, and residents have access to a resident lounge, theatre room, and exercise machines.

BELOW: The two buildings of the Nettleton, built 1949-1950, introduced a new modern vocabulary to the First Hill residential streetscape. shp_19252 1950, Seattle Public Library.

Other apartment buildings quickly followed. In the 1960s, demolition and construction crews again showed up on First Hill streets and razed more of the district's old homes, most of which had long ago been converted to rooming houses. Mrs. Frances Backus noted that these had served a valuable purpose and bemoaned their loss.

> *My father-in-law's house at Boren and University St. became a boarding house. And so many of the lovely big homes met that fate and then they were knocked down as the traffic situation worsened, they were made into parking lots and then some rather junky apartments were thrown up in their spots.*
>
> *It's too bad that the boarding house and the good sense and the kind times that must have taken place in the old Backus house could not have been maintained. There was a very pleasant community, a feeling with the shared meals and young people who came to the community not knowing anyone had an opportunity to make friends and to make a place for themselves. I've always thought it was a shame that teachers had to come home to a lonely apartment instead of a well-maintained boarding house where a good dinner was waiting for them.[104]*

The newcomers included apartment houses such as Panorama House (1100 University Street), Harborview Tower (600 Ninth Avenue), and Sutton Place, nicknamed "the purple palace" for its colored-tile facade (1221 Minor Avenue). Besides extolling the advantages of a near-in location and the best appliances, advertisements for these buildings called attention to a heated swimming pool, the latest in luxury living.

By the late 1970s, First Hill residents, advocates for low-income housing, and preservation-minded locals began serious negotiations to stop developers from building large apartments and condominiums without community input. In 1979 the First Hill Community Council, a neighborhood group formed to inform community members about neighborhood issues, signed an agreement with the Vancouver-based International Land Corp., the developer planning to build the Kelleher House condominiums. This "precedent-setting" agreement stated that the developer would replace the six demolished apartments with low-income apartments for 20 years. Furthermore, the company agreed to pay $350 in relocation expenses to the five tenants who were evicted.[105] The new 16-story Kelleher House at 1120 Spring Street opened in 1982. It was soon joined by 18-story Parkview Plaza, 1101 Seneca Street, and 33-story First Hill Plaza, 1301 Spring Street. Exercise rooms complete with bicycles, treadmills, and rowing machines added to the list of amenities. The 1980 buildings were condominiums, owner-purchased units that had begun appearing in Seattle in 1964.[106]

First Hill, once a neighborhood of beautiful homes, lush lawns, and towering trees, had been forever altered.

YESLER TERRACE: PROGRESSIVE PUBLIC HOUSING IN SEATTLE

TREVOR GRIFFEY AND LAWRENCE KREISMAN

IRENE MILLER ENDS HER REVEALING PERSONAL PORTRAIT OF THE CLEARING OF PROFANITY HILL FOR THE YESLER TERRACE HOUSING PROJECT:

> *Taking one last turn, I watched the orange-red streaks creeping up from behind the Cascades. As the colors grew stronger, they outlined the few remaining skeletons of old buildings on Profanity Hill. I took a deep breath that combined the smell of salt air and fresh timber. Then I looked over at Yesler Terrace's first completed building and thought of the happiness the new garden apartments would bring to needy families. Excitement filled me when I thought of Lisa, Tom and hundreds of other kids who would soon be living in warm safe homes.*[107]

Since its inception, Yesler Terrace's history has revolved around issues of race, displacement, and debates over the spoils of redevelopment. The 43-acre site on the south end of First Hill was first developed in the late 19th century as a suburban refuge for affluent Seattle residents to gain distance from the city's growing downtown. Originally called Yesler Hill, the area became more working class in the early 20th century as the city's affluent moved into other, more fashionable neighborhoods farther from downtown.[108]

With its mansions falling into disrepair, and an unusual patchwork of small businesses and wood-frame homes cropping up between them, the neighborhood increasingly accommodated a diverse collection of low-income residents and ethnic businesses. The nickname Profanity Hill, which supposedly referred to the expletives people would express while making the steep climb to its top from downtown, also came to refer to the underworld economy of drugs, crime, and 18 houses of prostitution that flourished there by the 1930s.

The federally funded Real Property Survey of city buildings in 1934 labeled the area as one of Seattle's worst slums. This survey, combined with an additional Seattle Housing Authority (SHA) survey in late 1937, put Yesler Terrace at the top of the city's list when local leaders sought federal funds for public housing and slum-clearance projects.

The 1,021 people who lived in the neighborhood cared, however. Their displacement, and the demolition of the neighborhood's 158 buildings—some of them Victorian mansions and more modest wood-frame architecture that could have been preserved—is the less publicized part of Yesler Terrace's history.

Irene Miller, the SHA social worker hired to help relocate residents out of the neighborhood and make way for its demolition, recalled in her book *Profanity Hill* that she was almost universally loathed when she started her work in the neighborhood. In her 1941 report to SHA, Miller described "an alarming shortage of decent homes at modest rentals" for Seattle's poor residents in 1940. Housing was even harder to find for the many people of color in the neighborhood, who were explicitly prohibited from living in most Seattle neighborhoods by racially restrictive covenants placed in property deeds.[109]

Rumors abounded among the area's residents that Yesler Terrace's construction would evict the poor from their homes so that wealthier people could have nice houses close to downtown. There was a grain of truth to those rumors. SHA required that applicants who lived in Yesler Terrace be families with U.S. citizenship, which effectively ruled out a number of immigrant families, single-parent families, and unmarried poor who lived on Profanity Hill. Many of these people ended up moving back down the hill to Seattle's Skid Row, living in more cramped quarters without their own private view lots or gardens. Yesler Terrace's housing catered to defense workers during World War II, and didn't explicitly serve low-income people until after the war.

SHA archives recorded that of the 359 families living in the south end of First Hill, 127 were Japanese. Yesler Terrace's construction not only displaced these families. It also displaced a number of significant Japanese institutions: three churches, four grocery stores, and four hotels. Japanese internment soon overshadowed this story.

If displacement is the largely untold history of Yesler Terrace, the often-repeated and just as important history of the site revolves around its significant accomplishments. At the center of these accomplishments is Jesse Epstein, the idealistic New Deal Democrat who as a graduate student effectively lobbied for Seattle to access federal funds for public housing construction. His efforts earned him the position of SHA's first director. His tireless leadership helped SHA overcome popular but disorganized opposition to public housing in Seattle. Epstein promoted Yesler Terrace as a way to stimulate housing construction after nearly a decade of the Depression, revitalize Skid Row, improve the condition of poor people's lives, help the poor eventually afford to buy their own homes, and promote racial integration. Yesler Terrace became the first public housing project in the state of Washington. Its cost of construction—$2,500 per unit—was one of the lowest in the nation. Most important, it was the first racially integrated public housing project in the nation.

In a radical move for a public agency of the time, SHA committed itself to having an integrated staff and fully integrated residential communities. Tenant applications were rejected if SHA believed that the applicant wouldn't support Yesler Terrace's nonsegregation policy.

The project's success rested on Jesse Epstein's decision to avoid the routine design guides issued by the federal housing division in favor of assembling a local team experienced in residential design—George W. Stoddard, J. Lister Holmes, William Bain Sr., and

William Aitken. John "Ted" Jacobsen was principal designer. According to the late Victor Steinbrueck, who worked with the design team, it was Jacobsen's study of Scandinavian housing models that most influenced the project's exterior appearance and overall site plan.

The plan consisted of groupings of attached two-story townhouses, all with flat roofs and wide overhangs, bands of casement windows, and horizontal cedar siding. According to William Bain, the flat-roof design had

BELOW: Dilapidated stairway on First Hill prior to Yesler Terrace redevelopment. Courtesy Seattle Housing Authority.

been a practical and economic decision, saving money for materials and controlling the collection of water on the site to stabilize a previously unstable hillside. Similar concerns dictated the location of parking and a central heating plant.

To enhance the residential character of the buildings and break up the monotony of a large number of similar units on the site, the designers varied the exterior colors. Each building's cedar siding was stained a different earth tone. Balconies were articulated with rounded, vertical battens. Covered entries personalized the units' designs,

as did the fact that each unit had its own yard to be shaped by its tenants.

Landscape designers Edwin Clair Heilman and Butler Sturtevant insisted on the value of open space and mature trees and shrubs to provide a parklike setting for the buildings. Each family in the community would have a separate plot of ground.[110]

Yesler Terrace consisted of over 850 units on 43 acres bordering Yesler Way east of downtown, a sloping site with exceptional views of Puget Sound and sunny south and southwest exposures. Instead of leveling the site, the designers took advantage of the natural grade changes to build retaining walls and create setbacks that allowed for a layering of units from the lowest to the highest points

BELOW: The immensity of the emerging Yesler Terrace housing project is seen from Beacon Hill, 1941. Seattle Housing Authority.

on the hillside. A great many units were oriented with living room, bedrooms, and balconies facing to the sun and views, with kitchens and bathrooms facing north or east. Gardens were also oriented to take advantage of the location. Parking on the periphery was separated from the pedestrian walks. Parkland and playgrounds, health and community centers, and laundry facilities were all designed into the project.

The original project, finished in phases from 1941-1943, underwent significant changes through continued use. In the 1960s, Interstate 5 construction took away 11 acres and over 260 units. Seattle Housing Authority rehabilitated and modernized 456 of its remaining 607 units from 1978 to 1982, and finished the other units during the 1990s. These renovations compromised the integrity of the original designs: replaced horizontal cedar siding with vertical wood cladding; replaced the buildings' modernist flat roofs with hipped roofs; and altered the original paint schemes. Yesler Terrace couldn't reform the rest of society by itself. While it has always been racially diverse, the pressures of residential segregation and employment discrimination, combined with increased African-American migration during and after World War II, made Yesler Terrace into an important refuge for people of color, as well as immigrants and the disabled. The result is that contrary to Epstein's dreams, Yesler Terrace has traditionally been disproportionately made up of people of color.

SHA is using HUD Choice Neighborhood Initiatives funding to replace the low-rise buildings at Yesler Terrace with 10 residential high-rise and mid-rise apartment buildings, two office towers, possibly a hotel, and as many as 5,000 parking stalls.

The new Yesler Terrace will have 3,200 market-rate units and over 1,000 units for people earning between 60 and 80 percent of the area's median income (between $35,000 and $45,000), while reserving 561 new units for those who make less than 30 percent of the median income. Construction began in 2013, and demolition began in 2014. The $300 million redevelopment, which

ABOVE: New housing unit, 1022 Yesler Way. Seattle Housing Authority.

has been contracted to Paul Allen's Vulcan Inc., is expected to take roughly five years. The City's Landmarks Preservation Board rejected a nomination of Yesler Terrace as a historic landmark in 2010, but did approve the preservation of its steam plant at 120 Eighth Avenue, which SHA is turning into a community center.

With all this change, in 2011 *Seattle Times* reporter Bob Young asked the question "What Would Jesse [Epstein] Do?" if he were alive to witness the redevelopment of the housing project that was his crowning achievement. Young found that everyone he spoke with lauded Epstein's ideals, while differing over how to adapt them to the 21st century. In this way, the history of Yesler Terrace is not just about the past, and it is not just located in the buildings that are about to be demolished. It is also a set of stories that people invoke as part of ongoing debates over the future of public housing in America.[111]

[CHAPTER] 5

SERVING THE PUBLIC

BROOKE V. BEST

ABOVE: The Geography Lesson, Summit School. June 18, 1913. Curtis 29968, Washington State Historical Society.

LEFT: The majestic King County Courthouse caps First Hill at upper left. The original Territorial University building is shown in middle center, and First Regiment Armory is in foreground right at Union Street between Third and Fourth Avenues. Mount Rainier is drawn into the photograph. Warner 190X, Photo Coll. 273, Special Collections, University of Washington Libraries.

FROM THE 1880S TO WORLD WAR I, First Hill served a diverse population ranging from mayors, judges, and timber barons to immigrants, nurses, and blue-collar workers. As the area's population grew, civic and institutional buildings followed. The most prominent was the King County Courthouse, perched on the south end and visible from Elliott Bay and nearly every vantage point downtown. From 1898 to 1932, Thomas Prosch's commercial building on Ninth Avenue was leased to the federal government and operated as the U.S. Assay Office. It had its heyday as the actual "gold" heart of First Hill's Golden Age. Fire Stations No. 3 and 25 were added in the early 1900s to service the neighborhood when the city switched from an all-volunteer fire department to a paid force.

Education of an expanding school-age population was a top priority for neighborhood residents. One public school was in place at the corner of Seventh Avenue and Madison Street by 1883. After burning to the ground in 1888, it was replaced with a larger Gothic-style school building. Over the next several decades, the area welcomed public and parochial schools, including Summit Grade School and Cathedral School. The first Catholic parish-constructed school came into existence between 1900 and

ABOVE: Corner grocery at James Street and Sixth Avenue. Jule Walter, watercolor. Collection of Milt and Sherry Smrstik, Seattle.

1910, in response to the 1884 decree of the Third Plenary Council of Baltimore: "Near every church a parish school; where one doesn't exist, it is to be built." Population shifts, industrial expansion, and changing socioeconomic conditions during the post-World War I period brought about an increase in the number of parish schools. The decade between 1920 and 1930 witnessed the construction of O'Dea, a high school for boys established under the direction of the Congregation of Christian Brothers.[112]

Early on, much of the hill's business activity was conducted out of people's homes or boarding houses. With the arrival of cable cars, retail hubs evolved along James, Madison, and Pike Streets and Broadway. The Pike-Pine corridor, later known as "Auto Row," became home to automobile showrooms, parts stores, and repair shops. Neighborhood restaurants, bars, and taverns were not commonplace. With growing density pressures in the 1920s, more services sprang up on formerly residential lots.

CIVIC AND INSTITUTIONAL BUILDINGS ON THE HILL

KING COUNTY COURTHOUSE, SEVENTH AVENUE AND ALDER STREET | 1890 (DEMOLISHED)

Rapid growth during the 1880s and statehood in 1889 spurred the county to replace its two-story wood, stone, and brick courthouse, built in 1876, with a more impressive structure. The site chosen was an imposing one:

> *It was filled with stately mansions with commanding views over the city. Most of its inhabitants were people who had made their fortunes on the sale of real estate to the railroad . . . The First Hill location of the courthouse showed the success of King County beside the success of its citizenry in a commanding position above the downtown area. Combining this significant event with Washington's new statehood, King County government found itself in a prominent position. What better way to convey this importance than in a new courthouse in a conspicuous location.*[113]

Architect Willis A. Ritchie, a newcomer to Seattle, won the design commission over many older and more experienced architects. He set out to create a beautiful, solid building that would convey the county's newfound power. Ritchie, who operated an office at Seattle's Union Block from 1889 to 1894, went on to design a number of courthouses in the state, including the Spokane County Courthouse, Whatcom County Courthouse in Bellingham, Jefferson County Courthouse in Port Townsend, Clark County Courthouse in Vancouver, and Thurston County Courthouse in Olympia.[114]

Completed in 1890 at a cost of $200,000, the Classical Revival building was constructed of Chuckanut sandstone, brick, iron, and cement. The three-story structure featured a central portico flanked by wings terminating in slightly projecting pediments. A tall clock tower supported by eight Ionic columns capped the central hall. The local press lauded it as one of the finest new buildings on the Pacific coast— the first major fireproof building erected in the state and the first to centralize all county offices under one roof.

Its design generated quite a bit of criticism. The restrained facade appeared unbalanced by its top-heavy tower, which was attacked as the county's "Gray Pile," "Cruel Castle," and "Tower of Despair." For better or worse, its value was short lived. By 1900 the courthouse could no longer accommodate the community's growing needs. The paneled courtrooms were remodeled for use as the county jail, and a *Seattle Daily Times* article from March 3, 1908, talked about plans for a wing addition designed by Saunders and Lawton. However, by 1917, courts were moved to a new, more accessible courthouse on the block between Third and Fourth Avenues and Jefferson and James Streets. Ten years later, Seattle Fire Marshal Robert Laing condemned the 1890 building as a fire-trap. The brick piers supporting the central tower were rotting and the foundation was failing. In 1931, the last of the county's prisoners were relocated to the newly expanded courthouse facility and the "old pile on Profanity Hill" was imploded in five seconds by 200 sticks of dynamite.[115]

BELOW: The Classical Revival courthouse with its overscaled cupola proved inadequate for increasing needs. Courtesy Ron Edge.

U.S. ASSAY OFFICE (PROSCH'S HALL), 613-619 NINTH AVENUE | 1893

The two-story Italianate masonry commercial building on Ninth Avenue between Cherry and James Streets was built by Thomas Wickham Prosch as an investment property, originally serving as Prosch's Hall. A noted newspaper publisher, civic leader, and secretary of the Chamber of Commerce, Prosch was appointed postmaster of Seattle and served as special agent in charge of the federal census. In the 1870s, he became publisher of the *Daily Pacific Tribune* and, later, the *Seattle Post-Intelligencer* (*P-I*). He made his fortune when he sold the *P-I* in 1886 and retired from the newspaper business, focusing instead on buying and selling property. This building was his first project and occupied a site next door to his residence at 611 Ninth Avenue.

As originally built, it housed two retail spaces on the first floor, with meeting space and ballroom above. Fixed plate-glass windows with clerestories defined the two storefronts. The upper facade featured arched windows and a decorative cornice along the parapet roof. City directories list Bate W. Alexander and John W. Seawright operating a bakery here in 1897.[116]

That same year, the Chamber of Commerce recognized the need for an assay office to test, weigh, and certify the massive amounts of gold flowing into the city from strikes in Alaska and the Yukon, and lobbied Congress to locate a new facility here. Prosch leased his building to the federal government, and the assay office opened on July 15, 1898, and operated over the next 34 years.

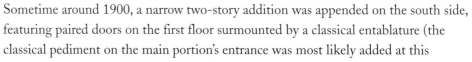

Returning Klondike miners, anxious to secure the best price for their gold, formed lines in front of the Assay Office that stretched back for blocks. Government officials weighed, melted and molded once-raw gold into bars, stamped the bars with Federal seals and sent them east to the mint in Philadelphia. The miners received certified government checks in exchange for the gold deposits that averaged over 20 million dollars during the early years.[117]

BELOW: Prosch's commercial building on Ninth Avenue served as the U.S. Assay Office for 34 years. Curtis 1313, Washington State Historical Society.

Sometime around 1900, a narrow two-story addition was appended on the south side, featuring paired doors on the first floor surmounted by a classical entablature (the classical pediment on the main portion's entrance was most likely added at this time).[118] In her book *Charlie Frye and His Times*, Helen Vogt recalled how the building's presence and activity were a big attraction during her childhood: "The dark, heavily-barred windows of the Assay Office, which we called 'The Mint' because there was so much gold inside, lured us on short walks south on Ninth."

The Assay Office ceased operations at this location in 1932, when it relocated to the U.S. Immigration Building, south of Chinatown. Since then, the building on Ninth Avenue has served as an officers' club and as the Deutches Haus (German House).

The German Society has retained ownership since 1947, using the upstairs hall for dances and other social engagements (see Chapter 3).

FIRE STATION NO. 3, 301 TERRY AVENUE | 1904

In the 1880s, Seattle's volunteer fire department consisted of a crude fire alarm telegraph system and two hose companies: Hose No. 1, at Columbia Street, and Hose No. 7, at Third Avenue and Pine Street. In April 1888, the department was put to the test when the three-story, frame Central School (Central II) at Seventh Avenue and Madison Street caught fire and burned to the ground, causing a great deal of criticism. Josiah Collins Jr., who became chief in May 1888, formulated plans to improve conditions, including "horses and drivers for the steamers, a new hose carriage in Belltown, new hose, new fire hydrants and a new fire alarm system."[119]

The Great Fire in June 1889 devastated roughly 50 square blocks, from University Street, south to a point near the old Moran shipyard, and eastward to Third Avenue. In its wake, the city passed an ordinance authorizing the creation of a paid force with a chief and five district fire stations. A two-story brick headquarters building was established at Seventh and Columbia. Fire Stations No. 3 and 25 were added to the First Hill neighborhood's infrastructure to support the increased density.

Fire Station No. 3 (301 Terry Avenue) is the city's oldest extant fire station and the first permanent one to be completed after the great fire. Prior to this, the station was housed in two locations, at Terry Avenue North and Republican Street (1883-1889) and 718 South Main Street (1890-1900s). On April 23, 1904, the company moved into its new First Hill quarters on Terry Avenue. Designed to accommodate a

ABOVE: Fire Department head-quarters, Columbia Street and Seventh Avenue, ca. 1900. SEA 1243, Special Collections, University of Washington Libraries.

BELOW: Fire Station No. 3, 1910, showing steam pumper and hose wagon. Courtesy Peter Rackers.

steam pumper and hose wagon, the station reflects the early era of horse-drawn fire-fighting equipment. The steam pumper was staffed by a driver and engineer, who rode in back and stoked the fire for the steam to pump the water. The hose wagon carried all the fire equipment, along with the officer, driver, and crew.

The architecture of these early stations was intended to complement the surrounding residential styles, materials, and scale so as to be "good neighbors." The design of this two-story, three-bay brick station was a modified English Tudor style featuring brick-work on the ground floor with stucco and half-timbering on the upper floor.

A combination hose-drying and training tower was housed in a tall brick tower rising on one side of the building. On the interior, stables and horse stalls occupied the main floor, with a hayloft above. Steel rails embedded in the brick floor of each bay allowed the horses to back up the apparatus to align it with the pipes coming out of the floor and hook it up to the building's steam system. When firemen responded to a fire, they would slip off the rubber hoses and turn the shut-off valves.[120] The rails were kept "well greased, allowing the horses an easier and faster start when the bell hit. When the firemen returned to the house the rails acted as guides for backing in the apparatus."[121]

The department's third ladder company went into service at this station in 1913. The building was never adapted for motorized vehicles and closed on April 21, 1921, when Engine 3 was relocated to its new quarters at 1400 Harvard Avenue. Seattle Parks Department used the former fire station for a brief period before it was adapted for use as security offices for Harborview Medical Center. The original hose-drying tower has been removed, the brick floor has been covered with carpet, and the names of the firemen on the lockers have been painted over.[122]

FIRE STATION NO. 25, 1400 HARVARD AVENUE | 1908

Fire Station No. 25 went into service on June 10, 1910, at 1400 Harvard Avenue, near the corner of East Union Street. Designed by the architecture firm Somervell & Coté, the two-story, four-bay structure survives as one of Seattle's first brick fire stations. The building, with features necessary to accommodate horse-drawn fire wagons, stands as a physical reminder of early-20th-century fire station operations. The interior housed stables and three horse stalls at the rear, dormitories and offices on the second floor, and the department's blacksmith shop at the basement level. A horse ramp was located along the rear alley that provided access to the stalls. The hillside location necessitated a terraced design for the equipment bays, featuring large arched doorways that opened automatically when the fire alarm rang. The four-bay stepped apparatus floor varied in height from 14 feet to 18 feet 6 inches, which required every pole to be a different length, and a railing and large wood posts were located between bays. The design proved impractical and dangerous to firefighters: "Numerous accidents led to the installation of individual fire poles for each bay, and even the placement of guardrails."[123]

A blacksmith shop operated at this location from 1910 to 1921, from which the "smithy" made his rounds to neighboring stations. By 1921, Engine 3, Engine 25, and Ladder 10 were stationed here. When Engine 3 disbanded in August 1932, the station adapted to changing

BELOW: Engines are ready and waiting at Fire Station No. 25. Historic Seattle.

times and was the city's first to be outfitted with motorized fire apparatus. By World War II, the last of the horse wagons were gone and modifications allowed the station to adapt to new requirements of contemporary fire equipment.[124]

Tom Gerbracht, a fireman stationed here from 1953 to 1956, remembered the station as one of the busiest in Seattle, with at least one run every day. "We had mostly residential fires . . . We . . . were responsible for about half of downtown Seattle, which would be all the commercial buildings there, and house fires, roof fires, garage fires, these kind of things." Shifts were 10-hour days and 14-hour nights. The top floor had a sleeping area for the firemen, he recounted, "kind of like a military barracks, basically. There was what we called the beanery, which was a kitchen where we cooked and prepared meals." The hose tower was also still in use in the 1950s. "Every time you would use the hose you had to dry it out or it would tend to rot. It was canvas with rubber insides and we could hang the hose at full length, 50 foot."[125]

By 1970, the station was no longer adequate to handle the size and complexity of modern-day equipment, and Engine 25 and Ladder 10 moved to new quarters at 1300 East Pine Street. The station was decommissioned, declared surplus by the city, and transferred to Historic Seattle in 1979. Historic Seattle, in turn, sold it to a developer with restrictions on exterior changes, and the interior was subdivided into 16 rental apartments.[126]

RIGHT: Fire Station No. 25 after its transformation to housing. Michael W. Romine.

PLACES OF LEARNING

ABOVE: The Classical Revival Territorial University building is incongruously sophisticated in its uncleared forested backdrop. Courtesy Lawton Gowey.

Seattle held its first public school classes at the new Territorial University Building in 1862, taught by Asa Mercer, one of Seattle's founding members and first president of the Territorial University of Washington. Several hastily erected "shack schools" were added to keep pace with the city's rapid growth, although these early schools were continually crowded and inadequate. Residents rallied to form a school board and in 1869 voted a tax to raise money for the district's first schoolhouse. One year later a two-story wood-frame school containing two classrooms for 120 students was completed on the east side of Third Avenue between Madison and Spring Streets. Mary Elizabeth ("Lizzie") Ordway was the only teacher when its doors opened; within days a second teacher, Mrs. C. M. Sanderson, was hired. At the close of the school year, enrollment had more than doubled, to 294 pupils.[127]

Additional school buildings were erected to handle the city's growing population, but provided only temporary relief. At a public meeting on April 1, 1882, a resolution was made for the construction of a second Central School. School board chair Judge J. R. Lewis proclaimed, "We have had saloon booms and real estate booms, and now for God's sake, let's have a school boom!" The appointed committee included Edward S. Ingraham, Rev. J. F. Ellis, William H. White, and Thomas Burke, who were to develop a plan for the new building. Residents passed a vote 345 to 97 on a $24,000 tax levy for its construction.[128]

Plans for the new Central School were ambitious. Located at the corner of Seventh Avenue and Madison Street, the elegant wooden structure was the largest in Washington Territory, measuring 112 by 128 feet. The six-room schoolhouse "boasted 1200 feet of blackboards, 600 iron framed seats, movable desks, a furnace, and sinks on each floor—luxuries never before seen in Northwest schools." The school opened on May 7, 1883, with O. S. Jones as its principal. Among its first teachers were Mr. Hollenbeck, Emma Shumway, Kate Cheasty, and Mrs. Nickels.[129]

Soon after Ingraham was appointed first superintendent of Seattle Public Schools in 1882, the first guidelines were established. The district continued struggling to accommodate the growing student population, which had increased to 1,478 students. Ingraham was replaced by Miss Julia Kennedy in 1888. That same year, the Central School burned to the ground, forcing relocation of its roughly 1,000 students. Two years later, Frank J. Barnard was brought in as superintendent, overseeing a wave of school building construction activity.[130]

The decades between 1890 and 1920 witnessed phenomenal growth in school-building as Seattle entered into a remarkably progressive era of public education. In

1919, Seattle boasted 64 grammar schools, six high schools, a school for the deaf, and nine "special schools." The school district's success was due in large part to the foresight of certain early school leaders, notably E. S. Ingraham and superintendent Frank B. Cooper, along with a forward-thinking school board and the expertise of the district architects James Stephen and Edgar Blair. They introduced a well-trained teaching staff, new and innovative programs, and state-of-the-art facilities.[131]

CENTRAL SCHOOL, SEVENTH AVENUE AND MADISON STREET | 1889 (DEMOLISHED)

One of the first buildings constructed during Barnard's "School Boom" was a new Central School, completed in 1889. Rebuilt in brick on the site of the second Central School, the three-story structure was designed by architects William E. Boone and George C. Meeker, with offices in Tacoma and Seattle. Among their works were the Annie Wright Seminary in Tacoma (1883-84), the Henry Yesler House in Seattle (1884, destroyed), and Seattle's South School (1889, demolished). The modified French chateau with its imposing mansard roof, clock tower framed by turrets, and tall central belfry provided the city with a distinctive downtown landmark that became a visual gateway to First Hill. Measuring 156 by 101 feet, the school building was touted as one of the finest on the Pacific coast, as described by author Clarence Bagley in his 1916 *History of Seattle*: "Its three towers, the middle one one hundred and thirty feet above the ground, and the graceful proportions of the building itself, are objects sure to arrest the attention of strangers as they near Seattle, whatever may be their avenues of approach."

Elementary classrooms occupied the first two floors, and the third floor housed the Seattle High School. During its second year, 22 teachers instructed 862 students. Salaries ranged between $70 and $130 per month. Improvements were under way for the lower grades during this period, as Bagley pointed out, where students were no longer required to " 'sit still and study,' but were given something to do to cultivate perception and imagination."[132]

BELOW: Central School, 1902, with a lone boy waiting in front on the corner of Madison Street. Curtis 317, Special Collections, University of Washington Libraries.

In 1890, the school hired H. P. Hollenbeck as high school principal. Orange and black were selected as the high school's colors, supposedly "because they were 'pretty together' and because the town's department stores carried plenty of ribbons in those colors." Edwin Twitmyer was listed as principal in the 1900 city directory along with 22 teachers, many of whom lived nearby. By the following year, J. M. Widmer was named principal and held that position until 1931. During his tenure, the school housed between 476 and 880 pupils. In 1902, the high school moved to a new location and the school was known briefly as the Washington School before returning to its original name.[133]

ABOVE: 1890 class photo at Central School. SEA 1424, Special Collections, University of Washington Libraries.

In a 1999 Historic Seattle panel discussion, Patsy Bullitt Collins recounted that, early on, everyone went to Central School since there were few private schools. Her mother, Dorothy Stimson Bullitt, who was eight when her family moved to First Hill, attended the school, and "she'd just run over there in the morning and run back for lunch, run back over and then run back, and didn't think it was far at all."

The school repeatedly expanded over the years with annexes and additions. A night class in shipbuilding was held in the school's assembly hall during World War I. By the early 1920s, school enrollment had declined, a result of several factors, including a shift in the neighborhood population. Office buildings and apartment houses began replacing single-family homes north of Madison Street. In 1933, when a storm damaged the school's north tower, it was removed.

Between 1935 and 1938, enrollment dropped from more than 400 students to 300. That year, the elementary school closed and the building was leased to the federal government for a youth center under the National Youth Administration (NYA). They also operated the Red Cross clinic, which provided medical and dental service to needy schoolchildren. Between 1939 and 1949, vocational classes for the Central Branch of the Edison Technical School operated out of this location. Extensive damage from the 1949 earthquake was the impetus to demolish the building in August 1953. The bell was donated to the Seattle Historical Society. The former site is now part of Interstate 5.[134]

SUMMIT GRADE SCHOOL, 1415 SUMMIT AVENUE | 1904-5

Perched near the crest of First Hill, Summit Grade School earned its name from its prominent location, overlooking downtown and Elliott Bay. The city purchased the former site of the old Grace Hospital in 1904, at a time when the population was growing and "view homes and gardens of the wealthy were taking over the wooded First Hill area."[135]

Built at a cost of $45,637, the wood-frame grade school was one of 11 designed by James Stephen, the school district's first architect and superintendent of construction, and illustrates the progressive development of public schools during this period. Stephen was the originator of Seattle's "model school plan" in 1901, which allowed for rapid expansion by using standardized floor plans with varied facades. Its basic design consisted of a two-story, rectangular frame-and-brick building with a raised brick basement and concrete floors. The interior contained four classrooms flanking a central

Above: Summit School raffia class, ca. 1909. Curtis 13741, Washington State Historical Society.

entry hall and staircase on each floor. The plan could be expanded in stages, by adding a four-room wing to create different plan configurations (an I plan became an H plan). Exteriors were finished in running bond brickwork and cedar lap siding, and Tenino sandstone was used for the basement windowsills, column bases, and entry steps. Interiors featured face-matched fir flooring, fir wainscoting, and turned oak balustrades (see Chapter 8).

Stephen's plan for Summit's 18-room building adopted a shallow H-shaped configuration due to the constraints of the sloping site. The school's modified Italian design featured a stucco exterior and Mission Revival parapets that differed from the more common Classical Revival school facades. Like John Hay and Latona schools, the building's two octagonal turreted towers dominated each side of the main entrance, housing ventilation stacks and spiral stairs. Inside, a generous 16-foot-wide central hall was flanked by classrooms on each side. Tall ceilings and generous windows lent a more spacious feeling, and provided an abundance of light and natural ventilation. A second-floor piano room occupied the space above the entrance between the circular-stairwayed turrets to provide music in the hallways. Other interior features included stairway railings, slate blackboards, varnished wall cabinets, and circular stairways with porthole windows.[136]

The school opened in 1905, with Mr. George Schoell serving as principal. During its first year, enrollment included 420 elementary students and 455 students in a Seattle High School annex. The annex had moved to another location by fall 1906, and was replaced by 7th- and 8th-grade classes. An addition constructed in 1914 accommodated two more classrooms. Beginning in 1920, a kindergarten operated here. Summit served both "well-to-do families and less affluent laborers living in dwellings ranging from mansions to boarding houses within blocks of one another."[137]

By the 1920s, the neighborhood surrounding Summit School had become more commercial. A 1923 district report recommended that the school be used for programs focusing on children with special needs. It became home to Seattle's first "Demonstration

Right: Summit School woodworking class. Curtis 13744, Washington State Historical Society.

School" from 1926 to 1930, with W. Virgil Smith serving as its principal. The program relocated to Seward School in 1931 because of declining enrollment.[138]

Starting in 1940 the School for the Deaf occupied the building, where children "who were totally deaf from birth were taught to speak and 'to read words on the lips of others.'" By the mid 1950s, the school accommodated five classrooms serving children ages 4 to 13. The program moved to University Heights in 1955, and in 1960, the intermediate pre-adjustment class moved to Bailey Gatzert School.[139]

Summit ranked second among Seattle's elementary schools in terms of an ethnically diverse student population, but a drop in enrollment to about 200 students in 1965 led to its closure. Summit's students were dispersed to other schools, including Bagley, Interlake, McDonald, and Greenwood.[140]

The school briefly served as a satellite to Seattle Community College before the Summit Alternative High School moved into the building in 1974. Operating out of the basement, it had roughly 100 students who came from all over the city to attend this alternative school, which emphasized "informal classes, group projects, and use of community resources."[141] The program moved to Horace Mann in 1977, and the building stood vacant and boarded up for a year before it was sold to a developer, Kemp Hiatt, with plans to convert the classrooms into offices. A 1979 *Seattle Times* article reported, "Hiatt is even leaving the pigeon roosts in the twin turrets flanking the main-entrance archway on Summit Avenue between Union and Pike Streets where generations of grade schoolers trod up until the 1965 closure."[142] In 1980, the Northwest School of the Arts, Humanities, and the Environment (now Northwest School) purchased the property and reopened it as a private facility for middle and high school students founded by three teachers: Ellen Taussig, Paul Raymond, and Mark Terry.[143]

ST. JAMES CATHEDRAL SCHOOL, 803 TERRY AVENUE | 1911

Sisters Mary Everildis (Directress), Mary Flora, Mary Rosella (music teacher), Mary Roswitha, and Mary Cyril founded the Cathedral School in 1911. The sisters, who were part of the Religious Order of Sisters of the Holy Names of Jesus and Mary, were given "a warm lunch at the noon hour and were paid per capita twenty-five dollars a month."[144] It was a free school, open to both Catholics and non-Catholics, with many of the children from poor working families. Classes were conducted out of spare rooms in St. Rose's Academy at Broadway and Madison Street for the first eight months, with an enrollment of 37 boys and 59 girls. Father Noonan announced on August 20, 1911, that ground was being cleared for a new building at the corner of Terry Avenue and Columbia Street. This prestigious commission was awarded to Beezer Brothers Architects, which proved lucrative for the firm and led to numerous other projects, including the rectory of St. Joseph Church and O'Dea High School.

The Cathedral Hall on the first floor of the new school opened on St. Patrick's Day, March 17, 1912. By Easter vacation, they had moved into their new state-of-the-art facility, with classes starting on April 15 and a formal blessing and dedication by Bishop O'Dea on April 21. The four-story building contained two floors of classrooms, an indoor gymnasium and a rooftop open-air exercise space at the top of the school, a large assembly hall with a stage, and a cafeteria in the basement. The school originally served as a grammar school for girls and boys connected with St. James Parish, and a girls' high school. Within the first year, enrollment jumped from 100 to 256 students, and by June 1914 to more than 400. By 1923, the average daily attendance was more than 600 students.[145]

A typical day at Cathedral School began with Mass in the Cathedral:

> *Those lucky enough to live close by might dash home for a quick cup of cocoa before school began. Then the children would line up in the street for the daily procession into the school, which usually happened to the accompaniment of recorded band music. In the classroom, the day began with the "Morning Offering" followed by the Pledge of Allegiance, and the first part of the day was devoted to recitations of learned material. Memorization was the basis of education in those days, and the children of the Cathedral School learned a great deal of poetry by heart, including passages from Longfellow's* Evangeline. *Lessons followed: math, civics, penmanship (following the Wesco system), religion, history, and "manual training" for boys and "domestic science" for girls; there were even classes in folk dancing."[146]*

BELOW: Students on the steps of Cathedral School, 1962. Courtesy Catholic Archdiocese.

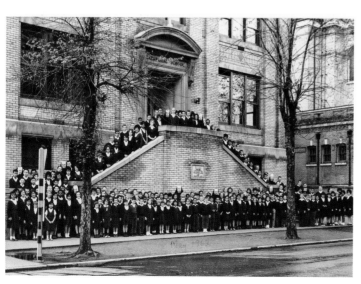

The sisters placed an emphasis on instrumental and vocal music. The children sang at Cathedral liturgies, including the weekly "children's Mass" on Sunday mornings. Margaret Downey, a first-grader in the 1920s, used to walk "a half-mile in her navy-blue uniform from her Bellevue homestead to catch a bus." Then she took a ferry across Lake Washington to Leschi Park. From there, she took the Yesler Way cable car to another streetcar to a third streetcar, before arriving at the Cathedral School. Her parents were devout Roman Catholics, and believed the school offered the best education.[147]

Roger Leed, another former student, recalled that O'Dea High School occupied the first floor of the building in those days but "there wasn't a great deal of interaction between the high school and the grade school, for all the reasons that we had between big kids and little kids." The Sisters reached out to a diverse student population, Leed recounted: "We had some Black children. We had some Filipinos . . . one of my best friends was Japanese . . . and all classes of children also because not too far away was Yesler Terrace."[148]

Shortly after O'Dea opened as a boys' high school in 1924, the girls' high school was discontinued at this location. A new gymnasium wing was added at some point and the original attic gym was converted into the library. With the city's changing demographics in the late 1960s, the school witnessed a sharp decline in its student population, and it was forced to close in 1971, 10 years after celebrating its Golden Jubilee.[149]

EDWARD O'DEA HIGH SCHOOL, 802 TERRY AVENUE | 1924

Reverend Father James Stafford, the pastor of St. James Cathedral from 1919 to 1935, purchased the half-block east of the cathedral to provide additional classrooms for the Cathedral School, with plans of establishing an all-boys' high school. His dream was to offer "young men an institution of learning equal to anything in the country." In one month alone, parishioners contributed $37,000 to the project.

ABOVE: The Catholic Archdiocese developed a campus on First Hill: St. James Cathedral (left), Cathedral School (to its right), and O'Dea High School (center right). Courtesy Ron Edge.

The school was to be an exceptional structure of "beauty and usefulness," built of all-steel construction, with plans drawn up by Beezer Brothers Architects. Constructed at a cost of roughly $200,000, it represented the firm's last major project in Seattle. They chose the Tudor collegiate Gothic style with a stairwell featuring impressive stained glass windows. The interior housed eight large, well-lit classrooms and two state-of-the-art laboratories. A large hall and library occupied about half of the first floor, and a gymnasium on the top floor was one of the largest in the city.

Dedicated on March 16, 1924, the new building was named for Edward John O'Dea, Bishop of Nisqually. Bishop O'Dea presided at vespers and Bishop John Carroll preached on catholic education. "Following the service at the Cathedral, prelates, priests, altar boys, students and teachers of the new school marched to the building in procession. There, his Lordship blessed the portables and rooms. The public was then invited to inspect the structure."[150]

The Congregation of Christian Brothers was responsible for running the Catholic high school, which admitted boys from seventh and eighth grades and the first two years of high school. A house at 1003 Marion Street had been purchased and renovated for use by the Christian Brothers.

JAMES PATRICK LEE PHOTOGRAPHED FIRST HILL BUSINESSES
BETWEEN 1909 AND 1911.

ABOVE: Businesses at 701-705 Seventh Avenue between Cherry and Columbia Streets, 1911. The building housed apartments above the drugstore and restaurant (lunch room). Lee 660, Special Collections, University of Washington Libraries.

ABOVE: Grahams Transfer & Storage (wood, coal and ice) at 807 Seventh Avenue, 1911. Lee 658, Special Collections, University of Washington Libraries.

ABOVE: The next step from working out of one's home was to build a shop addition, as shown by the T. L. Irving Shoe Shop at 1029 East Madison Street, 1909. Lee 660, Special Collections, University of Washington Libraries.

GOODS AND SERVICES

First Hill was close to nearly all the goods and services one would require in downtown shops—there was little need for the development of a retail center. Moreover, with the completion of the transcontinental railroad, Seattle shoppers were able to order by mail from a number of East Coast and Midwest companies advertising in the local papers for anything from the latest furniture and accessories to clothing, cookware, books, and periodicals. Soon they could order entire houses and instructions to build them. In the 1890s, skilled tradespeople, such as seamstresses and tailors, cobblers and accountants, designers and draftsmen, set up businesses out of their homes or boarding houses. Sometimes the increase in business led to building a one-story shop front onto an existing home. More often than not, groceries, milk and cheese, clothes, and pots and pans would be sold off a cart that came through the streets on a regular basis. Essentially the shop came to you. Paul Brown, who moved with his parents from San Francisco in 1915, lived at 1001 Columbia Street (site of today's Frye Art Museum), where his mother operated a boarding house. He recalled that time:

There were a lot of horses and buggies . . . in those days the post office had two horses together and big horses and clomp, clomp, clomp down the street. And besides that, we had a vegetable man, sold vegetables and fruit, and he had a cart with a white horse. He used to come up once a week and he'd stop and everybody would go down and see him and get stuff off the cart. He had a white horse. I'll never forget the white horse.[151]

BELOW: One of the most notable early businesses, the Madison St. Market & Grocery at 1021 Madison Street, has its delivery wagon ready and waiting, 1909. Lee 156, Special Collections, University of Washington Libraries.

With the advent of the telephone, the well-to-do could order foodstuff from any number of local vendors, and the commodities, such as ice for the icebox, would be delivered or house staff would pick it up.

With the arrival of the Pike Place Market in 1907, city residents had a variety of fish, meat, and vegetable stalls to visit, which allowed for comparison-shopping. Nevertheless, what later generations would refer to as "convenience stores" were scattered throughout First Hill, from small corner "mom and pop" shops to more expansive enterprises, such as the Madison Street Market and Grocery (1021 Madison Street), which had its own horse-drawn delivery wagon. With the large number of horses used for transportation, the hill also had its share of stables and blacksmith shops.

Edward B. Dunn's father, Arthur, and his friend Elton Ainsworth established Ainsworth & Dunn wholesale and retail fish canning, and their products were shipped nationwide. Dunn grew up on First Hill, and his family published his memoirs in a book entitled *1121 Union*. One of Ed's memories was of the local soda fountain:

> *Miss Downs's Bellevue Pharmacy at the corner of Pike and Bellevue served as the chief attraction, naturally, to all of us because of its large soda fountain and candy display. Ella Downs was a very kind and understanding woman and a great favorite in the neighborhood. One of the ailments so current or fashionable in those days was enlargement of the thyroid gland, or goiter, and Miss Downs had concocted a medication called Amber Goiter Cure, which was popular. Supposedly, the disease was caused by the lack of minerals in our melted snow water, and for that reason, we were all compelled to drink limewater to help our teeth.*[152]

RIGHT: The handsome terra-cotta facade of the offices of the *Seattle Star* newspaper, 1309 Seventh Avenue, 1909. Curtis 12743, Special Collections, University of Washington Libraries.

ABOVE: East Pike Street, "Auto Row." Courtesy Paul Dorpat.

The major retail streets evolved along the cable car and streetcar lines—James Street, Madison Street, Pike Street, and Broadway. With the increasing popularity of automobiles, Pike and Pine Streets built a reputation on their automobile showrooms and parts and repair shops, and became known as "Auto Row."

With a Packard showroom within walking distance, it was no wonder that Ed Dunn's father bought "what I think was the first Packard Twin-six sold in Seattle . . . It was with a sign of pride that we waved to the Perkins family the first time we drove past in screaming second gear. One could always recognize a Packard by that high whine of second, and our Minor Hill was just steep enough to require that gear."

Apart from hotel restaurants, places to "dine out" were not common during the early years. People ate at home with family, with fellow boarders (where your meals were included in the monthly rental), or if you lived in a residential hotel, you took your meals in the hotel dining room. Apartment dwellers ate in their efficient kitchens, as there were few options for "eating out" apart from downtown restaurants. Hospitals and nurses' housing included their own dining rooms and probably encouraged their staff to be "in house" rather than "out on the town." Bars and taverns were also few and far between, although they did appear on the fringes of First Hill.

With increasing density in the 1920s, more services became necessary. Formerly residential lots became more lucrative for retail. In one case, the entire north side of the block of Madison Street from Terry to Boren Avenues was replaced by two similar Gothic Revival style one-story terra-cotta-faced commercial shop fronts. In 1934, Mrs. Emily Carkeek's home at Boren Avenue and Madison Street was razed and replaced with a gas station—a sign of things to come.

RIGHT: American Automobile Company showroom, on the west side of Broadway at Madison Street, was where Stan Sayres promoted his Slo-Mo-Shun hydroplane. Seattle Municipal Archives.

ESTABLISHMENT OF A CULTURAL HUB

FRYE ART MUSEUM, 704 TERRY AVENUE, 1952

Iowa-born Charles H. Frye and his wife, Emma Frye (née Lamp), both children of German immigrants, made their wealth in the food industry. In 1891, Charles and his brother Frank, along with business partner Charles Bruhn, incorporated the Frye-Bruhn Company, a meat-packing plant located on Seattle's tide flats. Business boomed during the Klondike gold rush, and Charles expanded his business interests, acquiring large land holdings in Washington, Montana, and Alaska. In 1910 he bought out his partners and incorporated Frye & Company. He quickly became one of Seattle's wealthiest men.

Charles and Emma were devoted collectors and patrons of the arts. Charles reputedly saw his first oil painting at the 1893 World's Columbian Exposition in Chicago, which may have been his inspiration to begin their collection. The Fryes eventually amassed some 230 paintings, over half of them late-19th and early-20th-century German paintings from artists associated with the Munich Secession. By 1909 the Fryes had begun a collection of European paintings, and from 1914 until the late 1920s they visited Europe to acquire paintings for their collection. By 1915, they had built a specially designed exhibition space adjoined to their First Hill home (which stood at the southeast corner of Ninth Avenue and Columbia Street), where they hosted numerous concerts and charitable events.

Emma died in 1934, followed by Charles in 1940. In their wills, they specified that their estate be used to support a free public art museum. Their estate was managed by Charles's lawyer and close friend Walser Sly Greathouse, who set up a foundation to support the establishment of a museum. Their furnishings and possessions were sold at auction in July 1941, and the paintings were removed and temporarily stored at the Frye business offices, which were subsequently severely damaged in a plane accident during World War II.[153]

Over the next 12 years, Greathouse set about realizing the museum first proposed by Frye. In 1915, Frye had approached the

BELOW: Architect's rendering of the proposed home of Charles and Emma Frye, 722 Ninth Avenue, Bebb & Mendel. Frye Art Museum.

ABOVE: Interior of Charles and Emma Frye's home gallery, 1920s. Frye Art Museum.

Seattle Fine Arts Society with a plan to build a public art museum in Volunteer Park that would present major collections of art in Seattle, but the Society chose not to support the endeavor. In 1948, the Seattle Art Museum and the City of Seattle turned their back on the offer of the Frye Collection and funding to support its presentation.

Undaunted, Greathouse forged ahead without city support, becoming the museum's first director. The Charles and Emma Frye Free Public Art Museum

opened its doors on February 8, 1952, in a building designed by prominent local architect Paul Thiry.[154] At the opening celebration, visitors received a guide that described the schools of painting represented in the collection and included artists' biographies. The collection expanded over the years with acquisitions of 19th- and 20th-century European and American paintings. Prominent Seattle artists including Mark Tobey, Albert Fisher, and William Cumming were also represented. Educational programs were offered and the museum sent out monthly announcements, called *Frye Vues*, highlighting news about the artists and upcoming

ABOVE: Exterior of the Paul Thiry–designed Frye Art Museum, 1952. Frye Art Museum.

exhibits. After Greathouse's death in 1966, his widow, Ida Kay, took over "every detail of the museum, handling everything from its financial affairs to acquisitions to eagle-eye monitoring of the parking lot." Under her direction the permanent collection grew to encompass more than 1,200 paintings, including works by prominent women artists and regional artists from the Northwest and Alaska. Ida Kay retired in 1993.[155]

RIGHT: Ida Kay Greathouse and Norma Wissman seated in the Frye Art Museum gossip chair, ca. 1950s. Frye Art Museum.

As the collection expanded, the museum's original floor plan proved insufficient. In 1982, the museum began planning for an expansion that would include

additional work areas, painting storage, and a gallery/auditorium to present a number of Alaskan paintings that had been collected by Greathouse and to provide spaces for temporary exhibitions. Seattle's Callison Partnership was given the commission to design a two-story, approximately 13,000-square-foot wing appended to the museum's east side, along Boren Avenue. Callison designed the interior gallery so that it could be reconfigured, using "movable walls on ceiling tracks running lengthwise of the room," into a 200-seat recital hall.[156]

In 1997, the museum underwent a significant expansion and renovation designed by Olson Sundberg

BELOW: Olson Sundberg–designed museum addition, reflecting pool leading to the main entrance. Peter Eckert, Portland, courtesy Frye Art Museum.

Architects. The $12 million expansion, which won praise for its design, included a 142-seat auditorium, a two-story education wing with art studios, and a museum café. Well-known landscape architect Richard Haag designed the outdoor courtyard. Additionally, the museum's exhibition, storage, and work spaces were substantially upgraded to meet current standards for the display and care of works of art.

Rick Sundberg, who served as principal architect, skillfully applied his "love of ancient architecture," which can be seen in the oculus in the domed ceiling above the entry foyer. The oculus is positioned off-center and filters in natural light. The heavy 12-foot-high doors, which were designed by Oly Jensen, serve as bronze gates and feature a decorative "fence pattern" motif, which is repeated throughout the building. Sundberg took care to create an entry ramp along the Terry Avenue entrance that allows people with disabilities to share "exactly the same entry experience as anyone else." The interior color scheme was comprised of a deep and neutral paint palette to complement the canvases.

A *Seattle Times* article written by Robin Updike had this to say about the "new" Frye:

> If you don't get up to First Hill often, you may not have noticed. But the once-dowdy Frye Art Museum has had a makeover. There's a dramatic new rotunda at the entryway on Terry Avenue at Cherry Street, a lovely reflecting pool along the facade and a small outdoor courtyard that promises to become a treasured "secret" spot for summertime lunches. And that's just what you see from the outside.[157]

To this day, the museum remains free for all the public to enjoy.

FIRST · BAPTIST · CHURCH
SEATTLE · WASHINGTON

U · GRANT · FAY   ASSOCIATE ARCHITECT
RUSSEL · B · BABCOCK
SEATTLE · WASHINGTON

[C H A P T E R]

RELIGIOUS LIFE ON THE HILL

DENNIS A. ANDERSEN

Above: St. James in skyline.
Romans Photo Studio, courtesy
John Cooper.

Left: Rendering of proposed First
Baptist Church, designed by U.
Grant Fay, Russell & Babcock, ca.
1912. Courtesy First Baptist
Church.

SEATTLE'S RELIGIOUS COMMUNITIES INITIALLY FOCUSED their property and
ministries on the downtown core of the city. The first Christian houses of worship
were built on land huddled close to the business and retail core: the area between
Second and Fourth Avenues and Washington and Seneca Streets. Methodists,
Roman Catholics, Episcopalians, and Baptists all built their first structures between
the mid 1850s and the early 1880s in that central location.

These churches were all of wood-frame construction and with few exceptions
were designed by local builders. It was clear that church buildings would be subject to
adaptive reuse, removal to another location, or demolition in favor of other buildings.
They were structures of secondary importance to the city as it struggled for economic
survival. The so-called "White Church" building, constructed in 1855 at Second
Avenue and Columbia Street for a struggling Methodist congregation, served
subsequently as "gambling hall, saloon, restaurant, and vaudeville house" during its
lifetime. The congregation retained the property even after the building was moved
two blocks away, however, and sold it later at a tidy profit. The profit aspects of
property development were not lost on Seattle congregants who built churches.

Through most of the 1880s, worshipping communities remained well west—downslope of Fifth Avenue—even if residential development had begun to spread north toward Denny Hill and Belltown and east beyond the territorial university. It would be a slightly later generation that would embrace the concept of a "neighborhood" parish and leave behind a central downtown church.

Seattle citizens did not invest significantly in their houses of worship at this time. *West Shore*, a Portland monthly journal, reported condescendingly in June 1884: "There are several religious denominations possessing houses of worship, and though none of them are costly structures, they are all extremely neat and attractive."[158] The Great Fire of June 1889, the ensuing construction boom, and population growth slightly changed that pattern.

As the members of the Methodist Episcopal parish considered new construction after the fire, their building committee reported to the fledgling *Seattle Times*: "The exterior will be plain and substantial, it being the intention to convert the building into a business block when the site becomes too valuable for church purposes."[159] The commercial value of the occupied land became an important consideration for religious groups, often vying with issues of mission outreach, neighborhood proximity, and long-term commitment to a particular neighborhood context. That issue would become even more pressing after the turn of the century.

BELOW: Revival tent pitched for services in the block east of the Lowman house, viewed from Coppin's water tower. Arthur Churchill Warner, 1890. Private collection.

FIRST UNITARIAN CHURCH, 1420 SEVENTH AVENUE | 1889 (DEMOLISHED); NORTHWEST CORNER BOYLSTON AVENUE AND OLIVE WAY | 1905 (DEMOLISHED)

The first to move eastward from downtown were the Seattle Unitarians, who purchased a small lot on the north side of Seventh Avenue between Union and Pike in early 1889. Initially in rented quarters at Frye's Opera House on Front Street (now First Avenue), they had moved to the Pythian Hall on Yesler Way before the June 1889 fire. While they awaited construction of their uptown building, all of the

ABOVE: Unitarian Church, built 1889 at Seventh Avenue and Pike Street, ca. 1909. Courtesy Lawton Gowey.

congregation's records, ritual vessels, library, and instruments were lost in the fire.[160] But with generous support from out-of-town donors, they gathered sufficient funding to secure the property and commence construction, meeting during that time in a lecture hall at the university. Architect Herman Steinmann, who had arrived the previous year from St. Louis and was a member of the new congregation, donated architectural plans for a Shingle Style gathering place with a small tower. In outward appearance it was more cottage-like than ecclesiastical. Despite the building-material and labor shortages following the Fire of 1889, the new church was finished and dedicated in September of that year. Theirs was the first permanent house of worship outside the immediate downtown and on First Hill.

The congregation flourished and its members, among them the Hallers and Burkes, helped to create other Unitarian congregations in outlying neighborhoods. Its lecture series with nationally known speakers raised the intellectual bar for decades in Seattle. The shingled church served the congregation until they moved to a larger building (no longer extant) at Boylston and Olive in 1905. The Seventh Avenue building was sold to private owners who restyled it into Fern Hall, a lecture and multiuse structure. It was demolished in 1924 to make room for construction of the Eagles Auditorium. When the congregation left its Boylston building in 1920, it was occupied by the Central Seventh Day Adventist congregation. Damaged by fire, it was demolished in 1964. This Unitarian congregation is currently located in Des Moines, Washington.[161]

TRINITY EPISCOPAL CHURCH, 609 EIGHTH AVENUE | 1891-92; 1902

Next up the slopes of First Hill were the Episcopalians of Trinity Parish, whose downtown building at Third Avenue and Jefferson Street had burned in the 1889 fire. The site was sold and the congregation purchased property at the northwest corner of Eighth Avenue and James Street. Plans by Chicago architect Henry Fletcher Starbuck were accepted, Charles A. Alexander served as local supervising architect, and by 1892 the new church was dedicated.[162] Alexander also designed the first rectory, next door to the north. As originally built, the structure featured a long nave with rusticated stone walls. It was the first stone church in Seattle, its sandstone from the Wilkeson quarry, which opened in 1886. It was also a showcase for its Gothic lancet nave and clerestory windows, figural stained glass from the Franz Mayer Studio of Munich, Germany, and elaborate furnishings.[163] A fire in January 1902 gutted the roof and interior, but left the stone walls largely intact.

Architect John Graham Sr., who had recently arrived from England, refashioned the building. Graham added a transept, an extended chancel to the west, and a tower at the southeast corner. New windows were commissioned from the same Munich artisans, and more were subsequently added. Graham also designed the new rectory at the north end of the block. A parish hall and offices were added to fill in the middle of the block in 1930.

The parish served historically as the social center for leading families of First Hill and beyond—its members included the Prossers, Pellys, Scurrys, Snowdens, McDougalls, and Ferrys. But over time it also provided assistance services for ethnic and racial minorities and the homeless, as well as drug and alcohol rehabilitation.

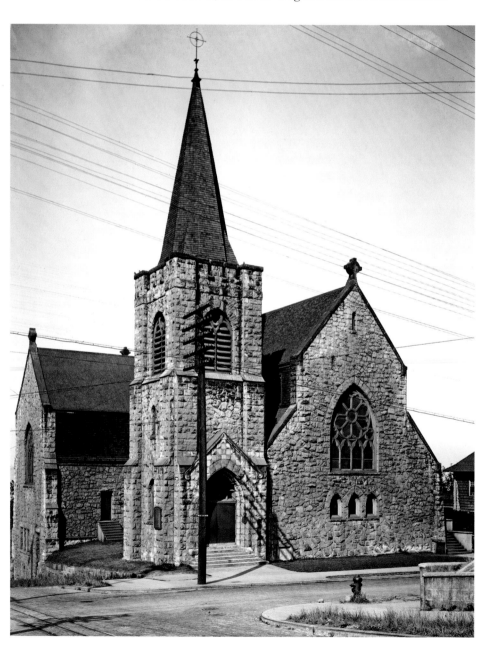

RIGHT: Trinity Parish Episcopal Church, rebuilt 1902. PEMCO Webster & Stevens Collection 1983.10.6494.1, MOHAI.

ABOVE: Trinity's stained glass windows. Historic Seattle.

RIGHT: Interior of Trinity Church, 2013. Walter White for SMR Architects.

Rector Herbert H. Gowen, who began his ministry at Trinity Parish in 1897, was a specialist in Asian and Middle Eastern languages, and founder of what was then the Department of Oriental Subjects at the University of Washington. He was also a prolific writer, and from Trinity Parish assisted in the creation of new neighborhood parishes throughout the Seattle area.

The changing nature of the neighborhood and the construction of Interstate 5 isolated Trinity Parish from its traditional membership; however, it remained a draw to multigenerational families with roots in its history. More than any downtown church of its era, it has continued to be diverse in its ministry and outreach. The 2001 Nisqually earthquake seriously compromised the stone structure of the sanctuary, and for two years the members met in the parish hall. A nearly three-year seismic rehabilitation secured the tower and strengthened the walls. At the same time, windows were restored, interior furnishings were updated, and the pipe organ was repaired. In 2013, a long-awaited repointing and cleaning of the exterior stone work and additional seismic work restored the outward appearance and inward strength of the building. At the same time, discolored protective window coatings were replaced. Trinity Parish remains the oldest continuously occupied church building in Seattle.

The cornerstone of Grace Hospital rests in the courtyard garden of Trinity Parish. Founded as a Protestant venture to counteract the healthcare monopoly of the Roman Catholic Sisters of Providence, the building at Summit Avenue and Union Street was ultimately a financial failure, closing in 1893 during a nationwide financial panic that seriously affected the Northwest economy (see Chapter 7).

OHAVETH SHOLUM/TEMPLE DE HIRSCH SINAI, NORTHWEST CORNER EIGHTH AVENUE AND SENECA STREET | 1891-92 (DEMOLISHED)

Seattle's first major Reform Jewish congregation was incorporated in November 1889, and secured a narrow site at the steep northwest corner of Eighth and Seneca. "Ohaveth Sholum" (spelled variously in local newspapers) was dedicated with city-wide interfaith participation in September 1892.[164] Architect Herman Steinmann followed the "Moorish Revival" examples of other contemporaneous West Coast synagogues (Victoria, B.C., Portland, San Francisco, and Los Angeles), even if he simplified the formula: a long wood-frame sanctuary fronted with two south-facing towers of unequal height, each capped with a stylized bulbous turret. A large Star-of-David window was set above the classical projecting porch, which was surmounted by carved Ten Commandments tablets. The congregation fell on hard times some months later and disbanded in 1895. The building was used for various secular purposes and served for some years as an auxiliary building for Seattle City Schools.[165] By 1908 it was partially rented out as an artists' studio and exhibition hall for sculptors Finn Frohlich and Anna Hatch.[166] The former synagogue was demolished in 1926 for the construction of the Exeter Apartments.

By 1900, the Reform Jewish community had reorganized and became Temple de Hirsch Sinai. Its members purchased property at the northwest corner of Boylston Avenue and Marion Street. Austrian-born architect Paul Bergfeld and his colleague Theobald Buchinger created plans for a sanctuary that was to be built in phases as a two-story synagogue with towers on Boylston Avenue.[167] A one-story masonry basement served the congregation on that site from 1901. By late 1905, all Jewish congregations in the city had experienced unexpectedly large growth rates, and it was determined that the planned structure and site would not be able to accommodate the larger congregation. The property and basement structure at Boylston and Marion were sold, and a new sanctuary was built farther east, at 15th Avenue and Union Street, in 1907.

One writer summarized the religious community's construction trends as Seattle's population grew and the narrow slopes of downtown were pressed for commercial development:

ABOVE: Ohaveth Sholum Synagogue at the corner of Eighth Avenue and Seneca Street. UW18708, Special Collections, University of Washington Libraries.

The feature of church affairs in Seattle during 1907 has been the removal of many of the central congregations to new sites, farther from the business center, their removal being deemed expedient because of the rapid rise in the value of the old sites. In every case the congregations have been able, with the proceeds of the sale of the old sites, to buy their new locations and to erect thereon new edifices far grander and more imposing than the buildings abandoned.[168]

The first decade of the 20th century was a rich one for church and synagogue construction and for the establishment of neighborhood congregations. First Hill became the next logical destination for some of those congregations, and for others it served as a temporary location on the way to sites farther out in the neighborhoods and suburbs. Because large single-family homes and some larger-scale apartments occupied land on First Hill, many congregations sought more generously sized plots of land on which to build elsewhere.

FIRST PRESBYTERIAN CHURCH, SOUTHEAST CORNER SEVENTH AVENUE AND SPRING STREET | 1907 (DEMOLISHED)

Seattle's First Presbyterian Church, organized in 1869, had permanent buildings in two successive downtown locations (Third and Madison, 1873; Fourth and Spring, 1893-94). The Byzantine-style Fourth Avenue building suffered from a disastrous fire in 1905, and during that year construction of the Great Northern Tunnel compromised its structural integrity. The Rev. Mark Matthews, who came to the pulpit in 1902, presided over these disasters with grace and energy, developing a congregational

RIGHT: Cincinnati architects Crapsey and Lamm designed the new First Presbyterian Church, dedicated in 1907. SEA 1859, Special Collections, University of Washington Libraries.

program of social ministry and urban activism scarcely matched into our own time. Matthews became known as a fiery preacher, an organizational genius, and a very visible civic personality. He involved himself in mayoral recalls, battles over city government corruption, and legislative affairs.

The fire and the building's structural destabilization provided timely excuses for a move farther uphill to Seventh and Spring and a massive institutional expansion. Matthews's organizational skills and endeavors—his energetic interest in the creation of hospitals, night schools, and day-care facilities, immigration, and reform of political and police agencies—all reflect a remarkable commitment to the social realities of urban industrial culture. Those same talents created the "institutional church," a phenomenon that current "church growth movement" congregations are attempting to recapture.[169]

The new First Presbyterian Church building itself, completed and dedicated in 1907, was of great significance in its architectural organization and plan and stood in contrast to other significant church buildings being constructed in the same neighborhood, at virtually the same time. Its Cincinnati-based architects, Crapsey and Lamm, were major-name designers of Protestant churches in the United States and created a building of great interest to both the church and the architectural communities nationally.[170] The "auditorium" reportedly seated 2,400 people on main floor and galleries, and was said to be the largest of its kind in the country. The basement Sunday school rooms offered space for 1,000 children. There were other classrooms, a gymnasium, and extensive work and social spaces. Matthews's office and personal library were on the third floor, over the entrance to the complex, and featured a view over the entire downtown—especially City Hall and the county offices. At its zenith in the 1920s, the

RIGHT: Interior of First Presbyterian Church. Courtesy Paul Dorpat.

congregation numbered more than 6,000 members and was the largest of its denomination in the country. The dramatic dimensions of ministry shifted with changing times. Matthews remained in the pulpit at First Presbyterian until his death in early 1940.

From 1967 to 1969, the old building was razed and a new sanctuary seating 1,300 was constructed on its site—a strongly shaped, sculptural building, set well back on the plaza. Its boldly textured "corrugated" exterior represented an interesting use of raw concrete at the time, and its freestanding campanile is a dramatic landmark. The austere Brutalist-style poured concrete sanctuary, designed by the firm Naramore, Bain, Brady & Johanson (later renamed NBBJ), was dedicated in late 1969.[171] Robert Tucci carved the sanctuary doors of Appalachian red oak; Willet Studios, founded in 1898, designed the spectrumlike stained glass windows. Recent membership decline and financial issues have stimulated proposals to demolish this still monumental complex and erect a mixed-use tower that would include worship, office, and educational facilities, as well as retail and residential space.[172]

ST. JAMES ROMAN CATHOLIC CATHEDRAL, SOUTHEAST CORNER NINTH AVENUE AND MARION STREET | 1907

Arriving in Washington in 1896, Roman Catholic Bishop Edward O'Dea worked initially from a cathedral seat in Vancouver, Washington. By 1903, he was able to announce the transfer of the diocesan seat to Seattle and initiated plans for the construction of a suitable cathedral. The nearest parish, Our Lady of Good Help, stood at that time at Fourth Avenue between Jefferson and James Streets.

Bishop O'Dea acquired property at Ninth Avenue and Columbia Street in 1904 and commissioned the construction of a small clapboard wood-frame church—St. Edward's Chapel—at the northwest corner of Terry and Columbia.[173] The first liturgy was held there in November 1904, and one year later the cornerstone was laid for what was to be Seattle's largest religious structure, St. James Cathedral. Bishop O'Dea and his committee hired the nationally prominent New York architectural firm Heins & LaFarge to design a domed sanctuary in what was described as "the Italian Renaissance" style, flanked on the west by two large towers. Heins & LaFarge were known for their winning design for the Cathedral of St. John the Divine in New York (partially built according to their plans) and for the Cathedral of St. Matthew the Apostle in Washington, D.C., and for many other large church buildings on the East Coast.[174] Their office sent Woodruff Marbury Somervell and Joseph Coté to supervise construction, and they became members of Seattle's new academically trained architectural establishment.

The finished cathedral was dedicated in December 1907, enriched with stained glass, sculpture, metalwork, and the city's largest pipe organ. Many of these major commissions came from prominent First Hill families, such as the Kellehers, Baillargeons, Pigotts, and Agens. A distinguished musical and choral tradition was firmly established within a short time. The Cathedral School, founded in 1910, opened for classes in 1911 and was ultimately expanded in 1923 to become O'Dea High School, and occupied the block east of the cathedral.

Disaster came during the great snowstorm of February 1916, when an accumulation of wet snow (and miscalculations by the construction contractors) caused the collapse of the cathedral's central dome, crushing the furnishings and blowing out most of the stained glass windows. Months later, the roof was repaired, albeit without

RIGHT: The New York architectural firm Heins & LaFarge designed the Italian Renaissance–style St. James Cathedral at the corner of Ninth Avenue and Marion Street. PEMCO Webster & Stevens Collection 1983.10.7640.1, MOHAI.

the dome over the crossing, and the interior was reconfigured. Figural stained glass windows by the distinguished Boston firm Charles J. Connick were installed between 1917 and 1919 and represent the largest collection of the firm's windows, for which founder Charles Connick himself did much of the painting.[175]

A major renovation in the early 1950s introduced baroque-style ornament and a color scheme typical of the period and also brought updated mechanical and structural improvements. Liturgical changes were left for a later generation. That time arrived during the tenure of Cathedral Pastor, the Very Reverend Michael G. Ryan. The extensive renovation of 1994 effectively gutted the interior and restored the original cruciform orientation and vividly reflected the worship understandings of the Second Vatican Council.[176] While it was not possible to reconstruct the vanished dome, a domelike interior space was recalled in the restored crossing oculus, and the main altar was placed there. Hans Gottfried von Stockhausen executed a new stained glass window in the Sacristy depicting Mary surrounded by texts by Hildegard of Bingen. Von Stockhausen also designed nine stained glass rondels in the east apse window spaces that were opened up by relocating organ pipes that had blocked the lower wall. Fixtures and furnishings from various periods were sensitively adapted to the new configuration. The Cathedral of St. James was set to resume its place, not only as the seat of the Archbishop of Seattle but also as a vibrant spiritual, cultural, and musical destination for the entire city.

FIRST BAPTIST CHURCH, HARVARD AVENUE AND SENECA STREET | 1912

First organized in 1869, the Baptist congregation had its first permanent home on the north side of Fourth Avenue, between James and Cherry Streets, designed by architect/builder Isaac Palmer and built between 1872 and 1874.[177] This structure was replaced by a larger wood-frame building dedicated in 1899. The regrading work of Fourth Avenue marooned the church entrance more than 25 feet above street level, and the search for a more stable and accessible property drove members uphill. They first considered a lot at the corner of Broadway and Madison, but some women in the church were quite adamant that the streetcar line would be noisy and disturb worshippers. Ultimately they opted for a site at Seneca Street and Harvard Avenue. Between 1908 and 1911 the congregation used the unfinished basement shell of the Temple de Hirsch Synagogue.

ABOVE: First Baptist Church made its temporary home at the Temple de Hirsch Synagogue before moving to its new sanctuary farther east. PEMCO Webster & Stevens Collection 1983.10.7844, MOHAI.

The cornerstone of the building was laid in October 1910, and the Gothic Revival sanctuary was dedicated in 1912. Described at the time as "an excellent example of Tudor gothic in brick and terra cotta,"[178] it was designed by the architectural team Fay, Russell & Babcock. The brick-and-copper steeple with its terra-cotta crockets, the hook-shaped decorative elements, is a significant feature. The story has been passed down that Pastor Hootland, who orchestrated construction, became ill and was hospitalized at Swedish Hospital and could see the church under construction. There was some controversy about whether to put the spire on the building. From his hospital bed, he insisted it be built because it would be the highest spot on First Hill—and it was. Sadly, the pastor died before the building was completed.

Stained glass windows by the Belknap Company of Seattle were framed by terra-cotta surrounds and quoins. The interior included balcony seating on three sides. Pews were arranged to face the pulpit, centered at the southeast axis corner of the building. The complex plan included offices, downstairs social hall, and classrooms. Classroom and meeting room additions were made during the next three decades. For years, this was the second-largest Baptist congregation on the West Coast. Changes to the sanctuary were made in 1953, new windows were added in the late 1960s, and further remodeling occurred in the early 1990s. During the ministry of the Rev. Dr. Rodney Romney (1980-2000), First Baptist became a center of social activism and openness to all people and was frequently at odds with stated policies of the national denomination, especially regarding issues of human sexuality.[179]

The 2001 Nisqually earthquake dislodged two of the tower's crockets, which tumbled into the building—fortunately with no injuries to building occupants. Because the main construction of the building was steel frame, major damage was minimal. The fallen terra-cotta ornamental pieces were replicated and replaced with fiberglass copies.[180]

RIGHT: First Baptist Church. PEMCO Webster & Stevens Collection 1983.10.4519, MOHAI.

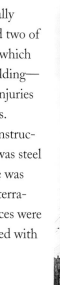

RIGHT: St. Mark's Church, formed in 1889, was Seattle's second Episcopal church. The new Gothic-inspired wood-frame building on Harvard Avenue, between Seneca and Spring Streets, was dedicated in 1905 and served until the congregation moved to its larger north Capitol Hill building. PEMCO Webster & Stevens Collection 1983.10.7523, MOHAI.

FOURTH CHURCH OF CHRIST, SCIENTIST, 1119 EIGHTH AVENUE | 1916-23

BELOW: Fourth Church of Christ, Scientist, 1119 Eighth Avenue. Courtesy Lawton Gowey.

Followers of Mary Baker Eddy first held gatherings in 1896, initially meeting in the downtown area. Congregations were organized after the turn of the century, ultimately building on Capitol Hill, in Ballard, and in the University District.

Members of the Fourth Church of Christ, Scientist, first met in rented halls in the downtown area, then purchased property at the southwest corner of Eighth and Seneca (opposite the 1891 Ohaveth Sholum building) in 1914. The congregation engaged architect George Foote Dunham, from Portland, Oregon, himself a Christian Scientist, who specialized in designs for Christian Scientist church structures.[181] Construction began in 1916 and was completed in stages by 1923.[182]

The Classical Revival exterior is clad in cream-colored terra-cotta, and a large-scaled colonnade lines the main entrance on Eighth Avenue. The dramatic domed main

ABOVE: Stained glass windows in the sanctuary were designed and executed by Povey Brothers Glass Company, Portland. Lawrence Kreisman.

auditorium is on the second floor and originally accommodated more than 1,100 worshippers; other meeting rooms and gathering spaces line the main floor and the basement. Acoustics were excellent—always a strong prerequisite for churches of this tradition. Nonfigural stained glass windows by the Povey Brothers Glass Company of Portland transmit filtered light to the interior.[183] The congregation was able to make sensitive upgrades and improvements in the 1960s, but was challenged by declining membership and maintenance costs by the late 1980s. In 1990 they decided to sell the property.

David Brewster, the founding publisher of the *Seattle Weekly*, contacted Historic Seattle to assist with the negotiation process for the purchase of the Fourth Church of Christ, Scientist. Brewster envisioned it as a community music, lecture, and meeting place on the order of New York's Town Hall. Historic Seattle convened a group of possible users to examine the potential of the project as a performance venue, and in 1997 the parties successfully negotiated a purchase and sale agreement for the property. Historic Seattle's offer was chosen over other development proposals, including a plan to demolish the structure and create a surface parking lot. Today, now called Town Hall, it is maintained and operated by the nonprofit group Town Hall Association, and has undergone a multiyear process of upgrades and rehabilitation, even as it successfully serves as a performing arts center.

PLYMOUTH CONGREGATIONAL CHURCH, NORTHWEST CORNER SIXTH AVENUE AND UNIVERSITY STREET | 1912 (DEMOLISHED)

Congregationalists organized their church in 1869 and located initially on Second Avenue, between Spring and Seneca Streets, in a wood-frame structure dedicated in 1873. While the building survived the Fire of 1889, the congregation had already outgrown the building and site, and purchased a prominent lot at the northeast corner of Third and University. Architects William Boone and William Willcox designed and built an exuberant Gothic Revival sanctuary with a tall corner tower, other square and round turrets, and elaborate stained glass windows that was dedicated in 1891.[184] By 1910, the site was crowded on the north side by the Federal Building and to the east by the Cobb Building and the development of the Metropolitan Tract. As with other downtown churches, eventually the "old location grew so valuable that a price of

more than $300,000 induced the congregation to sell, buy larger space and build anew."[185] The Victorian-era church (scarcely 20 years old) was demolished to make way for the sumptuous Pantages (later Palomar) Theater (itself demolished for a post office and parking garage structure years later).

New church property was found on the west half-block of Sixth Avenue between Seneca and University Streets, at the gateway to First Hill. The John Graham Sr.-designed church complex, described as "a fine example of Colonial Classic," was dedicated in May 1912 and had a seating capacity for 1,400 worshippers and space for classrooms, meetings, and various social services. In plan and function it, too, followed the institutional lead of First Presbyterian's architects and clergy. During the mid 1960s, the congregation resolved to remain in the upper downtown area, despite the construction of Interstate 5 and development of a Minoru Yamasaki–designed IBM Building on the half-block along Fifth Avenue to the west.

Architects Naramore, Bain, Brady & Johanson drew plans for a new church—the first downtown church to feature garage parking. The 1912 sanctuary was demolished and its four fluted Ionic columns were relocated to the triangular park at the eastern edge of Interstate 5 between Pike and Pine Streets. The new sanctuary was dedicated in 1967.[186] Plymouth's Chapel is used by downtown Roman Catholics for daily Mass during the week—a unique example of ecumenical partnership in the midst of the city.

[CHAPTER] 7

HOSPITALS

DOTTY DeCOSTER

SCIENTIFIC MEDICINE WAS STILL IN ITS INFANCY IN 1880. Throughout
Europe, the eastern United States, and Canada, scientists and physicians were
beginning to associate the spread of disease with what we would call public health
issues: polluted water, rotten food, disease in animals, stinking air, overcrowded
conditions, and rats. In Seattle, as in other new West Coast cities growing so rapidly,
the development of public health facilities and the legal frameworks for enforcing
public-health rules and regulations were just beginning to emerge. Seattle's Great Fire
in 1889 unleashed not only a major building boom downtown but also a movement to
provide clean drinking water and proper sewage facilities, immunize citizens and live-
stock with such vaccines as were available, and provide laboratory services to local
doctors and veterinarians.

People often believed that it was the stink itself—the miasma—that was the source
of disease. Smallpox, diphtheria, typhoid, cholera, measles, influenza, venereal diseases,
and tuberculosis were all prevalent in early Seattle. Until well into the 1900s only
careful nursing was efficacious in these cases. Downtown Seattle, especially the
entertainment district, was considered the hotbed (sometimes called the "lava beds") of

disease and vice, devoutly to be shunned—along with those who lived there (including Native Americans and Asians, who were not allowed to live in the new residential communities up the hills). Public-health measures were the major civic focus at the turn of the 20th century, along with an ongoing campaign to "clean up downtown."

One thing people seemed to agree on was that sick and injured people should receive plenty of fresh air and good food to recover. Florence Nightingale, that most famous of English nurses, required fresh air and cleanliness in all her army hospital designs and protocols in the mid 1800s. This departure from the earlier fear of night air and too much bathing had become part of the public consciousness well before Seattle became a city. "Up the hill" came to mean up in the clean air away from the miasma and sin of downtown in Seattle.

Hospital care was a missionary service of all the religions during the 19th century. Hospitals provided nursing for those recovering from surgery, accidents, and disease—often as the result of war—and were staffed, operated, and administered by nurses. People who could afford medical care were served at home by physicians and volunteer or professional nurses associated with the family physician. Nurses, like most physicians, were trained through apprenticeships. Professional nursing schools as well as medical schools did not become widespread in the United States until the 20th century.[187]

SEATTLE'S FIRST HOSPITALS

Seattle's first hospice (not yet a hospital) was the King County Poor Farm, out in the country south of Seattle, in what is now called Georgetown. In 1877, the acting pastor of Our Lady of Good Help Church, at the request of a King County councilman, invited the Sisters of Charity of Providence at Vancouver, Washington, to

RIGHT: King County Hospital, Georgetown. PEMCO Webster & Stevens Collection 1983.10.6577, MOHAI.

request the King County contract for care of the county poor at the poor farm. The
Sisters had founded and maintained the hospital in Vancouver, along with several
others in the West, and were experienced nurses and hospital administrators.

Three sisters arrived in May of that year to give service to the poor, but moved in
July 1878 to a new location at Fifth Avenue and Madison Street, which had more
room and came to be called Providence Hospital.[188] Until 1887, the Sisters cared for
the poor in both locations—at the farm and in their hospital under contract from the
county. In 1893, a new King County Hospital was built in Georgetown, and a staff was
hired when it opened the following year. This became the major charity hospital for
King County residents and also the hospital for those with contagious diseases. Providence Hospital was rebuilt facing Spring Street in 1882, where it remained until 1910,
when the hospital moved up to Second Hill at 17th Avenue and Jefferson Street. It has
been Swedish Medical Center Seattle–Cherry Hill Campus since 2000.

GRACE HOSPITAL, SUMMIT AVENUE AND UNION STREET | 1885-87 (DEMOLISHED)

Grace Hospital was First Hill's first hospital, a progressive initiative by the
Episcopalian congregation of Trinity Parish, who started the hospital and first
administered it. Grace Hospital was the culmination of the hopes of the Protestant
matrons of the parish who wished to have a private hospital, far away from downtown's miasma and the sins of alcohol. Unfortunately, Trinity Parish did not have any
experience in professional nursing or hospital administration. The group of doctors
who tried to manage the place were already extremely busy downtown, both in private

ABOVE: Grace Hospital at Summit Avenue and Union Street. The building was demolished in 1905. Courtesy Kurt Jackson.

practice and as volunteer medical advisors in the public health movement. They did, however, come to practice regularly at the private Seattle General Hospital once it was rebuilt between Fourth and Fifth Avenues on Marion Street in 1900. At that time, Seattle General was taken over by the Deaconess Home Association, a Protestant missionary organization with nursing and hospital administration experience. Grace Hospital was not able to weather the depressed economy of 1893. A group of doctors attempted to maintain it until 1899. The building stood vacant for a time, and then operated as a boarding house and hotel. In 1905 the building was demolished to make room for Summit Grade School (see Chapter 5).[189]

1900 – 1910 SEATTLE

Murray Morgan described the economic growth of the time:

> *In Seattle gold spurred growth, and growth battened on growth. Bank deposits surged from $4.6 million in 1897 to $7 million in 1898 and $12.3 million in 1899; bank clearings in the same period went from $36 million to $92 million. Shipments to foreign points rose from $2.8 million in 1897 to $4 million in 1899; imports more dramatically from $1.1 million in 1897 to $5.3 million in 1899.*
>
> *When the federal census was taken in 1900, the state had grown from 357,232 to 518,103—an increase of 44 percent. Seattle's population had jumped from 42,837 to 80,676—an increase of 98 percent . . .[190]*

In addition to a number of new settlers, now there were funds to proceed with both public and private enterprises simultaneously. One of the new public enterprises was a City Hospital, to be part of a new Seattle Public Safety Building between Fourth and Fifth Avenues and Yesler Way and Terrace Street. It didn't happen overnight, but in 1909, it did open with a new City Emergency Hospital, laboratories in the basement, and an ambulance underneath.[191] For decades, the area around Fourth and Yesler included both Seattle General Hospital and the City Emergency Hospital. It also included the Seattle General Hospital Nursing School, which became essential for the operation of both hospitals. This was Seattle's first hospital zone.

In 1910, Seattle had a population of 237,194. Economic activity continued to be brisk. While the automobile had made an appearance, most transportation was still tied to the waterfront or to railway and streetcar lines. By this time, most settlers with families did not live downtown unless they were quite poor or excluded from uphill neighborhoods.

PRIVATE HOSPITALS ON FIRST HILL, 1906-1912

T. T. MINOR HOSPITAL, 1414-24 SPRING STREET │ 1906

BELOW: Minor Hospital. PEMCO Webster & Stevens Collection 1983.10.7543.1, MOHAI.

The first private hospital, organized and built by physicians and administered by specially trained nurse superintendents, was T. T. Minor Hospital, built in 1906 and named for the prominent early Seattle physician (see Chapter 2). Heins & LaFarge of New York designed it, with construction supervised by Somervell and Coté, who had come to town from New York to supervise the building of St. James Cathedral.[192]

ABOVE: Minor Hospital had spotless preparation, anesthetic, operating, and recovery rooms. PEMCO Webster & Stevens Collection 1983.10.7544, MOHAI.

Curiously, the story of the development of Minor Hospital is somewhat obscure. Contemporary building permits and newspaper reports indicate that real estate entrepreneur and local wholesale grocer Nelson Grimsley bought the property, and he was listed on the building permits. A much later newspaper report listed the St. Anthony Association, a group of physicians and surgeons, as the motivating and later managing group. Perhaps this was a sufficiently radical idea that the founders wished to keep it quiet until it was built; or perhaps the physicians involved were simply very busy and relied on Grimsley to do the paperwork. In any case, we do know that Dr. Alfred Raymond (1860-1919) was president of the St. Anthony Association in 1913, and Dr. Caspar W. Sharples (1866-1941) held that position in 1921. Both were distinguished surgeons, early and active members (and presidents) of the King County Medical Association, and active volunteers in many public health and charitable efforts.[193]

Minor Hospital was unusual in Seattle when it was built. *Pacific Building and Engineering Record* in July 1906 featured it, pointing out the new hospital's virtues, lauding the architects, and detailing the building suppliers.

> *A full basement extends along the Harvard avenue end, and contains the main kitchen, laundry, refrigerator, boiler-room and servants' sleeping rooms and bath. It is entirely cut off from the floors above, and is supplied with separate suction fan ventilation, so as to carry away all odors . . .*
>
> *The first and second floors contain the private rooms, of which there are 45, arranged single and en suite with or without private bath; also the office, reception room, sun room for convalescents, doctors' preparation rooms and diet kitchens. The third floor is given over to the operating suite and to the quarters for the nurses, so that each floor is isolated from the others and from the rest of the building.*[194]

The article went on to describe the two operating rooms with sterilizing and general preparation room between, and anesthetic and recovery rooms. Since ether was used for anesthetic at this time, ventilation was critical and special flues were installed in the floor to remove the fumes before they permeated the building. Many details were described, such as rounded corners to prevent dust accumulation, floor deadeners, special tile lavatories and baths, pipes set away from walls for careful cleaning, etc. Both high- and low-pressure steam were used for sterilization and laundry, and heating.

The *Seattle Daily Times* noted, "The hospital is strictly a private hospital and only private cases will be received. All diseases will be accepted except pulmonary tuberculosis, contagious and mental diseases. Special facilities will be given for surgical, obstetrics and rest cure cases. A separate group of rooms will be set aside for obstetric cases with a special head nurse in charge."[195]

The first superintendent of the hospital was Margaret Leary of New York. Miss Pringle of Cleveland was in charge of the operating rooms, and Miss Underwood from Buffalo was her assistant. All the nursing staff upon opening were professional nurses. There was also a resident physician and an assistant. (A small house was also provided northeast of the hospital for the resident.)

Eventually, Minor Hospital opened a nursing school as well, and occupied the old Alexander B. Stewart home at 1102 Boylston Avenue as a nursing residence. In 1920 the hospital was sold to Bethesda Association, and in 1929 it closed abruptly after filing for bankruptcy in federal court. There was a dream project floated in 1925 to build a new, larger hospital on the corner (where the Stewart house was located), using the existing hospital for the nurses, but it did not come to pass.[196] First Baptist Church acquired the property in 1929. The building remains, now the Spring Street Early Learning Center.

SUMMIT AVENUE HOSPITAL, 803 SUMMIT AVENUE | 1911-12 (DEMOLISHED)

Summit Avenue Hospital at 803 Summit Avenue became the third hospital on the hill. Dr. Edmund Marburg Rininger (1870-1912), a surgeon, came to Seattle after spending time in the Yukon and Alaska. In 1905, he and his wife purchased the home of C. J. Smith at 803 Summit Avenue. By 1911, Dr. Rininger had decided to build his own hospital on the site of his home. He purchased a house for his family next door (1214 Columbia), took an extensive tour of hospitals around the country looking for ideas and equipment, and hired J. S. Coté to design the building. The plans are similar to the descriptions of Minor Hospital, modified to include the entrance, front foyer, and staircase of the Smith house and configured to the site.[197]

The neighbors rebelled, taking him to court to enjoin him from building a hospital in their neighborhood. Reporting on Dr. Rininger's day in court, the *Seattle Daily Times* quoted him:

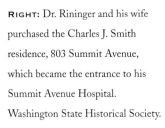

RIGHT: Dr. Rininger and his wife purchased the Charles J. Smith residence, 803 Summit Avenue, which became the entrance to his Summit Avenue Hospital. Washington State Historical Society.

I propose to erect a white brick and terra cotta building that will cost $50,000 and one that will increase rather than decrease the value of surrounding property . . . It will not be a hospital at all in the generally accepted sense of the word. It will be strictly private, for the exclusive use of my patients and those of my associate, Dr. O. F. Lamson [Dr. Otis Floyd Lamson, 1876-1956, also a surgeon] . . . We will have no contagious diseases there and no mental diseases . . . That property values deteriorate in the vicinity of a hospital is more or less of a myth. It has not been the case with Minor Hospital. A beautiful church has been built next to it, the Masonic cathedral has been built across the street from it and all around it people are living undisturbed by its presence and almost unaware of its existence.[198]

The City had already issued a building permit in February, and excavation was under way, Dr. Rininger won the court case, and Summit Avenue Hospital at 803 Summit Avenue was built. Sadly, Dr. Rininger was killed in an automobile accident on July 25, 1912. The hospital and house were sold to the Swedish Hospital Association in December 1912.

SWEDISH HOSPITAL, 1733 BELMONT AVENUE | 1910
803 SUMMIT AVENUE | 1911-12 (DEMOLISHED)

Swedish Hospital had leased a new residential hotel building at 1733 Belmont Avenue in 1910. Dr. Nils A. Johanson (1872-1946), a surgeon newly arrived in Seattle from Denver, was the major initiator of the project, although Scandinavian Seattleites had long sought to build a hospital of their own. (Elmer Nordstrom

RIGHT: By 1943, Swedish Hospital included a former apartment building and a newer "streamlined moderne" building that was more factorylike. PEMCO Webster & Stevens Collection 1983.10.14697.10, MOHAI.

married Dr. Johanson's daughter Kitty soon thereafter.) Their new hospital was bursting at the seams by 1912, and the Swedish community went into fundraising high gear to purchase Summit Avenue Hospital. They raised the funds, and moved there in early 1913. Mrs. Rininger donated Dr. Rininger's X-ray machine, along with his medical library.[199]

Swedish had a nursing school from the beginning; the nurses' residence was the house on Columbia Street. Swedish student nurses were affiliated with Children's Orthopedic Hospital (then on Queen Anne Hill) for clinical training (as had been the student nurses at Minor Hospital). Hildur Newberg was superintendent of Swedish Hospital in this period.[200]

The original apartment building used by Swedish is still standing but not the original Summit Avenue Hospital/Swedish Hospital building. Swedish Hospital became Swedish Medical Center and is still on First Hill, with a greatly expanded footprint.[201]

THE TEENS AND TWENTIES

COLUMBUS, LATER CABRINI, HOSPITAL, 1019 MADISON STREET | 1916 (DEMOLISHED)

BELOW: Sisters of the Sacred Heart ran the Columbus (renamed Cabrini) Hospital, which operated as the fourth hospital on the hill. Photo by Max Loudon, courtesy Grace McAdams.

In 1916, Mother Cabrini (Saint Frances Xavier Cabrini, 1850-1917) came to Seattle and purchased the Perry Hotel at 1019 Madison Street (see Chapter 4). She intended to found a boys' home but chose instead to open a hospital. Bishop Edward John O'Dea (1856-1932), Roman Catholic bishop of Seattle from 1896-1932, did not feel that another Catholic hospital was needed here, and so the facility opened as a sanitarium. By 1918, during the influenza pandemic, Columbus Sanitarium was serving patients. Columbus, later Cabrini, Hospital became the fourth hospital on First Hill. It was demolished in 1996 and replaced with Cabrini Senior Housing, a mission of the Sisters of the Sacred Heart, offering 50 units of subsidized housing.[202]

In a September 1916 article in *Pacific Builder and Engineer*, Frederick Heath, Heath & Gove, architects, Tacoma, discussed the complicated issues in planning for efficient and effective facilities in "The Hospital Problem."

Much has been published in the past few years on the planning of hospitals . . . The units and elements that make a modern hospital suggest immediately a group of buildings, combining a greater or less [sic] number of units according to the size of the institution. In studying the units that make up the main body of the plan, the following appointments are considered: Administration. Patients' rooms with service rooms. Hospital supplies and distribution. Dispensary with distribution. Kitchen, food service and distribution. Accident and emergency department. Operating department. Provision for nurses and employees. Laundry. Heating and power plant.

One cannot depend too much for information from doctors, nurses or superintendent, as each views a hospital from a different viewpoint . . .

In all hospitals the nursing or direct care of the patient is necessarily the greater importance, and the plan should be considered almost wholly from that standpoint, both the efficiency of service and salary cost, and the main problem in designing a hospital is to determine the size of unit for housing this element . . .[203]

RIGHT: The former Ranke/Thomsen home became a nurses' home for Columbus Hospital. Pierson Photo Co., courtesy Dennis Andersen.

Minor and Swedish Hospitals were busy serving patients, many of them new babies. Swedish began expanding almost immediately. With the Peterson addition, designed by Bebb & Gould, the hospital grew to 130 beds in 1917.[204]

By the 1920s, scientific medicine had won the support of the public majority and hospitals were more widely used. Other forms of health care and disease management—osteopathy, chiropractic, naturopathy, Christian Science nursing, midwifery, etc.—were available in Seattle, but became less popular as surgical techniques and scientific ways of managing infectious diseases improved.

VIRGINIA MASON HOSPITAL, 1101 TERRY AVENUE | 1920

ABOVE: Bebb & Gould designed the Italian Renaissance–style Virginia Mason Clinic, which had the appearance of an upscale apartment building to fit into its residential setting. Curtis 46808, Washington State Historical Society.

Virginia Mason Hospital, the fifth hospital on First Hill, opened its doors in 1920 in an Italianate beige brick and terra-cotta trimmed building designed by Charles H. Bebb (1856-1942) and Carl F. Gould (1873-1939) at 1101 Terry Avenue extending from Spring to Seneca Street. The hospital included a clinic on the ground floor (six doctors' offices), an 80-bed hospital, and nurses' quarters upstairs. It looked much like the elegant apartment buildings that would soon share space on the adjoining blocks. Virginia Mason expanded soon, opening a nursing school in 1922. Anna J. Frazer was superintendent.

Virginia Mason was founded to take the concept of group physician practice a step further: to provide a physician team effort and hospital services for their patients on-site. Founders were: Dr. James Tate Mason (1882-1936), a surgeon; Dr. John M. Blackford (1887-1945), internal medicine; and Dr. Maurice F. Dwyer (1889-1944), a radiologist.[205] The name for the new hospital had its genesis in two young girls. Both Mason and Blackford had daughters named Virginia. Coincidentally, both physicians had graduated from the University of Virginia.[206]

Dr. Mason, who was president of the board and founder of Virginia Mason, had served as King County coroner from 1913 to 1917, and in 1917 was appointed head of staff at King County Hospital, serving until the end of 1922. He is credited with founding the King County morgue. Dr. Blackford came to Seattle in 1917 after serving on the staff of the Mayo Clinic in Minnesota for six years, and Dr. Dwyer interned at Providence Hospital before joining the Virginia Mason crew. Virginia Mason Medical Center remains on First Hill, and the original hospital building is visible from Spring Street and (closed) Terry Avenue. It has been overshadowed by additions starting with the 1950s-era Buck Pavilion, major hospital additions in the 1970s, and later, the Benaroya Research Institute, Lindeman Pavilion, and most recently, a new hospital and emergency wing along Boren Avenue between Seneca and Spring Streets called the Jones Pavilion.

RIGHT: Nurse Kathryn Perrine with X-ray machine at Virginia Mason Hospital, 1937. The hospital was the first on the West Coast to have advanced X-ray equipment. PEMCO Webster & Stevens Collection 1986.5.9563.1, MOHAI.

RIGHT: Virginia Mason Public Library station (undated). Seattle Public Library had an outreach program to serve patients in the area hospitals. shp_12262, Seattle Public Library.

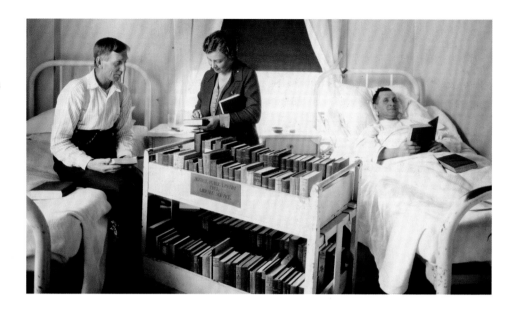

NORTHWESTERN HOSPITAL (LATER MARTHA WASHINGTON HOSPITAL AND MAYNARD HOSPITAL) 1309 SUMMIT AVENUE | 1929 (DEMOLISHED)

Just as Minor Hospital was closing in 1929, the sixth First Hill hospital was opening a few blocks away at 1309 Summit Avenue. Designed by Victor W. Voorhees (1876-1970) and owned by Dawnland Maternity Inn, Inc., this was to be a private maternity

RIGHT: Maynard Hospital, named for the city's first doctor, opened in 1933 and closed in 1971. PEMCO Webster & Stevens Collection 1983.10.14696.8, MOHAI.

hospital. Original plans called for a seven-story building, with kitchens and nurseries on each floor, two elevators, and three operating rooms on the top floor. A frame building on the site was razed. The Northwestern Hospital opened in 1929 in an apartment-building-sized hospital facility.

It was renamed Martha Washington Hospital in 1931 and became Maynard Hospital in 1933 when a group of physicians—Doctors William A. Glasgow, James E. Hunter, Hulett Wyckoff, J. C. Moore, E. Weldon Young, and Gordon G. Thompson—purchased it and renamed it after pioneer doctor David S. Maynard. During the 1930s the superintendents were Miss McKenzie, Tyra Asplund, Henrietta Bronsema, and Coralee Steele. Maternity care remained a specialty throughout Maynard Hospital's life, although it was a general hospital.

Maynard Hospital was purchased by Seattle General Hospital in 1970, closed in 1977, purchased by Fred Hutchinson Cancer Research Center in 1980, and then razed. The site is now the home of The Summit at First Hill, 1200 University Street, a Kline Galland senior community.[207]

THEN CAME THE TOWERS – THE THIRTIES

HARBORVIEW HOSPITAL, 325 NINTH AVENUE | 1931

Dreams of new public hospitals in Seattle came to fruition at almost the same time. The new King County Hospital, on First Hill, was designed by Thomas, Grainger &

ABOVE: Model of the proposed Harborview Hospital campus, Thomas, Grainger & Thomas, architects. Lot 149, Washington State Historical Society.

Thomas, and patients were moved in March 1931. At the time, the *Seattle Daily Times* ran an article to name the hospital, offering a $100 award. Elva Patterson submitted the winning name, "Harborview." The U.S. Marine Hospital, on Beacon Hill, was designed by Bebb & Gould with John Graham and opened in 1932-33. These were vertically oriented towers, Modernistic/Art Deco in style, in brick with terra-cotta ornament, with plans for smaller auxiliary buildings in a campus setting. They were Seattle's first medical centers.

Harborview, as the new King County hospital was named, was authorized in 1925, and construction was paid for with a public bond issue in 1928 and operating funds from the State Department of Public Assistance.[208] It was anticipated at the time that this would be the nucleus of a major medical center. Only the hospital building and Harborview Hall, the nurses' residence, were built at the time. Harborview was the seventh First Hill hospital.

The new facility had 350 beds in 15 stories. It was designed for those who could not afford care by private doctors and hospitals. It included clinics, dispensary, X-ray and EKG facilities, pathology, bacteriology, and biochemistry laboratories, operating

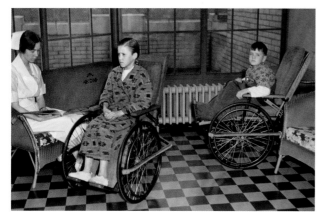

ABOVE: Nurse reading to boys in wheelchairs at Harborview. PEMCO Webster & Stevens Collection 1986.5.9399.2, MOHAI.

rooms, "psychopathic" wards, a maternity and pediatric facility, communicable disease wards, and regular hospital wards. It was a nursing school affiliated with the University of Washington nursing school and provided for interns and paid residents. The first black professional nurse, Ida Gordon, was hired at Harborview in 1943.[209]

Expansion was the norm. In 1925, Columbus Hospital purchased the old Ranke house at Terry Avenue and Madison Street for a nurses' residence, and in 1931 obtained the Stetson Hotel, adjoining the hospital to the south on Boren Avenue (now the Cabrini Medical Tower, built in 1973). Bebb & Gould designed additions for Swedish Hospital in the early 1930s: a new laboratory, housing for radiation therapy technology, and patients' quarters for the new Tumor Center. An orthopedic wing was also added. Virginia Mason also expanded. John Graham Sr. provided much of the architectural expertise for these additions, joined in the late 1930s by Perry Johanson.

Extraordinary changes came to Seattle with World War II, including a big jump in population[210] (and consequent housing shortage), a considerably expanded federal

RIGHT: Harborview Hospital, view from downtown. P. D. Wade Stevenson, ca. 1961.

presence, smallpox and polio epidemics, and the replacement of street rails by rubber-tired trolleys. On First Hill, the large number of hospitals spurred a variety of specialty office buildings adjacent to them to accommodate small private medical, dental, and optical practices. Some of these professionals took over older single-family residences, adapting them for offices and examination rooms; others hired local architects to design new one- and two-story buildings. These new buildings embraced streamlined modern and International Style modernism in their street appearance and efficient division of interiors for reception, waiting rooms, and consulting rooms.

DOCTOR'S HOSPITAL, 909 UNIVERSITY STREET | 1944; ADDITION 1967

An eighth new hospital opened on First Hill in 1944: Doctor's Hospital, between Ninth and Terry Avenues, and University and Seneca Streets, the site of the old Rolland Denny home. Designed by George Wellington Stoddard (1896-1967), this was a project of the King County Medical Service Corporation, financed by federal funds and matching funds saved over time by the nonprofit corporation. Originally, it was two floors with basement and sub-basement, including an emergency entrance. The first floor was dedicated to maternity and childbirth; the second floor included

THE FORTIES

DeLena Cresto was a student nurse at Columbus Hospital, 1941-1944.

[The school was run by] Missionary Sisters of the Sacred Heart. We were affiliated with Seattle University at that time for a little while—Seattle College—for a few years, and then the Sisters became independent again, and it stayed just as Columbus Hospital training school. We did a lot of overtime. We had to. We were going to school. We took five [classes] at Seattle College and had classes right here at the hospital or in the nurses' home. We worked just about eight hours a day. When we were seniors we were running the floors . . . When we were seniors they put us in the Cadet Nurses Corps—the federal

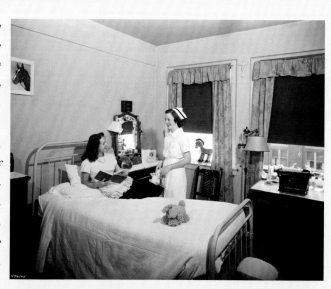

ABOVE: Student nurses in a dormitory room, Columbus Hospital, 1947. Until the 1950s, the Sisters of the Sacred Heart ran a nursing school as part of the hospital program. 1983.10.16686.1, MOHAI.

government did—and Nazleh Vizetelly, who was our director, made sure that we all got into the Cadet Nurses Corps so we could get some money. So we all got, I think it was, $10 a month . . . from the Cadet Nurses Corps . . . Yes, I joined the service. I was in the Army Nurse Corps.

DeLena M. Cresto

1st Lieutenant, Charter member Army Nurse Corps 1945-48; Reserves 1948-61.[211]

five surgeries, two wings of rooms for 80 patients, X-ray, laboratories, "frozen-section" rooms, and special facilities for bone surgery and urology procedures. Physicians of the King County Medical Society who belonged to the bureau (reported to be 480 in May 1944) had use of the hospital. Patients were subscribers to the bureau, some 40,100 in 1940. Doctor's affiliated with the University of Washington School of Nursing for student nurses. Dr. Karl H. Van Norman was superintendent of the hospital.[212]

The building and its 1967 addition, designed by Naramore, Bain, Brady & Johanson, are still visible, now part of the Virginia Mason Medical Center. Local artist and sculptor Dudley Pratt designed the *bas relief* panels executed by his family in preparation for the hospital opening in 1944.[213]

New nurses' residences were opened for Virginia Mason Nursing School (Blackford Hall, 1945) and Swedish Nursing School (Eklind Hall, 1946, designed by Naramore, Bain, Brady & Johanson). All the nurses' residences had classrooms and or meeting spaces—there were no separate school buildings. Blackford Hall is located at the northeast corner of Seneca Street and Terry Avenue; Eklind Hall was at the northeast corner of Columbia Street and Boren Avenue (formerly site of the home of Mary and James Lowman). All three nurses' residences—Blackford, Eklind, and Harborview Hall—became research laboratories in the early 1960s. Eklind became an early facility of the Fred Hutchinson Cancer Research Center and was also the first home of Northwest Kidney Centers.

In October 1946, the University of Washington opened a medical school as part of the new School of Health Sciences, which would soon expand to include a new School of Dentistry, absorbing the School of Nursing (founded in 1922) and the School of Pharmacy (founded in 1894). The first class of the School of Medicine graduated in 1950.

BELOW: Doctor's Hospital Dudley Pratt *bas relief*. PEMCO Webster & Stevens Collection 1986.5.9399.2, MOHAI.

"FIRST HILL IS APARTMENT, MEDICAL CENTER"

"Walking about First Hill today one finds many of the pedestrians are graduate nurses in their stiffly starched, white uniforms, or student nurses in blue, with big white aprons and bibs, who have an hour off duty. Ambulances dash past on emergency duty and Catholic nuns hurry on their way."[214]

This long-awaited event began by transforming Harborview:

> *In May 1946, the Board of Trustees of Harborview granted the medical school authority to establish a united program for clinical supervision and patient care. Patients were segregated according to their problems in wards designated for individual medical specialties, and record-keeping was revised in compliance with standards of the American Medical Association.*
>
> *A closed staff of university faculty and a few selected town physicians was drawn up . . . Affiliation agreements were also reached within the year with the Seattle Marine Hospital, Firlands Tuberculosis Sanatorium, and Children's Orthopedic Hospital. All affiliated hospitals accepted the principle that the training of house staff and students would be under university auspices, and that staff appointments would be approved by the medical school.[215]*

Harborview remained a county hospital serving only those in need, but it was no longer incumbent upon local physicians to volunteer their time.

THE FIFTIES AND BEYOND

If there was a golden age of First Hill hospitals, it was the 1950s. Hospital architects continued to innovate to provide for sterile surgeries, efficient organization of nursing services, accommodating fathers in maternity facilities, and new technological diagnostic and treatment machines. And now that automobiles were ubiquitous, parking garages were essential.

Harborview Hospital regularly began to offer positions to African-American professional nurses and, slowly, other hospitals followed suit. Nursing schools accepted female nurses of color as well. Physicians often specialized, but most families who could afford health care still had family doctors. Private hospitals continued to be selective about which physicians could use their hospitals—Jewish, Asian, and African-American physicians were not always welcome. Harborview and Providence continued to offer care for the needy regardless of background.

Dr. William B. Hutchinson founded the Pacific Northwest Research Foundation in 1956. Located at, but independent of, Swedish Hospital, this set the stage for several major medical research efforts to come. In 1956 also, Virginia Mason opened a research center. The Reconstructive Cardiovascular Research Laboratory was founded by Lester R. Sauvage, M.D., at Providence in 1959. Decades later it would move to Virginia Mason on First Hill. Although Swedish had a Tumor Center earlier, this was the time when First Hill hospitals began to develop medical research facilities and treatment pavilions.

Further isolated from downtown by the construction of Interstate 5, First Hill came to be called "Pill Hill," and the rise in downtown land values helped drive the last downtown hospital (Seattle General) up the hill, as well as the long-term group medical practice called The Polyclinic (founded in 1922).[216] Numerous other physicians and hospital-serving businesses joined them. A few new small hospitals were also built on First Hill during this time; the only one that survives today is the First Hill Convalescent Home, at 1318 Terry Avenue, built in 1964.

Seattle General bought Maynard Hospital at the end of 1970, and moved uphill. In June 1980, Seattle General (formerly Maynard) and Doctor's Hospital merged into Swedish—their patients, staff, and programs became part of a new pavilion attached to the Swedish Medical Center. The old Maynard hospital facility was sold to Fred Hutchinson Cancer Research Center and later razed, and the Doctor's Hospital facility became part of the Virginia Mason Medical Center.[217]

Today the remaining medical centers on First Hill—Harborview, Swedish, and Virginia Mason—look from the outside as if they had grown over time in the way a coral colony grows.[218] Now spatially confined, they are a hodgepodge of styles, additions, sky bridges, tunnels, pavilions, laboratories, physicians' offices, parking facilities, and occasionally a fountain or sculpture. From inside, a maze of facilities offers a myriad of health and research services, interspersed with the hospitals' art collections. Swedish and Virginia Mason are nonprofit corporations. Each has decentralized over the past few decades, purchasing and leasing facilities outside their First Hill confines not just in the next neighborhood but much farther afield. Harborview, which is managed by the University of Washington, is also part of a network of facilities.

It is hard to predict what will be next for the First Hill medical centers that began as hospitals. It is equally hard to predict what will happen to the many other First Hill facilities providing health-related services and spaces.

SOMERVELL & COTÉ

W. Marbury Somervell (1872-1939) was sent to Seattle by the well-known architecture firm Heins & LaFarge of New York City to supervise construction of St. James Cathedral (1903-07). Joseph S. Coté (1874-1957), of the same firm, came to Seattle as his assistant. Trained in Beaux-Arts classicism, they chose to stay in Seattle and formed a partnership in 1906 that lasted until 1910, after which they practiced individually or with others until joining the military in World War I. After the war, Coté returned to practice in Seattle until about 1948; Somervell returned to the West Coast,

working individually or with other architects from Vancouver, B.C., to Los Angeles for the next decade.

The partnership was quite successful, working on both private and public commissions, designing and building residences, libraries, firehouses, and hospitals. David Rash noted:

When Architectural Record *published its first survey on Seattle architecture in July 1912, four of the twenty-two published buildings were wholly or partly the work of Somervell & Coté . . . At a time when American architecture was judged primarily by East Coast standards, Somervell & Coté helped Seattle come of age as "unquestionably the city of most considerable promise in these United States."* [219]

LEFT AND BELOW LEFT: Portraits of Somervell and Coté in *Pacific Builder and Engineer*. UW 7250 and UW 14478, Special Collections, University of Washington Libraries.

Hospital design seems to have been one of Coté's contributions to the firm, although they worked together on many Seattle hospitals. The first of these was Minor Hospital (1906), built to designs by Heins & LaFarge, on Spring Street at Harvard Avenue. Contemporary accounts mention that Coté had previously been involved in construction at Vassar Brothers Memorial Hospital in Poughkeepsie, New York. They designed and built the second Providence Hospital at 528 17th Avenue in 1907-1912. In 1908-9, they did an addition to St. Joseph Hospital in Bellingham. Children's Orthopedic Hospital (1911) at 100 Crockett on Queen Anne followed (later King County Hospital, now Queen Anne Manor); and Coté designed Noble Hospital on Woodland Park

BELOW: Perry Apartments, Somervell & Coté. Curtis 25615, Special Collections, University of Washington Libraries.

Avenue in Fremont (1911, later Norwegian Hospital) for Dr. G. S. Peterkin and Summit Avenue Hospital for Dr. Rininger at 803 Summit Avenue (1911-1912, later Swedish Hospital). The firm also designed the Perry Apartment Hotel at 1019 Madison Street (1907), which later became Columbus/Cabrini Hospital. Of these buildings, Minor Hospital, Providence Hospital, and Children's Orthopedic Hospital survive, all altered.

The partners seem to have cultivated the potential patrons they met through their early work over time. For instance, they designed a home for Clare E. Farnsworth at 803 East Prospect in 1909-10. Later, Coté designed the Sunset Club at 1021 University Street for Mrs. Farnsworth in 1914-15, as well as a 1923 extension. (He also designed a small Lighthouse for the Blind workshop for her charity in 1924, *pro bono*.) The partners supervised design and construction of Minor Hospital in 1905-6. In 1912, Coté designed a mansion for Dr. Alfred Raymond at 702 35th Avenue. Raymond was president of St. Anthony's Association, which ran Minor Hospital.

(Both the Farnsworth and Raymond homes are extant.)

Somervell & Coté designed the Florence Henry Memorial Chapel in The Highlands, which opened in 1911. Numerous other commissions followed for each of them, designing residences in The Highlands and at the country club at Restoration Point on Bainbridge Island—major residential commissions for the well-to-do—as well as homes, apartment buildings, and business buildings downtown and throughout Seattle. In 1912, Somervell was able to take advantage of these relationships in a different way: he was reported as a patient in Minor Hospital recovering from appendicitis.

Surviving examples of the partnership's work on First Hill include Minor Hospital, the Sunset Club, St. James Cathedral and the Bishop's House next door, and Fire Station No. 25 at East Union Street and Harvard Avenue (an adaptive reuse project by Historic Seattle in 1979).[220]

BELOW: Providence Hospital, Somervell & Coté. Curtis 23959, Special Collections, University of Washington Libraries.

[CHAPTER]

THE MODERN ERA AND PRESERVATION OF THE HILL

DOTTY DECOSTER AND LAWRENCE KREISMAN

SURROUNDED

ABOVE: Protesters march across Spring Street demonstrating opposition to freeway construction, June 1961. PEMCO Webster & Stevens Collection 1986.5.4018.1, MOHAI.

LEFT: *Looking West on First Hill.* Leon Derbyshire (American, 1896-1981), oil on linen. Captures the small-scale frame housing north of Yesler Way prior to demolition for the freeway in the early 1960s. Frye Art Museum.

DURING THE 1960S, CHANGES AROUND FIRST HILL BEGAN to have a significant impact on the neighborhood. Sutton Place, a tile-faced high-rise apartment block that gained the nickname "the purple palace," replaced single-family homes on the west side of Minor Avenue across from the Stimson-Green Mansion in 1962. It was a sign of renewed confidence in the city's growth but also signaled the fragility of the earlier residential scale with increasing property values. The most dramatic change was the demolition of seven blocks of buildings along the western edge of First Hill to build Interstate 5. By 1969, when the entire length of I-5 was completed, First Hill was cut off from downtown by a river of traffic along a ditch separating the two. Access to downtown was now by bridges over the noisy freeway.

While the Norton Building, completed in 1959, was the first of the city's International Style skyscrapers, its 21 floors were hardly comparable to the 50-story Seattle-First National Bank tower, which debuted in 1969 at Fourth Avenue and Madison

Street. The Seafirst Tower would reign as the tallest building in Seattle until 1985 and block the view from the top of the Sorrento Hotel, on Madison Street and Terry Avenue. Locals dubbed it "the box the Space Needle came in" since the Space Needle, at the former Century 21 Exposition grounds, now Seattle Center, was the other significantly tall landmark of the era, built in 1962. Over time, skyscrapers were built throughout downtown, obscuring most Sound and mountain views from older First Hill buildings.

At the same time, just to the east of First Hill across Broadway, Seattle College grew dramatically, becoming Seattle University. Its adjacency to the official First Hill boundary has made it a valuable contributor to the neighborhood. The university provides First Hill residents and visitors with cultural, religious, and educational

BELOW: Madison Street, looking east from Sixth Avenue, 1961 and 1975. Lawton Gowey.

BELOW: A year of demolition, earth-moving, and construction created enormous changes and disruption to daily life on First Hill. Left: 1963; right: 1964.

RIGHT: The great freeway divide was partly moderated by the award-winning Freeway Park, its series of waterfalls, and a connecting pedestrian corridor to First Hill, 1976. Frank Shaw, courtesy Paul Dorpat.

programs, a beautiful campus, security, employment for area residents, and service projects. In return, Seattle University gets access to shops and restaurants, availability of a range of housing, jobs for students, access to healthcare facilities, and use of public transportation systems and streets.

Seattle Central Community College (now Seattle Central College) was founded in the late 1960s as well, just northeast of First Hill in the old Broadway High School building at Broadway and Pine Street and the Edison Technical School building next door. It was rebuilt during the 1970s. Faculty and students found First Hill apartments desirable.

BELOW: The former Anderson residence served as a women's dormitory for Seattle University students. Courtesy *Seattle Times*.

INFLUENCES FROM ELSEWHERE

Farther afield, the University of Washington Health Sciences complex was beginning what became a massive construction project along the north side of the Lake Washington Ship Canal, and the nursing program expanded significantly. As training for nurses and hospital affiliations changed, the First Hill nurses' residences were repurposed.

In 1961, when the National Housing Act allowed FHA mortgages to be used to purchase condominiums, Washington State began to allow condominium ownership. This opportunity led to some preservation efforts. Some First Hill apartment buildings were converted from rentals to condominium ownership. Two examples are The Gainsborough, on Minor Avenue between Madison and Spring Streets, and the 1223 building at 1223 Spring Street.

BELOW: The floor plan for The Gainsborough shows variants in each of the four apartments on a floor. Courtesy Diana James.

TYPICAL FLOOR PLAN OF THE GAINSBOROUGH

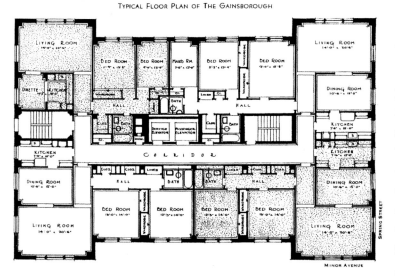

NEIGHBORS WORK TO SHAPE FIRST HILL

By the 1970s, First Hill had begun to feel somewhat isolated, and many residents and property owners were concerned that the neighborhood was on a path to becoming an institutional ghetto. Two efforts were undertaken during the 1970s to address these issues: (1) to preserve the best of the historic heritage of the neighborhood, and (2) to constrain the educational and medical institutions from continuing to expand over the landscape, resulting in the City of Seattle Major Institutions Policies and Code of 1981 and 1983, respectively.

HISTORIC PRESERVATION

The demolition of vestiges of the historic First Hill community during the 1950s and 1960s did not go unnoticed by those who lived there and by a small contingent of history buffs and preservationists. Certainly the razing of hundreds of buildings for the freeway had an enormous impact in terms of relocation of homeowners and renters. But there were very few avenues available at the time to address the losses apart from the occasional newspaper article or editorial.

That began to change in 1973 with the enactment of an ordinance establishing a means by which individual buildings and sites of historic and architectural importance could be designated landmark properties with a degree of protection from significant alterations and demolition. Some of the earliest buildings to be reviewed and designated were on First Hill—the Stimson-Green Mansion, Trinity Church, First Baptist Church, St. James Cathedral, and Fire Station No. 25.

Even with a landmarks ordinance in place, blocks of single-family residences that had been important fixtures in the community during its Golden Age were often considered expendable given the value of land and zoning that encouraged mid- and high-rise apartment towers. The Pelly, Waterhouse, and Peters houses, on the east side of Minor Avenue between University and Union Streets, were razed. So too were the shingled Colonial Revival Kelleher house, at the corner of Minor Avenue and Spring Street, Josiah Collins's Arts and Crafts home at the corner of Minor Avenue and University Street, and others. In the case of the Collins house, community activists pushed for a vest-pocket park on the site. In another case—the A. A. Denny Tudor Revival home at the corner of Boren and Seneca Street—the replacement was a surface parking lot for the Sunset Club.

To protect a neighborhood that was rapidly losing its integrity called for a more comprehensive historic district designation. In the fall of 1979, Arthur Skolnik, principal of The Conservation Company, with historians Gwendolyn A. Lee and Miriam Sutermeister, submitted a draft National Register Historic District nomination that was thematic, focusing on the remaining residential resources on First Hill. They assembled information on contributing single-family and multifamily buildings to make the case that these were significant and valuable to protect. The initial draft

RIGHT: The Waterhouse home, along with the Pelly and Peters residences, was turned down for city landmark designation and demolished. Seattle Public Library.

was sent back for additional information and corrections but was never resubmitted to the State. While a state designation would not necessarily have protected these buildings from demolition, it would likely have been the first step in requesting that the City of Seattle create a First Hill historic district. Over 35 years later, so many primary and contributing buildings have disappeared that it is unlikely there are enough extant resources to qualify for district designation.

Only recently have additional buildings been brought forward for individual designation, the Baroness Apartment Hotel in 2010 and the Sorrento Hotel in 2011. In the former case, Virginia Mason Medical Center presented three adjacent interwar buildings to the Seattle Landmarks Preservation Board, including the Rhododendron (Inn at Virginia Mason) and Casselton, partly to respond to neighborhood criticism around the loss of the Hungerford and the Northcliffe apartment buildings for a new hospital addition fronting Boren Avenue. Only the Baroness received landmark designation.

In the early 1970s the city passed enabling legislation for the establishment of public development authorities to accomplish specific public functions that the City of Seattle cannot undertake. Of these, the one with the broadest influence has been Historic Seattle Preservation and Development Authority, created in 1974 to preserve historic properties. The authority has acted as a catalyst to identify significant local landmarks that are neglected or threatened with destruction but which possess the potential to be reused and again successfully compete in the marketplace. Over 40 years of stewardship and risk-taking have resulted in approximately 45 important projects that have turned fragile and underutilized properties into attractive, income-producing components of city neighborhoods. They were big projects and small, in the downtown and scattered throughout the city: the Mutual Life Building in Pioneer Square; Queen Anne High School and West Queen Anne Elementary School on Queen Anne Hill; the Home of the Good Shepherd in Wallingford; an old fire station on Ballard's Russell Way and another one on First Hill's Harvard Avenue.

RIGHT: William Phillips double house, at 711 East Union Street, during renovation. Historic Seattle.

NORTH

FIRST HILL

LEGEND

Above: Inventory map of First Hill from *An Inventory of Buildings and Urban Design Resources*. Historic Seattle.

Historic Seattle's efforts on First Hill were significant, and its role has varied depending on the situation. Some involved purchase, establishment of protection to the exterior and interior, and resale, such as the timely acquisition by Historic Seattle of the Stimson-Green mansion in 1975, which saved it from an uncertain future. For Fire Station No. 25, the City transferred ownership to Historic Seattle, which then transferred ownership to a development team. In the case of the Ward House, on Boren Avenue, Historic Seattle worked with an interested owner to assure that the building could be relocated to a safe site on East Denny Way.

For the William Phillips (Heg-Phillips) and Bel-Boy Apartments, Historic Seattle took on the role of developer, partnering with low-income housing groups. To preserve the Fourth Church of Christ, Scientist, Historic Seattle prepared a feasibility study that justified the establishment of a community performing space that has been highly successful. Since 1997, Historic Seattle has been headquartered in the H. H. Dearborn House, one of only four major residences that are left on First Hill. It had been preserved largely through its use as medical offices from 1953 until 1997, and the downturn in the market for new condominiums in the 1990s. The previous owner's interest in preventing the razing of the house, along with a $1.3 million contribution toward the purchase price by Priscilla Bullitt Collins,

Right: H. H. Dearborn House, Historic Seattle's headquarters. Marissa Natkin.

ABOVE: The six buildings in the Bel-Boy restoration and adaptive reuse project were painted their original exterior colors. Historic Seattle.

ultimately saved the property. Collins, granddaughter of C. D. Stimson, had purchased the Stimson mansion in 1986 when it appeared it might be the latest victim of high-rise development on First Hill. In 2001, she gifted the Stimson-Green mansion to the Washington Trust for Historic Preservation.

MAJOR INSTITUTIONS POLICIES AND CODE

The second preservation effort was begun by citizens on First Hill and in other neighborhoods being significantly impacted by the expansion of educational and medical campuses. In 1981, the City of Seattle adopted policies and set boundaries for the future development of major institutions. Then in 1983, the first major institution codes became part of the City's Land Use Code. The idea was to provide actual boundaries to each institution's growth over time, offering specialized zoning (including more height) and creating a requirement for master plans for each campus. A Citizens Advisory Committee was established for helping to develop each master plan. The code has been amended periodically, but master planning still shapes the growth of all of Seattle's major institutions, including those on or near First Hill: Seattle Central College and Seattle University among the educational institutions, and Swedish, Virginia Mason, and Harborview among the medical institutions. Swedish was the first major institution to submit a Master Plan.

OTHER POLICY CHANGES AFFECTING FIRST HILL

During the 1960s and 1970s, federal legislation and policy changes began to influence the way people could live on First Hill, and also the ways in which work was conducted here.

The Civil Rights Act of 1964 transformed employment practices and set the stage for fair housing policies locally that prevented discrimination in renting and selling property.

At the same time, the federal government began to view seniors (those over age 65) as a protected class. Passage of the federal Medicare legislation beginning in 1965 also provided funding for medical care for seniors in an unprecedented way. Now it was possible to provide housing in exclusive residential communities (or buildings) for seniors of any income, close to the newly affordable medical services. From the 1980s onward, residential communities for seniors began to develop on First Hill, some subsidized for low-income seniors, and some operating as private, although usually nonprofit, institutions on their own. Among these are Exeter House, The Summit, and Skyline at First Hill.

GGLO/HRG, architects of Tate Mason House, at 1100 Minor Avenue, made efforts to respect the scale of lower-rise apartment buildings and homes adjacent to it in their 1998 project that provided replacement of senior units lost when the Waldorf Apartments was razed for the north extension of the Washington State Convention and Trade Center.

One progressive institution, Horizon House, was an early model that set the bar high for those senior residences to come, such as The Summit and Skyline. Starting with a wish list in 1958 by civic leader Myrtle Edwards, she and a senior citizens committee in discussion with the University Congregational Church developed plans for a senior residence community "to provide elderly persons on a nonprofit basis with housing facilities and services specifically designed to meet [their] physical, social and psychological needs." Developer Loren Baldwin's offer to sell his 18-story apartment tower at 900 University Street, built in 1956, moved the dream to reality in record time. By 1961, with architect Robert Durham planning an annex to accommodate the common rooms, Horizon House opened. Additions and new buildings have expanded its housing, assisted living, and community facilities significantly.

Medicare began transformation of the way medical services were to be delivered, and by whom—the hospital and medical center industries had to face radical changes in terms of both provision of service and increased regulation of their facilities and activities. These changes, along with others based on new information and techniques of medical care, created an era of consolidation and resulted in the closing of several hospital facilities on First Hill. Former hospital buildings adjacent to medical centers defined by the Major Institutions policies and code, such as Doctor's Hospital, were absorbed into the existing medical centers. Others, such as Maynard Hospital, were razed and the land became available for reuse.

By the 1960s, the Seattle School Board concluded that northern First Hill could not sustain an elementary school, and Summit School was closed in 1965. The Northwest School of the Arts, Humanities, and the Environment (now Northwest School) developed during the 1970s in the former Summit School building on north First Hill, and continues as a private day and boarding college-preparatory school at that site, serving middle- and high-school students from the region and abroad. Adjoining the southern part of First Hill, Bailey Gatzert elementary school, originally located at 615 12th Avenue South, was closed in 1984 (and demolished, apart from preserving the entrance portal) and reopened in a new building at 1301 East Yesler in 1988.

BELOW: The Baldwin Apartments became the core of a thriving senior residential community.

RIGHT: The Northwest School was developed in the 1970s and continues as a private school serving middle- and high-school students. Historic Seattle.

BELOW: First Hill Neighborhood Plan, November 1998.

First Hill Neighborhood Plan
Master Plan Map

Environmental concerns also surfaced during the 1970s. In Washington State, 1000 Friends of Washington, a citizens' group, began to advocate growth-management legislation for the state. In 1990, the legislature adopted Washington's Growth Management Act, which was amended in 1991. This act called for concerted planning to target areas where growth should occur, and areas that should be preserved, especially for open space and agriculture. While the act focused on protecting the state from costly urban sprawl, it also forced existing populous areas to become more densely populated. With the Comprehensive Plan required by the Growth Management Act adopted by the City, a follow-on planning effort called Neighborhood Planning was conducted between 1994 and 1998. First Hill's 220 acres became a target of planning for what came to be known in Seattle as an urban center village.

The First Hill Improvement Association was established as a community service organization in 1958. As a coalition of both residents and members of the business community, the association was active in a two-phase planning project. The first phase was to gauge what the neighborhood wanted, and the second phase was to put together a conceptual proposal. According to John Dolan, speaking for the First Hill Neighborhood Planning Committee at a Historic Seattle panel in the spring of 1999:

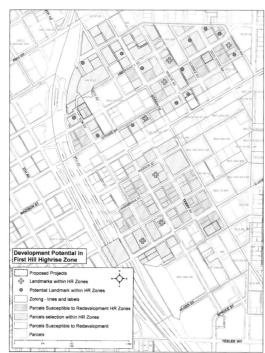

ABOVE: Development Potential in
First Hill Highrise Zone, ca. 2006.
City of Seattle.

*First Hill was most difficult to plan for, particularly due to
the wide uses of occupants on the hill. The central core was
undergoing a renaissance and incredible amount of growth,
drawing a range of regional institutions—medicine, education, sports, entertainment, business, etc. That brings its
challenges, which we attempted to address in neighborhood
planning. It also took into account residential growth.
Affordable housing was one of the biggest challenges.*

Citizens worked hard to grapple with the changing demands
upon their neighborhood, but much of the focus was on the then
anticipated Sound Transit light rail connections and station, which
would have linked First Hill to the University District on the north,
Beacon Hill and eventually the airport on the south, and downtown.
Subsequent planning for the underground light rail route bypassed
First Hill.

Seattle Housing Authority had long sought to redevelop the
Yesler Terrace housing project of the 1940s, in the southern part of
First Hill. Today that redevelopment is under way. First Hill is also experiencing
construction of a number of new towers—residential towers with mixed-use facilities
on the ground floor—perhaps reclaiming some of the hill's views while completing
replacement of many of the remaining older buildings.

In recent years, citizens and City
government have focused attention to
the north edge of First Hill and the
south edge of Capitol Hill—East Pike
Street and East Pine Street—with considerable success. New housing and
retail have been stimulated. Repair and
renovation of old automobile showrooms and repair shops is evident,
although the more common approach
has been keeping the primary facade
and reattaching it to a new building
base. In general, genuine efforts are
being made to maintain mixed uses and
smaller-scale streetscape character while
accommodating residential growth at
various income levels.

RIGHT: First Hill aerial map, 2012.
Courtesy Ron Edge.

VISION FOR FIRST HILL

The authors of *Tradition and Change on Seattle's First Hill* have made a concerted effort to explore and reveal the essential nature of one of the richest and most diverse historic neighborhoods in the city. It was no easy task. We have found ourselves at times frustrated by the large number of razed and extant buildings of distinction we would have liked to discuss, wonderful newspaper clippings, gossipy, often cutting magazine articles, colorful oral histories, and facts and figures that could not be included in a limited space. For the same reason, hundreds of evocative and telling images of First Hill had to be put aside. Nevertheless, this book is a marvelous starting point for urban understanding and exploration. We hope it will encourage long-time and newly settled residents, workers, and users to do some critical thinking about what it is that makes this place special and worthy of preservation. Here are a few questions to start you on your First Hill journey.

What makes it a livable place?

What gives it a sense of place?

What presently unprotected and threatened buildings deserve to be designated?

Where are the opportunities for sharing resources?

Are there opportunities for a central "gathering space"?

How can we strengthen linkages?

How can we nurture retail businesses?

Where are the opportunities for collaboration for making it a better place?

Finally, we urge you to put down this book, go out in the street, and walk around First Hill with your newly found perspective. Take it all in and enjoy it!

RIGHT: View west and northwest from First Hill Plaza toward Elliott Bay shows the change in scale of buildings on First Hill, from the residences of the Dearborn and Stimson families to pre-Depression era apartment buildings to post-World War II high-rises, hospitals, and recent condo and mixed-use buildings. Alan Axelrod.

VIEWS OF FIRST HILL FROM 1874, 1913, AND 2012

This 1874 watercolor view of Seattle from Elliott Bay shows the few streets of the downtown that have been cleared for businesses and residences. The prominent white building is the Territorial University (future University of Washington) on Denny's Knoll (Fourth Avenue between Seneca and University Streets, the site of the Fairmont Olympic Hotel). Forest still defines the western edge of First Hill. Courtesy © R. Denny Watt, Jr., great-great grandson of Arthur A. Denny, who commissioned the painting.

Compare the 1913 panorama taken from the Smith Tower, courtesy Loomis Miller, Webster & Stevens, with a 2012 view by Jean Sherrard. With the freeway and high-rises, it takes some effort to find surviving landmarks: The Rainier Club (Fourth Avenue) and First Methodist Church (Fifth Avenue) (left foreground); St. James Cathedral (left of center); and domed King County Courthouse (right of center), replaced by the Art Deco Harborview Hospital tower, now with multiple additions. Yesler Way still skirts the 1909 Municipal Building (now 400 Yesler Way) on its path to Lake Washington (right foreground).

ENDNOTES

CHAPTER 2. THE RESIDENTIAL GOLDEN AGE: 1885-1910

[1] General information about the homes in this section is drawn from a number of sources: Margaret Pitcairn Strachan, "Seattle's Pioneer Mansions," a series of 52 weekly articles for the *Seattle Sunday Times*, 1944; Paul Dorpat, HistoryLink Essay 3095, "Seattle Neighborhoods: First Hill – Thumbnail History," www.historylink.org; Frank Calvert, ed., *Homes and Gardens of the Pacific Coast*, Vol. I (Seattle: Beaux Arts Society, Beaux Arts Village, Lake Washington, 1913).

[2] Information provided by Dennis Andersen.

[3] Ibid.

[4] Lawrence Kreisman, *Bloedel Reserve: Gardens in the Forest* (The Arbor Fund, 1988), 23.

[5] After living at the Lincoln and Perry hotels and traveling to Europe, Mrs. Ranke bought the Henry Dearborn House and filled it with furniture from both her Pike Street and Terry Avenue homes.

[6] *Sketches of Washingtonians* (Seattle: Wellington C. Wolfe & Co., 1907), 290.

[7] Clarence B. Bagley, *History of Seattle from the Earliest Settlement to the Present Time* (Chicago: The S. J. Clarke Publishing Company, 1916), 485.

[8] Paul Dorpat, *Seattle Now & Then, Vol. III*, Second Edition (Paul Dorpat, 1989), 135.

[9] *The Seattle Daily Times*, June 26, 1891, 6.

[10] Excerpt from Lawrence Kreisman, *The Stimson Legacy: Architecture in the Urban West* (Willows Press, Seattle, 1992), 59-76.

[11] See *Kelleher House at Thirty: Looking Back*, prepared by the Kelleher House 30th Anniversary Committee.

[12] Excerpt from Lawrence Kreisman and Brooke Best, Hofius House Open to View Tour, Historic Seattle, August 2012.

[13] Mabel Lisle Ducasse clipping archive, Martin-Zambito Fine Art.

CHAPTER 3. SOCIAL AND CULTURAL LIFE

[14] Walt Crowley and Ronald M. Gould, *The Rainier Club, 1888-1988* (Seattle: Crowley Associates, 1988), 15-18, 23.

[15] Excerpt from "History of the Woman's Century Club, Seattle, Washington," a history book created by club members in 1893, Woman's Century Club Archives, Seattle.

[16] *The Seattle Sunday Times*, "Men Now Prominent Were in Seattle's First Tennis Club," August 25, 1912, 29.

[17] A McDonald's fast-food restaurant has occupied this corner since the mid 1970s.

[18] In December 1895 the Seattle City Council passed legislation that changed over 300 street names. The name of 12th Street, from Broadway to Depot Street, was changed to Minor Avenue.

[19] James R. Warren, *A Centennial History of the Seattle Tennis Club* (Seattle: Seattle Tennis Club, 1990), 5-6. The equivalent today would be about $2,170. The Gainsborough was built in 1930 at 1017 Minor Avenue.

[20] Ibid., 21.

[21] *Seattle Post-Intelligencer*, "New Buildings in Prospect," January 12, 1893, 3 *Seattle Post-Intelligencer*, "The New Buildings," January 23, 1893, 5.

[22] City directories indicate that Bate W. Alexander and John W. Searight ran a bakery and lived in this building in 1897.

[23] *The Seattle Sunday Times*, November 28, 1948, 56.

[24] *The Seattle Sunday Times*, "New Name of Lodge to be Open in Fall," July 23, 1933, 13; *The Seattle Daily Times*, "German Clubs to Open Headquarters Here on Sunday," December 7, 1934, 15.

[25] *The Seattle Sunday Times*, "Old Assay Office Transformed into New Officers' Club," July 18, 1943, 1, 32.

[26] *The Seattle Sunday Times*, "Women Transform Assay Office Into Modern and Charming Social Center," July 18, 1943, 32. The article describes the decorations and furnishings, along with the women who played a role in transforming the building. The same issue, on p. 24, includes a list of paid positions to staff the facility, including a cook, assistant cook, 3 waitresses, 2 maids, 2 dishwashers, bartender, janitor, night watchman, and 2 errand boys.

[27] This phrase was taken from *History of the University Club of Seattle* (Seattle: The Club, 1963), 1. In a later rendition of the club's history (Sidney S. Andrews, *Another Year Has Rolled Around: The University Club of Seattle Centennial*. Seattle: Sasquatch

Books, 2005), it states "a place where like-minded educated men could gather and talk."

28   The maximum membership was raised to 225 in 1952, and continues to be so today.

29   *The Seattle Star*, "Plans Big Addition," February 28, 1902, 2.

30   Dorpat, *Seattle Now & Then, Vol. III*, 134.

31   A complete list of former presidents and deceased members can be reviewed in the 1963 publication *History of the University Club of Seattle*. It also contains brief notes on some former club members.

32   *The Seattle Daily Times*, December 21, 1901, 31. The initial board of management was made up of Messrs. E. Ferneaus, E. Sinclair, H. Hatheson, D. Cameron, C. Thornber, and C. Matheson.

33   *Seattle Sunday Times*, "Mr. P. E. Newberry Entertained by Fellow Club Members at the Crescent Club," August 30, 1903, 9.

34   *The Seattle Times*, "Alums Sing Farewell to Monks Club," May 16, 1962, 2.

35   *The Seattle Daily Times*, July 7, 1913, 5. "Women Organize Club Exclusively for Sex."

36   *The Seattle Daily Times*, "Woman Now Has Her Own Club," March 26, 1907, 30.

37   Barbara Stenson Spaeth, *Sunset Club History, 1913-1998* (Seattle: Sunset Club, Inc., 1998), 15, 16, 18.

38   Ibid., 11, 20, 23.

39   In the 1884-85 Seattle City Directory, Gasch is listed as the proprietor of the Fountain Beer Hall (saloon) and as residing at the corner of Seventh and Union. The 1888-89 City Directory lists him living at the northwest corner of Fifth and Terrace.

40   *The Seattle Daily Times* published a classified ad on July 4, 1906 (p. 14, col. 2) announcing a "monster auction sale of elegant furniture Thursday July 5, at 10am sharp on the premises, 1402 Seventh Ave…on sale is the entire contents of 12 large and well-furnished rooms. Among this fine lot of furniture are brass mounted beds, elegant bed sets (one set of mahogany, cost $95) springs, mattresses, large quantity of bedding in splendid condition, fancy chairs and rockers, morris chair, fine extra bureaus and commodes, carpets and art squares, dressing table, sanitary couch, lady's desk and chair, library table, extra heavy center table, round extension table, dining chairs, elegant sideboard, stair and hall carpet, swell front folding bed, willow rocker, gas heaters and reading lamps, gas grange, cooking utensils, crockery, draperies, curtains, toilet ware, etc. E. G. Bickerton, Auctioneer."

41   *The Seattle Sunday Times*, "Bert Farrar's Auditorium," June 24, 1906, 52.

42   *The Seattle Daily Times*, "Fifteen Hundred Hear Sermon at Dreamland," March 7, 1910, 7.

43   *The Seattle Daily Times*, "Judge Asks Jury to Probe Cafes," February 25, 1910, 17.

44   Sources include *The Seattle Star*, January 31, 1912, 4; "Mike Fisher and Dreamland," July 31, 1912, 5; "Now, if Santa Claus will Bring the Toys the Small-Chimney Kids will have Big Time," November 30, 1912; "Billy Williams Can't Fight O'Leary," April 4, 1913.

45   John Caldbick, "Cornerstone for new Seattle lodge of Fraternal Order of Eagles, Aerie No. 1 is placed on February 22, 1925," HistoryLink Essay 10168, August 29, 2012, www.historylink.org.

46   National Register of Historic Places Inventory Nomination, prepared by Randall Potter, CHG International, Inc., Federal Way, WA, 1979.

47   Capitol Hill Seattle Blog, "The Past – and future – of the stairway to nowhere at Broadway and Harvard," Dotty DeCoster and jseattle, September 10, 2010.

48   *The Seattle Daily Times*, "Temple's Cornerstone Will be Laid December 14," December 1, 1910, 2.

49   *The Seattle Sunday Times*, "Masons Install Cornerstone of Temple," October 2, 1960, 39.

50   *The Seattle Sunday Times*, "Knights of Columbus," June 22, 1902, 24.

51   Knights of Columbus Council 676 History (www.kofc676.org/about.htm).

52   *Seattle Sunday Times*, "Mrs. Foss Donates Beautiful Site to Be Used for Home," October 13, 1912, 5.

CHAPTER 4. APARTMENT LIVING ON FIRST HILL

53   Oral Interview, Karen Harris and Barbara Olsen, June 27, 1999, Historic Seattle First Hill History Project. James and Mary Lowman, noted Seattle citizens, moved into the home in 1891.

54   Quintard Taylor, *The Forging of a Black Community: Seattle's Central District from 1870 Through the Civil*

Rights Era (Seattle: University of Washington Press, 1994), 86-7, 178-9. A notice in the *Seattle Daily Times* classified dated January 1, 1958, said: "There are in Seattle many apartments for rent today that are not being advertised because it is so easy for landlords to select suitable tenants from the 'Wanted to Rent' column. If you are seeking an apartment be sure your message appears there daily."

[55] Janet Ore, *The Seattle Bungalow: People & Houses 1900-1940* (Seattle: University of Washington Press, 2006), 103-104.

[56] *Seattle Daily Times*, April 20, 1905; *Seattle Sunday Times*, January 6, 1907.

[57] Until 1883, F. H. Whitworth, a renowned land surveyor, owned the entire block occupied by the Belmont-Boylston Houses. He sold the block to Bailey Gatzert, president of both Puget Sound National Bank and Schwabacher Brothers and Company. Gatzert sold the lots prior to any development activity. Seattle Landmark nomination, prepared by Megan Meulemans for Historic Seattle, January 28, 2014.

[58] *Seattle Post-Intelligencer*, October 21, 1906, 3.

[59] *The Week-End,* Seattle, December 7, 1907, Vol. #49, 10.

[60] *Seattle Post-Intelligencer*, August 28, 1910, Real Estate, 2. One tenant who did remain was William Boeing. Five years before he took his first airplane ride, Boeing called the Perry home. Today the term "transient" has a pejorative connotation. In the early 1900s it simply meant a person seeking a room in a hotel for a short time.

[61] Kate Stoner, HistoryLink Essay 2325, "Cabrini, Mother Francesca Xavier (1850-1917)," www.historylink.org.

[62] Leslie Jackson, "Sauntering Seattleite: The Sorrento Hotel," cited in *Seattlife*, February 1940, 57-58. Jackson was vice president of the corporation that operated the Sorrento.

[63] Norman J. Johnston, "Harlan Thomas," in *Shaping Seattle Architecture: A Historical Guide to the Architects* (Seattle: University of Washington Press, 1994), 126-28; Katheryn H. Krafft, "Sorrento Hotel," City of Seattle Landmarks Preservation Board Landmark Nomination Application, revised January 22, 2008.

[64] The Rookwood Pottery Co. was established in Cincinnati, Ohio, in 1880 at the outset of the American Arts and Crafts Movement. It is considered one of the most innovative and influential art pottery companies in the United States. The Kellogg Company was the major local supplier of Rookwood tile.

[65] *Hotel News of the West*, November 21, 1925.

[66] Jackson, 57-58.

[67] *Seattle Post-Intelligencer,* October 23, 1937, 1.

[68] *Seattle Post-Intelligencer*, October 1, 1905, 5.

[69] Doris Pieroth, *Seattle's Women Teachers of the Interwar Years* (Seattle: University of Washington Press, 2004), 66-67.

[70] *Seattle Post-Intelligencer*, February 17, 1907, August 17, 1907, classifieds.

[71] Pieroth, 67.

[72] *Seattle Daily Bulletin,* May 16, 1902, 1.

[73] *Seattle Post-Intelligencer*, July 16, 1905, classifieds; February 17, 1907, August 17, 1907, classifieds.

[74] *Seattle Post-Intelligencer*, April 6, 1902, classifieds; *Seattle Post-Intelligencer*, August 17, 1907, classifieds; *Seattle Daily Times*, May 6, 1906. For more on the Greystone see Jeffrey Karl Ochsner and Dennis Alan Andersen, *Distant Corner: Seattle Architects and the Legacy of H. H. Richardson* (Seattle: University of Washington Press, 2003), 243.

[75] *Seattle Sunday Times*, August 13, 1911; July 7, 1912; *Seattle Daily Times* July 15, 1912. The City of Seattle Landmark Nomination Form survey calls the Acirema a "turn of the century apartment house" and a "modest, but fashionable hotel [that] provided temporary housing for many families until they could acquire private residences."

[76] See Diana James, *Shared Walls: Seattle Apartment Buildings, 1900-1939* (McFarland & Co., 2011) for the most comprehensive information about Seattle apartments. For this chapter Williams is using James's definition of apartments: "a self-contained unit that includes a kitchen and bathroom within a building of more than four such units." Jacqueline Williams worked with Diana James on *Shared Walls*. Much of the information in that book's chapter about First Hill apartments was based on an earlier draft written by Williams.

[77] Prices began rising in 1906, causing reformers to begin questioning middle-class spending. For more on these very complicated studies, see Daniel Horowitz, *The Morality of Spending: Attitudes Toward the Consumer Society in America*

(Baltimore: Johns Hopkins University Press, 1985), 86.

78 Thomas J. Schlereth, *Victorian America: Transformations in Everyday Life, 1876-1915* (New York: Harper Perennial, 1992).

79 See Anne Vernez Moudon, *Built for Change: Neighborhood Architecture in San Francisco* (Cambridge: MIT Press, 1986), 117, for a discussion of the use of bay windows.

80 Margaret Reed interviews, HistoryLink Essay 2265, April 7, 1999, www.historylink.org.

81 *Seattle Daily Bulletin*, February 21, 1901; *Seattle Daily Times*, February 23, 1901; *Seattle Post-Intelligencer*, May 26, 1901; *Seattle Sunday Times*, July 22, 1906, 40.

82 Seattle Department of Plans and Development, permit #34050; *Seattle Daily Times*, December 28, 1905.

83 *Seattle Daily Bulletin*, February 20, 1905.

84 *Seattle Post-Intelligencer*, July 1, 1906, Real Estate, 9; August 21, 1910.

85 Oral interview, Frances Backus, Historic Seattle First Hill History Project.

86 The 1937 Property Record Card lists 32 apartments, divided among five- and four-room apartments, and three two-room apartments in the basement. Today there are 41 apartments, including six single rooms in the basement, sharing two bathrooms. See also James, *Shared Walls*, 133.

87 Mary Bard, *The Doctor Wears Three Faces* (Philadelphia: J. B. Lippincott, 1949).

88 For more about the Maxmillian, see James, *Shared Walls*, 135-6.

89 *Seattle Sunday Times*, March 8, 1925, 21.

90 "Progressive Dinner on First Hill," tour brochure prepared by Historic Seattle; "A Tour of Stained Glass on Seattle's First Hill," prepared by Lawrence Kreisman, Program Director, Historic Seattle, September 2012.

91 "Progressive Dinner on First Hill."

92 Seattle Municipal Archives, Ordinance #74516, provided for widening and repaving Boren Avenue from Denny Way to Broadway. 1893 Sanborn maps show that Boren Avenue was originally named Moltke Street.

93 Interview with Frances Backus, "First Hill History Project" brochure prepared by Historic Seattle, 1999.

94 Landmark Nomination Report prepared by BOLA Architecture + Planning, January 2004.

95 *Seattle Sunday Times*, July 26, 1925, 13; August 23, 1925, classifieds.

96 *Seattle Daily Times*, July 18, 1925, 3; Oral interview, Shirley Fuller, February 21, 2008, Historic Seattle First Hill History Project. Ms. Fuller began work as a switchboard operator and rose to become manager.

97 *The Washington State Architect*, May 19, 1927, 11. Building plans, dated June 3, 1927, and permit #268704, 1927, on file at Seattle Department of Plans and Development show Morrison's name.

98 Description of apartments in *Seattle Daily Times*, May 29, 1927, 21; February 5, 1928, 17; September 22, 1929. In 2008, Live Historic updated the interiors and turned the apartments into condominiums.

99 *Seattle Sunday Times*, January 6, 1929, 24; "An Apartment of Distinction," *Pacific Builder and Engineer*, May 4, 1929, 37-38.

100 Baroness description is from City of Seattle Landmark Nomination, July 2009, prepared by BOLA Architecture + Planning, and *Seattle Sunday Times*, March 15, 1931; July 25, 1931.

101 *Seattle Daily Times*, November 15, 1949, 11.

102 Oral interview, Roland and Dorothy Brennan, September 1999, Historic Seattle First Hill History Project.

103 Oral interview, Roland and Dorothy Brennan; *Seattle Daily Times*, May 25, 1958.

104 Oral interview, Frances Backus.

105 *Seattle Times*, September 24, 1979. The tenants were evicted from the old Kelleher House, home of prominent attorney and bank president Daniel Kelleher.

106 According to the *Seattle Sunday Times*, July 5, 1964, the Highlander at 505 Belmont East was Seattle's "first new condominium."

107 Irene Burns Miller, *Profanity Hill* (Everett, WA: The Working Press, 1979), 139.

108 Trevor Griffey, "Preserving Yesler Terrace," *Preservation Seattle*, January 2004, Historic Seattle's online monthly newsletter.

109 Miller, 139.

110 Lawrence Kreisman, "Going Public: Architectural solutions break from stereotypes of public housing," *Seattle Times Pacific*

Magazine, March 12, 1989, 20.

111   Sources include Bob Young, "Seattle's Yesler Terrace faces the future," *Seattle Times*, March 19, 2011; Bob Young, "Housing board picks Vulcan to redevelop Yesler Terrace," *Seattle Times*, January 22, 2013; Vanessa Ho, "Historic landmark bid for Yesler Terrace shot down," *Seattle Post-Intelligencer*, August 18, 2010; Aubrey Cohen, "Historic steam plant to become community center," *Seattle Post-Intelligencer*, November 19, 2012.

CHAPTER 5. SERVING THE PUBLIC

112   Catholic Schools, Archdiocese of Seattle, 1856-1987, Sister Kathleen Gorman Oral History Collection.

113   The King County Courthouse: A History, http://www.kingcounty.gov/about/contact-us/locations/Courthouse/courthouse History.aspx.

114   Pacific Coast Architecture Database (PCAD), University of Washington Digital Collections; Rev. H. K. Hines, D.D., *An Illustrated History of the State of Washington* (Chicago: The Lewis Publishing Co., 1893), 362-363.

115   Dorpat, HistoryLink Essay 3095; Priscilla Long, Paul Dorpat, HistoryLink Essay 7038, "Seattle's First Hill: King County Courthouse and Harborview Hospital – A Slideshow," www.historylink.org.

116   Robert Ketcherside, "CHS Re:Take – Berlin bakery beatdown at Ninth and James, 1905 and 2011," Capitol Hill Seattle Blog, December 4, 2011.

117   "German Club/Assay Office," National Park Service website, http://www.nps.gov/nr/travel/seattle/s19.htm.

118   Pacific Coast Architecture Database (PCAD), "Structures – Prosch, Thomas, Office Building and Hall, First Hill, Seattle, WA," ID 8081.

119   Stephen Sanislo, *50 Years of Fighting Fires: Organization and Development of the Seattle Fire Department* (Seattle: Northwestern Mutual Fire Association, n.d.), 8.

120   Personal communication with Galen Thomaier, Seattle Fire Department historian, March 18, 2013; Jim Stevenson, *Seattle Firehouses of the Horse Drawn and Early Motor Era* (1972), 4; Alan Stein, HistoryLink Essay 3938, September 2, 2002, www.historylink.org; Sanislo, 7-8, 11-12; Glen W. Garvie, *Seattle Fire Department Centennial: 1889-1989* (Portland: Taylor Publishing Co., 1989), 37, 72; Lawrence Kreisman, *Made to Last* (Seattle: University of Washington Press, 1999), 44.

121   Stevenson, 14.

122   Kreisman, *Made to Last*, 44; Garvie, 72; Last Resort Fire Department private collections; First Hill DVD, Part 3, "History on the Hill, Role in Community, Current Stake," Debby Gibby.

123   "First Hill City Walks," Self-Guided Walking Tour, Seattle Architecture Foundation, 1999; Kreisman, *Made to Last*, 151; Personal communication with Galen Thomaier, March 18, 2013; Garvie, 86.

124   "First Hill City Walks"; Kreisman, *Made to Last*, 151; Last Resort Fire Department private collections; Garvie, 86.

125   Oral interview, Thomas (Tom) Kirk Gerbracht, February 5, 2000, by Connie Schnell, Historic Seattle First Hill History Project.

126   "First Hill City Walks"; Kreisman, *Made to Last*, 151.

127   Nile Thompson, *Building for Learning: Seattle Public School Histories, 1862-2000* (Seattle School District, 2002), 50; Greg Lange, HistoryLink Essay 1509, www.historylink.org; "Seattle Public Schools: Historic Building Survey," prepared by Patricia Erigero for Historic Seattle, August 1989, 2; Welford Beaton, *The City That Made Itself: A Literary and Pictorial Record of the Building of Seattle* (Seattle: Terminal Publishing Co., 1914), 139.

128   Bagley, 166-168, 326-327; Beaton, 139.

129   Seattle Schools exhibit; Bagley, 168; Thompson, 52; Archives and Records Management Center, Seattle School District No. 1, Box 94 – Central School Photos.

130   Erigero, 3; "Good Public Schools: A Celebration of Seattle School History."

131   S. E. Fleming, *Civics (supplement): Seattle King County* (Seattle: Seattle Public Schools, 1919), 41; 1919 Polk's Seattle City Directory; Seattle Schools exhibit.

132   Archives and Records Management Center, Seattle School District No. 1, Record No. 2, November 2, 1889 – June 21, 1983 minutes; Bagley, 171.

133 1900 City Directory; Thompson, 3-4.

134 Thompson, 54-55.

135 Boyd Burchard, "1905-style office space for the old Summit School," *Seattle Times*, September 13, 1979.

136 Erigero, 12-13; Thompson, 286; "First Hill City Walks"; Kreisman, *Made to Last*, 46.

137 Thompson, 286; Kreisman, *Made to Last*, 46.

138 SPS, Histories of the Seattle Public Schools, 1961; Thompson, 285.

139 SPS, Histories of the Seattle Public Schools, 1961; Thompson, 287.

140 Thompson, 287.

141 Ibid.

142 Burchard, *Seattle Times*, September 13, 1979.

143 Paul Dorpat, "Two Landmarks on Summit," in "Then and Now," Pacific Magazine, *Seattle Times*, May 10, 1987.

144 Catholic Schools Archdiocese of Seattle 1856-1987, Sister Kathleen Gorman Oral History Transcript.

145 *Golden Gleanings: 1881-1931* (Seattle: Academy of the Holy Names, 1931), 35, 45.

146 Excerpt from the "House Chronicles," Archives of the Sisters of the Holy Names of Jesus and Mary, Washington Province.

147 Vanessa Ho, "St. James marks 100th year: Celebration of founding of parish begins this weekend," *Seattle Post-Intelligencer*, Thursday, November 11, 2004.

148 Oral interview, Roger Leed, November 23, 1999, Historic Seattle First Hill History Project.

149 Oral interview, P. J. Callahan, November 15, 1999, Historic Seattle First Hill History Project.

150 "St. James Cathedral: Years of Change," August 9, 1992, 2; *Golden Gleanings* 1931, 53.

151 Oral interview, Paul Brown, July 12, 1999, Historic Seattle First Hill History Project. Brown's father was manager of the newly opened Arctic Club.

152 Edward Dunn, *1121 Union: One Family's Story of Early Seattle's First Hill* (Seattle: E.B. Dunn Historic Garden Trust, 2004).

153 Cassandra Tate, HistoryLink Essay 3711, "Frye Art Museum (Seattle)," www.historylink.org; Robin Updike, "Frye Art Museum: Framing the Future," *Seattle Times*, September 15, 1994, E4; Helen E. Vogt, *Charlie Frye and His Times* (Seattle: SCW Publications, 1995), 282.

154 Thiry also designed the museum for the Seattle Historical Society (later MOHAI) at Montlake, which opened the same year.

155 *Seattle Times*, September 15, 1994, E4; Tate, HistoryLink Essay 3711.

156 Record Group 2, Box 9, Folder 7, Ida Kay Greathouse – Addition to Museum, "Functional & Architectural Program for an Addition to the Frye Art Museum," May 14, 1982, Frye Art Museum Archives.

157 Robin Updike, " 'New' Frye to be filled with energy and style," *Seattle Times*, December 16, 1996.

CHAPTER 6. RELIGIOUS LIFE ON THE HILL

158 *West Shore*, Vol. 10, No. 6, June 1884, 169.

159 *Seattle Daily Times*, August 10, 1889, 8.

160 Esther McDowell, *Unitarians in the State of Washington, 1870-1960* (Seattle: Frank McCaffrey, 1966), 51.

161 McDowell, 92.

162 *Washington Churchman*, April 1892, "Trinity Church, Seattle, is rapidly nearing completion. Its style of architecture approximated the Early English. Henry F. Starbuck, architect, of Chicago submitted plans for the building, which were accepted by the vestry in 1890. Subsequently he associated himself with Mr. C. A. Alexander, of Seattle, to whom he entrusted the details, and their adaptation to local conditions."

163 "New Trinity Church. Its construction being rapidly pushed forward – the new rectory," *Seattle Post-Intelligencer*, January 25, 1892, 7, col. 3.

164 "Their Holy Temple," *Seattle Post-Intelligencer*, September 18, 1892, 13.

165 "Sales by John Davis & Co," *Seattle Daily Times*, February 13, 1904, 7.

166 *Seattle Sunday Times*, July 26, 1908, 22.

167 *Seattle Daily Bulletin*, April 4, 1901, 3.

168   *Seattle of To-Day: Illustrated* (Seattle: National Publishing Company, 1908), 72.

169   Dale Soden, *The Reverend Mark Matthews: An Activist in the Progressive Era* (Seattle: University of Washington Press, 2001).

170   "First Presbyterian Church, Seattle" [illustration and description], *Pacific Builder and Engineer*, July 28, 1906, 3; "Dedication of Presbyterian Church," *Pacific Builder and Engineer*, December 21, 1907, 3.

171   Robert Welsh, *The Presbytery of Seattle, 1858-2005* (privately published, 2006), 263.

172   "Church seeks redevelopment ideas," *Seattle Times*, January 24, 2009, B3.

173   "Catholics will build," *Seattle Daily Times*, August 19, 1904, 9.

174   "Cathedral of the Sacred Heart as It Will Appear When Completed," *Seattle Daily Times*, December 10, 1905, 35.

175   Information furnished by Dr. James Savage, Music Director of St. James Cathedral in "A Tour of Stained Glass on Seattle's First Hill," Historic Seattle, September 15, 2012.

176   O'Ryan, Jackie, ed. *House of God, Gate of Heaven: Seattle's St. James Cathedral* (Strasbourg: Éditions du Signe, 2000).

177   "Another Church Building," *Seattle Intelligencer*, April 22, 1872, 3.

178   "The First Baptist Church, Seattle, Wash," *Pacific Builder and Engineer*, October 12, 1912, 297-302.

179   Obituary: " 'Transformational' Rev. Rod Romney Welcomed All Spiritual Paths," *Seattle Times*, July 4, 2012.

180   "Towering beauty," *Seattle Times*, May 3, 2003, B1.

181   Richard Ellison Ritz, *Architects of Oregon* (Portland: Lair Hill Publishing, 2002), 118.

182   "Fourth Church Ready," *Seattle Daily Times*, September 22, 1923, 5.

183   Considerable correspondence regarding the design and technical issues of these Povey windows exists in the Mary Baker Eddy Library, Boston.

184   *Seattle Sunday Times*, June 26, 1891, 6.

185   "The New Institutional Church for Seattle," *Pacific Builder and Engineer*, May 11, 1912, 397.

186   "New Plymouth Church Opens," *Seattle Times*, September 9, 1967, 7.

CHAPTER 7. HOSPITALS

187   The major print sources for this chapter included *Saddlebags to Scanners: The First 100 Years of Medicine in Washington State*, Nancy Rockafellar and James W. Haviland, eds. (Seattle: Washington State Medical Association Education & Research Foundation, 1989); *A Century of Service, 1858-1958*, John Bigelow, ed. (Seattle: Washington State Hospital Association, 1958); *Seattle Times Historical Database*; *King County Medical Society, 1888-1988* (Seattle, 1998); Presentation by Chuck Kolb, Principal/Architect at NBBJ, and Laura Dushkes, MLIS, Librarian, NBBJ, February 2013; "The Hospital Problem," Frederick Heath, *Pacific Builder and Engineer*, September 29, 1916, 24-25.

188   John Bigelow, ed., "King County Hospital System" and "Providence Hospital," in *The First Hundred Years: A Century of Service, 1858-1958.*

189   Pacific Magazine, *Seattle Times*, May 10, 1987.

190   Murray Morgan, *Puget's Sound: A Narrative of Early Tacoma and the Southern Sound* (Seattle: University of Washington Press, 1979), 301.

191   Dotty DeCoster, HistoryLink Essay 9339, "400 Yesler Way: Seattle Municipal Building 1909-1916, Seattle Public Safety Building 1917-1951," www.historylink.org, accessed May 2013.

192   T. T. Minor Hospital was named after former mayor and physician Dr. Thomas T. Minor (1844-1889).

193   *Seattle Daily Times* article many years later (May 11, 1922, 3, "Hospital Day Will be Observed," also June 4, 1913, May 11, 1922), bio of Sharples, and King County list of past presidents. Note: J. S. Coté designed Raymond's home in Madrona, which is now a Seattle landmark: Dave Wilma, HistoryLink Essay 3248, www.historylink.org.

194   *Pacific Building and Engineering Record*, July 14, 1906, 3-4.

195   *Seattle Sunday Times*, June 17, 1906, 42.

196   *Seattle Daily Times*, February 26, 1925, 1.

197   The plans for Summit Avenue Hospital are still extant in the Swedish Hospital Archives. We are grateful to Chuck Kolb, Principal/Architect at NBBJ, for sharing the plans and a host of information about the architectural development of

Swedish Hospital with us in February 2013.

198   *Seattle Daily Times*, April 6, 1912, 4. A list of the complainants can be found in the *Seattle Daily Times*, April 3, 1912, 19.

199   Photograph, *Seattle Times*, April 15, 1968, 39. This photograph, greatly enlarged, is also featured in the lobby display of First Hill and Swedish Hospital history located in the 1101 Madison Building.

200   *Proceedings, National League of Nursing Education*, held in San Francisco, Vol. 21, June 24, 1915.

201   Jennifer Ott, HistoryLink Essay 9572, "Swedish Medical Center (Seattle)," www.historylink.org, accessed December 23, 2012. Also see *Seattle Sunday Times* articles "Rininger's Estate Sells New Hospital," February 16, 1913, 5, and "Association Buys Rininger Hospital," March 2, 1913, 4.

202   The Missionary Sisters of the Sacred Heart offer a lovely historic display of the history of Mother Cabrini, Cabrini Hospital, and the block on which it stood, located in the lobby of the Cabrini Tower Building, on the west side of Boren Avenue a half block south of Madison Street. The display is not signed, but inquiries are directed to SUHRCO Management Inc., 425-455-1950. We were referred to this excellent display by librarians at the Lemieux Library of Seattle University.

203   *Pacific Builder and Engineer*, September 1916.

204   T. William Booth and William H. Wilson, *Carl F. Gould* (Seattle: University of Washington Press, 1995), 64.

205   Dwyer photograph, http://radiology.rsna.org/content/42/6/599.2.full.pdf; plans on UW Digital website; "Dr. Blackford Dies at Age 56," *Seattle Daily Times*, September 12, 1945, 13; C. H. Hanford, ed., *Seattle and Environs, 1852-1924*, Vol. 2. (Seattle: Pioneer Historical Pub. Co., 1924), 234.

206   https://www.virginiamason.org/OurHistory, May 15, 2013.

207   *Seattle Daily Times*, June 11, 1931, 16; *Seattle Daily Times*, March 30, 1933; "Maynard Hospital (1933-1971)," by Betty T. Parry, 1207 Spring St., C-1, Seattle, WA 98104, April 1977, manuscript (typescript) WX 28 AW2 S4 M471p 1977, University of Washington Libraries Special Collections, 3-5.

208   Dr. William H. Walsh, a hospital consultant from Chicago, was hired to oversee the planning, and the architects began work in January 1929, designing the hospital and Harborview Hall across the street and preparing a site plan.

209   Lois Price Spratlen, *African American Registered Nurses in Seattle: The Struggle for Opportunity and Success* (Seattle: Peanut Butter Publishing, 2001), 59.

210   Seattle population 1940: 368,302; 1950: 467,591.

211   Oral interview, DeLena Cresto by C. Schnell, February 16, 2000, Historic Seattle First Hill History Project.

212   *Seattle Daily Times*, November 14, 1943, 11; May 31, 1944, 5.

213   *Seattle Sunday Times*, "Sculptor's Game Taking Shape: Pratt Family Works on Hospital Panels," June 4, 1944, 11.

214   *Seattle Daily Times*, "First Hill is Apartment, Medical Center," Margaret Pitcairn Strachan, March 3, 1946, 2.

215   Clement A. Finch, M.D., "Academia at Last," in *Saddlebags to Scanners*, 177.

216   The partnership that became the Polyclinic began in the American Bank Building downtown in 1917. Dr. Homer J. Davidson (surgeon) and his brother Dr. Cline F. Davidson (internal medicine) began to share facilities with physicians with a range of specialties. In 1922, the group became known as The Polyclinic, and included the following physicians: H. J. and C. F. Davison, C. L. Templeton, Kenneth J. Hotz, Homer Wheelon, and Earle F. Ristine. The Polyclinic was strictly private, although all of the associated physicians provided volunteer medical services to charitable hospitals. Patients and/or individual physicians chose their own hospitals if hospital care was needed. In 1965, the Polyclinic moved up First Hill to Harvard Avenue, and in 2012, leased space at Seventh Avenue and Madison Street as well. This information comes primarily from the Polk's Seattle Street Directories.

217   *Seattle Times*, December 23, 1970, 6; June 11, 1980, 39.

218   For the past few decades, NBBJ has supplied most of the architects for all the First Hill medical centers.

219   David A. Rash, "Somervell & Coté" in Jeffrey Karl Ochsner, ed., *Shaping Seattle Architecture: A Historical Guide to the Architects* (Seattle: University of Washington Press, 1994), 123.

220   George Lewis Heins (1860-1907) and Christopher Grant LaFarge (1862-1938), firm founded 1886; Rash, 120-125, 331; Historic Seattle website, "Fire Station #25," accessed March 10, 2013, www.historicseattle.org/projects/fire25.aspx; Pacific

Coast Architecture Database, ID #4791, accessed February 2013; *Pacific Building and Engineering Record*, "Minor Hospital," July 14, 1906, 3-4; *Pacific Builder and Engineer*, February 17, 1912, 151; March 2, 1912, 190; and July 13, 1912, 25; Records of various building projects of Somervell and Coté in the *Seattle Daily Times*, November 19, 1905, 63; February 18, 1906, 38; February 27, 1906; March 4, 1906; May 13, 1906; August 12, 1906, 43; September 30, 1906, 54; June 10, 1906, 53; "Suburban Homes," October 14, 1906, 59; October 21, 1906, 54; March 28, 1907, 13; April 7, 1907; November 24, 1907, 27; August 9, 1908, 59; November 7, 1908; December 24, 1908; February 28, 1909; March 2, 1909, 19; March 28, 1909, 32; April 9, 1909; May 14, 1909, 18; June 13, 1909; September 5, 1909, 32; November 14, 1909, 37; November 28, 1909, 18; January 2, 1910, 29; February 21, 1912, 3; July 19, 1914, 22; June 10, 1917, 61; January 25, 1920, 26; July 29, 1923, 12; August 31, 1924, 59. Note that many projects are mentioned in these articles that are not mentioned in this text.

BIBLIOGRAPHY

SELECTED REFERENCES

Andrews, Sidney S. *Another Year Has Rolled Around: The University Club of Seattle Centennial* (Seattle: Sasquatch Books, 2005).

Axelrod, Alan. *The International Encyclopedia of Secret Societies & Fraternal Orders* (New York: Checkmark Books, 1997).

Bagley, Clarence B. *History of King County, Washington* (Chicago: S. J. Clarke Publishing Company, 1929).

Bagley, Clarence B. *History of Seattle from the Earliest Settlement to the Present Time* (Chicago: The S. J. Clarke Publishing Company, 1916), 3 volumes.

Bagley, Clarence. *Pioneer Seattle and Its Founders* (Seattle, 1925).

Bass, Sophie Frye. *Pig-Tail Days in Old Seattle* (Portland: Binfords & Mort, 1937).

Bass, Sophie Frye. *When Seattle Was a Village* (Seattle: Lowman & Hanford Co., 1947).

Beaton, Welford. *The City That Made Itself: A Literary and Pictorial Record of the Building of Seattle* (Seattle: Terminal Publishing Co., 1914).

Berner, Richard C. *Seattle in the 20th Century* (Seattle: Charles Press, ca. 1991), 2 volumes.

Bigelow, John, ed. "King County Hospital System" and "Providence Hospital," *The First Hundred Years: A Century of Service, 1858-1958* (Seattle: Washington State Hospital Association, 1958).

Booth, T. William, and William H. Wilson. *Carl F. Gould: A Life in Architecture and the Arts* (Seattle and London: University of Washington Press, 1995).

Broderick, Henry. *The "HB" Story: Seattle's Yesterdays* (Seattle: Frank McCaffrey Publishers, 1969).

Broderick, Henry. *Mirrors of Seattle's Old Hotels* (self-published, 1953).

Broderick, Henry. *A Slice of Seattle History by "HB"* (Seattle: Frank McCaffrey, Dogwood Press, 1960).

Calvert, Frank, ed. *Homes and Gardens of the Pacific Coast*, Vol. I. (Seattle: Beaux Arts Society, Beaux Arts Village, 1913). Republished in 1974 by Christopher Laughlin.

Capitol Hill Seattle Blog, "The Past—and future—of the stairway to nowhere at Broadway and Harvard," by Dotty DeCoster and jseattle, September 10, 2010.

Carkeek, Emily Gaskill. "Historical-sketch of the Seattle Public Library" manuscript (Seattle, 1919).

Cayton, Horace Roscoe. *Autobiographical Writings of Horace R. Cayton, Sr.,* published in *Cayton's Weekly*, 1917-1920 (Awali, Bahrain: R.S. Hobbs, 1987).

Chung, Justine Hae. "First Hill Place: A Mixed-Use Development Which Responds to Neighborhood Context" (Thesis, University of Washington, 1989).

Collins, Bertrand. *Rome Express* (New York and London: Harper & Brothers, 1928).

Conover, Charles Tallmadge. *Mirrors of Seattle: Reflecting Some Aged Men of Fifty* (Seattle: Lowman & Hanford Co., 1923).

Crowley, Walt. *National Trust Guide Seattle: America's Guide for Architecture and History Travelers* (New York: John Wiley & Sons, 1998).

Crowley, Walt, and Ronald M. Gould. *The Rainier Club, 1888-1988* (Seattle: Crowley Associates).

De Barros, Paul. *Jackson Street After Hours* (Seattle: Sasquatch Books, 1993).

DeCoster, Dotty. "400 Yesler Way: Seattle Municipal Building 1909-1916, Seattle Public Safety Building 1917-1951," HistoryLink.org

Essay 9336.

Denny, Emily Inez. *Blazing the Way* (Seattle: Seattle/King County Historical Society, 1984).

Dorpat, Paul. "Seattle Neighborhoods: First Hill – Thumbnail History," HistoryLink.org Essay 3095.

Dorpat, Paul. *Seattle Now & Then, Vol. II* (Seattle: Tartu Publications, 1984).

Dorpat, Paul. *Seattle Now & Then, Vol. III*, Second Edition (Seattle: Tartu Publications, 1989).

Dunn, Edward B. *1121 Union: One Family's Story of Early Seattle's First Hill* (Seattle: The E. B. Dunn Historic Garden Trust, 2004).

Ferguson, Robert L. *The Pioneers of Lake View: A Guide to Seattle's Early Settlers and Their Cemetery* (Bellevue, WA: Thistle Press, 1996).

"First Hill Neighborhood Plan: Final Plan" (November 1998) and "First Hill Neighborhood Plan Phase I Summary" (January 1997).

Fleming, S. E. *Civics (supplement): Seattle King County* (Seattle: Seattle Public Schools, 1919).

Frye Art Museum Archives, Record Group 2, Box 9, Folder 7, Ida Kay Greathouse – Addition to Museum.

Grant, Frederic James. *History of Seattle, Washington* (New York: American Publishing & Engraving Co., 1891).

Greater Seattle, Illustrated: The Most Progressive Metropolis of the Twentieth Century (Seattle: National Publishing Company, 1909).

Hanford, C. H., ed. *Seattle and Environs, 1852-1924* (Seattle: Pioneer Historical Publishing Co., 1924), 3 volumes.

Heritage of Seattle's Hotels 1853-1970. Fashion Group of Seattle, Inc. 1970. Uncatalogued Northwest Material. Museum of History and Industry.

History of the University Club of Seattle (Seattle: The Club, 1963).

Hobbs, Richard Stanley. "The Cayton Legacy: Two Generations of a Black Family, 1859-1976" (Dissertation, University of Washington, 1989).

Hotel Sorrento brochure, 90th-anniversary edition, 1909-1999.

Hotels and Apartment Pamphlet File. Pacific Northwest Collection, University of Washington Libraries.

Jackson, Leslie. *Seattlelife.* Sorrento, February 1940, Pacific Northwest Collection, University of Washington Libraries.

James, Diana E. *Shared Walls: Seattle Apartment Buildings, 1900-1939* (Jefferson, NC: McFarland & Company, Inc., 2012).

Jones, Nard. *Seattle* (New York: Knopf Doubleday, 1972).

Kelleher House 30th Anniversary Committee. *Kelleher House at Thirty: September 1982–September 2012.*

King County Department of Planning and Community Development, *King County Survey of Historic Places*, 1979.

Knights of Columbus Council 676 History, www.kofc676.org/about.htm.

Kreisman, Lawrence. *The Bloedel Reserve: Gardens in the Forest* (Bainbridge Island: The Arbor Fund, 1988).

Kreisman, Lawrence. *Made to Last: Historic Preservation in Seattle and King County* (Seattle: Historic Seattle Preservation Foundation in association with University of Washington Press, 1999).

Kreisman, Lawrence. *The Stimson Legacy: Architecture in the Urban West* (Seattle: Willows Press, 1992).

Kreisman, Lawrence, and Andrea Divoky. "First Hill Neighborhood Tour" (Seattle Architecture Foundation, 1999).

Kreisman, Lawrence, Judy Donnelly, Mimi Sheridan, and Margaret Aebersold. Progressive Dinner on First Hill tour brochure, prepared for Historic Seattle.

Kreisman, Lawrence, and Glenn Mason. *The Arts and Crafts Movement in the Pacific Northwest* (Portland: Timber Press, 2007).

Laughlin, Corinna. *Century of Grace: Stories of St. James Cathedral* (St. James Cathedral, 2007).

Luxton, Donald, ed. *Building the West: The Early Architects of British Columbia* (Vancouver: Talonbooks, 2003).

Marsden, Al. "Dearborn House." Unpublished manuscript. University of Washington, Built Environments Library.

McDowell, Esther. *Unitarians in the State of Washington, 1870-1960* (Seattle: Frank McCaffrey Publishers, 1966).

Meier, Gary and Gloria. *Those Naughty Ladies of the Old Northwest* (Bend, OR: Maverick Publications, 1990).

Miller, Irene Burns. *Profanity Hill* (Everett, WA: The Working Press, 1979).

Morgan, Murray. *Puget's Sound: A Narrative of Early Tacoma and the Southern Sound* (Seattle: University of Washington Press, 1979).

Morgan, Murray. *Skid Road: An Informal Portrait of Seattle* (New York: Ballantine Books, Inc., 1973).

Nyberg, Folke, and Victor Steinbrueck. *First Hill: An Inventory of Buildings and Urban Design Resources.* Historic Seattle Preservation and Development Authority, 1977.

Ochsner, Jeffrey Karl, ed. *Shaping Seattle Architecture: A Historical Guide to the Architects* (Seattle: University of Washington Press, 1994).

Ochsner, Jeffrey Karl, and Dennis Alan Andersen. *Distant Corner: Seattle Architects and the Legacy of H. H. Richardson* (Seattle: University of Washington Press, 2003).

O'Dea, E. J. *The Golden Sheaf, A Short Sketch of Providence Hospital, Seattle, Washington: Golden Jubilee Years 1877-1927* (Seattle, 1927).

Ore, Janet. *The Seattle Bungalow: People & Houses 1900-1940* (Seattle: University of Washington Press, 2007).

O'Ryan, Jackie, ed. *House of God, Gate of Heaven: Seattle's St. James Cathedral* (Strasbourg: Éditions du Signe, 2000).

Ott, Jennifer. "Swedish Medical Center (Seattle)," HistoryLink.org Essay 9572, September 13, 2010.

Pieroth, Doris. *Seattle's Women Teachers of the Interwar Years* (Seattle, University of Washington Press, 2004).

Polk's Seattle City Directories.

Proceedings, National League of Nursing Education, held in San Francisco, Vol. 21, June 24, 1915.

Prosch, Thomas W. *A Chronological History of Seattle from 1850-1897, Prepared in 1900-1901* (unpublished manuscript, ca. 1935).

Quense, Nancy Anne. "First Hill Plaza: A Multi-Use Development" (Thesis, University of Washington, 1981).

Ritz, Richard Ellison. *Architects of Oregon* (Portland: Lair Hill Publishing, 2002).

Rockafellar, Nancy, M.A., and James W. Haviland, M.D., eds. *Saddlebags to Scanners: The First 100 Years of Medicine in Washington State* (Seattle: Washington State Medical Association Education & Research Foundation, 1989).

Sale, Roger. *Seattle, Past to Present* (Seattle: University of Washington Press, 1978).

Schwantes, Carlos. *The Pacific Northwest: An Interpretive History* (Lincoln: University of Nebraska Press, 1996).

Seattle Chamber of Commerce. *Seattle Illustrated* (Chicago: Baldwin, Calcutt and Blakely, ca. 1890).

Seattle Department of Community Development, Draft First Hill Neighborhood Improvement Plan, 1976.

Seattle Public Schools. Histories of the Seattle Public Schools, 1961.

Seattle of To-Day: Illustrated. (Seattle: National Publishing Company, 1908).

Sherwood History Files, Seattle Parks and Recreation.

Sketches of Washingtonians (Seattle: Wellington C. Wolfe & Co., 1907).

Social Register, Seattle 1919.

Soden, Dale. *The Reverend Mark Matthews: An Activist in the Progressive Era.* (Seattle: University of Washington Press, 2001).

Spaeth, Barbara Stenson. *Sunset Club History, 1913-1998* (Seattle: Sunset Club, Inc., 1998).

Speidel, William. *Sons of the Profits* (Seattle: Nettle Creek Publishing Co., 1967).

Spratlen, Lois Price. *African American Registered Nurses in Seattle: The Struggle for Opportunity and Success* (Seattle: Peanut Butter Publishing, 2001).

Steinbrueck, Victor. *Seattle Cityscape* (Seattle: University of Washington Press, 1962).

Steinbrueck, Victor. *Seattle Cityscape #2* (Seattle: University of Washington Press, 1973).

Stoner, Kate. "Cabrini, Mother Francesca Xavier (1850-1917)," HistoryLink.org Essay 2325.

Strachan, Margaret Pitcairn. "Seattle's Pioneer Mansions," a series of 52 weekly articles for the *Seattle Sunday Times*, 1944-1945. Northwest Collection of the Seattle Central Library.

"Swedish Hospital Medical Center and Fred Hutchinson Cancer Research Center Master Plan 1975-1995," including the First Hill Hospital Merger Consolidated Pavilion Final Environmental Impact Statement (Seattle: Dept. of Buildings, 1977).

Tate, Cassandra. "Frye Art Museum (Seattle)," HistoryLink.org Essay 3711.

Taylor, Quintard. *The Forging of a Black Community: Seattle's Central District from 1870 through the Civil Rights Era* (Seattle: University of Washington Press, 1994).

Vogt, Helen E. *Charlie Frye and His Times* (Seattle: SCW Publications, 1995).

A Volume of Memoirs and Genealogy of Representative Citizens of the City of Seattle and County of King, Washington, Including Biographies of Many of Those Who Have Passed Away. (New York, Chicago: Lewis Publishing Company, 1903).

Warren, James R. *A Centennial History of the Seattle Tennis Club* (Seattle: Seattle Tennis Club, 1990).

Watt, Roberta Frye. *Four Wagons West: The Story of Seattle* (Portland: Metropolitan Press, ca. 1931).

Welsh, Robert. *The Presbytery of Seattle, 1858-2005* (Privately published, 2006).

Williams, Jacqueline B. *The Hill with a Future: Seattle's Capitol Hill 1900-1946* (Seattle: CPK Ink, 2001).

Woman's Century Club history book, created by members in 1893.

Woodbridge, Sally. *A Guide to Architecture in Washington State* (Seattle: University of Washington Press, 1980).

REPORTS & EXHIBITS

"Building for Learning: Seattle Public School Histories, 1862-2000."

"City Walks," Self-Guided First Hill Walking Tour, prepared by Lawrence Kreisman and Scott Souchock for Seattle Architecture Foundation.

First Hill, a three-part lecture and panel series on its past, present, and future produced by Historic Seattle, 1999. VHS and DVD.

"The First Hill Exhibit – Seattle's Boom Years: 1880-1925," installed at 1101 Madison Street. Designed and curated by Olson/Sundberg Architects and fabricated by Turner Exhibits.

First Hill History Project brochure, Historic Seattle, 1999.

"First Hill Neighborhood Tour" (unpublished), prepared by Lawrence Kreisman, Seattle Architecture Foundation, 1999.

"Good Public Schools: A Celebration of Seattle School History" traveling exhibition. Text and design by Lawrence Kreisman. Seattle School District, 2002-2003.

Historic Seattle Belmont/Boylston Historic Houses Project.

Historic Seattle Preservation and Development Authority. *An Inventory of Buildings and Urban Design Resources* (Seattle: The Authority, commenced 1975).

"Hofius House Open to View Tour," prepared by Lawrence Kreisman and Brooke Best, Historic Seattle, August 2012.

Krafft, Katheryn H. "Sorrento Hotel," City of Seattle Landmarks Preservation Board Landmark Nomination Application, revised January 22, 2008.

National Register of Historic Places Inventory – Nomination Form, "Residential Properties on Seattle's First Hill," prepared by Gwendolyn A. Lee and Miriam Sutermeister for The Conservation Company, July 1979.

"Seattle Public Schools: Historic Building Survey," prepared by Patricia Erigero for Historic Seattle, August 1989.

"Swedish Hospital Medical Center: 75 Years of Caring, 1910-1985."

"A Tour of Stained Glass on Seattle's First Hill," prepared by Lawrence Kreisman, Historic Seattle, September 15, 2012.

ORAL HISTORIES

Catholic Schools, Archdiocese of Seattle, 1856-1987. Sister Kathleen Gorman Oral History Transcript.

Historic Seattle First Hill Oral History Project (1999-2012):

Frances Backus, April 28, 1999.
Paul Brown, July 12, 1999.
P. J. Callahan, November 15, 1999.
Thomas K. Gerbracht, February 5, 2000.
Karen Harris and Barbara Olsen, June 27, 1999.
Roger Leed, November 23, 1999.
Leonard Saari, 1999 (no date).
Sister Kathleen Gorman, January 25, 2000.
DeLena Cresto, February 16, 2000.

NEWSPAPERS AND PERIODICALS

The Argus
Broadway Whims
Building News
The Capitol Hill Times
Hotel News of the West
Pacific Builder and Engineer
Pacific Building and Engineering Record
Seattle Daily Bulletin
Seattle Daily Intelligencer

The Seattle Daily Times
The Seattle Sunday Times
The Seattle Times
Seattle News-Letter
Seattle Post-Intelligencer
The Seattle Star
Seattle Sun
The Town Crier
Washington Churchman

Washington State Architect
The Week-End
The Weekly (later *Seattle Weekly*)
West Shore
The Western Architect

INDEX

Note: Page numbers in *italic* indicate photographs.

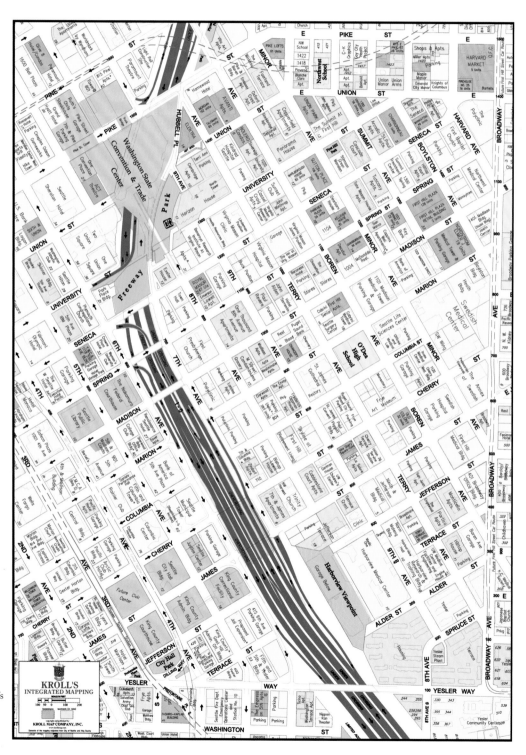

RIGHT: First Hill, 2014. Kroll's Integrated Mapping. Kroll Map Company, Inc.